RESEARCH IN ACCOUNTING
IN EMERGING ECONOMIES

RESEARCH IN ACCOUNTING IN EMERGING ECONOMIES

Series Editors: R. S. Olusegun Wallace, Managing and Joint Editor

John M. Samuels, Richard J. Briston and Shahrokh M. Saudagaran, Joint Editors

RESEARCH IN ACCOUNTING IN EMERGING ECONOMIES

EDITED BY

R. S. OLUSEGUN WALLACE

*Department of Accounting and MIS College of Industrial Management,
King Fahd University of Petroleum & Minerals, Saudi Arabia*

JOHN M. SAMUELS

Department of Accounting and Finance, University of Birmingham, UK

RICHARD J. BRISTON

Department of Accounting and Finance, University of Hull, UK

SHAHROKH M. SAUDAGARAN

*Department of Accountancy, College of Business Administration,
Oklahoma State University, USA*

2003

JAI
An Imprint of Elsevier Science

Amsterdam – Boston – London – New York – Oxford – Paris
San Diego – San Francisco – Singapore – Sydney – Tokyo

ELSEVIER SCIENCE Ltd
The Boulevard, Langford Lane
Kidlington, Oxford OX5 1GB, UK

First edition 2003

Library of Congress Cataloging in Publication Data
A catalog record from the Library of Congress has been applied for.

British Library Cataloguing in Publication Data
A catalogue record from the British Library has been applied for.

ISBN: 0-7623-0901-6

∞ The paper used in this publication meets the requirements of ANSI/NISO Z39.48-1992 (Permanence of Paper).
Printed in The Netherlands.

CONTENTS

PART III. ACCOUNTING IN SOUTH ASIA

ix

LIST OF CONTRIBUTORS

Ajay Adhikari

Kogod School of Business, American
University, Washington, D.C., USA

Gilda M. Agacer

Monmouth University,
West Long Branch, New Jersey, USA

Taha Eltayeb Ahmed

Bahrain Institute of Banking and
Finance, Manama, Bahrain

Hasan Al-Bastaki

Ministry of Education, Manama,
Bahrain

Khalid Al-Khater

University of Qatar, Qatar,
United Arab Emirates

Nabeel E. Al-Loughani

Department of Finance and Financial
Institutions, College of Administrative
Sciences, Kuwait University, Safat,
Kuwait

Ahmad Abdullah Al-Meghanes

Department of Accounting,
College of Administrative Sciences,
King Saud University, Riyadh,
Saudi Arabia

Abdulridha Al-Shawaf

College of Administrative Sciences,
Kuwait University, Safat, Kuwait

Casimir I. Anyanwu

School of Business, Department of
Accounting, Howard University,
Washington, D.C., USA

John A. Brierley

Sheffield University Management
School, University of Sheffield, U.K.

Jeselito G. Diga	University of the Philippines and SGV Arthur Andersen & Co., Manilla, Philippines
Hussein M. El-Nafabi	Al-Madina Al-Munawarah College, Al-Madina Al-Munawarah, Saudi Arabia
David R. Gwilliam	School of Management and Business, Cledwyn Building, University of Wales, Aberystwyth
John Innes	Department of Accounting and Business Finance, University of Dundee, Dundee, Scotland
Mustapha Bakar Mahmud	Accounting Department, Faculty of Economics, Garyounis University, Benghazi, Libya
Sayel Ramadhan	Department of Accounting, College of Business Administration, University of Bahrain, Bahrain
Alex Russell	Faculty of Law and Accountancy, University of Dundee, Dundee, Scotland
Robert W. Rutledge	Department of Accounting, College of Business Administration, South West Texas State University, San Marcos, Texas, USA
Shahrokh M. Saudagaran	College of Business Administration, Oklahoma State University, Stillwater, Oklahoma, USA
Daniel T. Simon	Department of Accounting, University of Notre Dame, Notre Dame, IN, USA

Mark H. Taylor   Department of Accounting,
                                   College of Business, Creighton
                                   University, Omaha, NE, USA

Chuibuke Ugochukwu Uche   Department of Banking & Finance,
                                   University of Nigeria, Enugu Campus,
                                   Nigeria

P. W. Senarath Yapa   School of Management Technology
                                   and Environment, LaTrobe University,
                                   Bendingo, Victoria, Australia

PREFACE

Since the publication of the last volume in the year 2000, many accounting debacles and events across the world have drawn attention to the need for greater transparency in corporate financial reporting. Although these debacles and events have come to light predominantly in the developed world, there is anecdotal evidence that similar scandals are waiting to be unearthed in the group of countries often described as emerging economies. Not only is transparent accounting and corporate financial reporting of prime importance today, but the myriad of problems and issues concerning corporate governance, behavior of financial analysts and their attempts to talk-up the value of stocks also demand the attention of scholars. It is obvious from the current scandals that when one discusses accounting and financial reporting, one is discussing conflicts between private prosperity and national and international financial security, and conflicts between rival modes of political and economic organizations. The accommodation of these competing claims requires not only passion and bureaucratic or business or technical skill, but it also requires intensive rational thought and a commitment to liberal values. It is my hope that those who read this volume will respond to this spirit of intelligent and humane inquiry. While the chapters brought together in this volume do not address the recent scandals, they draw attention to the accounting (broadly defined) needs, problems and solutions of countries situated in three regions of the world – Gulf, Africa and Asia. The topics in the volume include: the relationship between moral intensity and information ethics in a Gulf country, accounting education and certification process, the market for audit services, internal auditing in the public sector, perceptions on auditors' independence, the relationships between the returns of stocks of large and small firms, internal transfer pricing of bank funds, academic and professional cooperation in accounting education environment, management accounting practices, a critique of the relevance of historical cost accounting model to Sub-Saharan Africa, the absence of accounting and auditing provisions in the rules governing banks in colonial Nigeria, and accounting harmonization options for emerging countries. The countries in which the studies reported in the volume are set come from three separate geographic regions: (a) Gulf (Bahrain, Kuwait, Oman, Qatar, Saudi Arabia, and United Arab Emirates); (b) Africa (Libya, Nigeria and Sudan); and (c) Asia (Brunei Darussalam, Indonesia, Malaysia, Philippines, Singapore, and Thailand).

There are six chapters in Part I. The first chapter, by Adhikari and Alshawaf, focuses on ethical issues around information technology. They conclude that IT decisions are contingent on the magnitude of consequences and their interaction with gender effects. The second chapter, by Rutledge et al., reports on the results of a study of the perceptions of auditors and financial analysts domiciled in Kuwait, Saudi Arabia and United Arab Emirates on the independence of auditors. The authors examine, specifically, the role which the size of the client, the provision of management accounting services by the auditor to the same client, unpaid client fees, and the employment of a member of the auditor's family by the client, plays on auditor independence. The results suggest that auditors and financial analysts from the Gulf do not differ in their perceptions of auditor independence.

Al-Loughani examines, in the third chapter, the relationship between stock prices of large and small firms in Kuwait. He concludes that the stock prices of large firms are more value relevant than those of small firms in the short run during the bull phase. This superior performance of large firms is believed to arise from differences between large and small firms in their ownership structure, quality of their information and the role of institutional investors. In Chapter 4, Ahmed uses Islamic banking to illustrate the pricing of internal fund transfers. The chapter provides insights into how Islamic banks use Mudabaha or Mudaraba principles in internal transfer pricing. Al-Bastaki and Ramadhan examine in Chapter 5 how to enhance the cooperation between the accounting department at the University of Bahrain and auditing firms operating in the Kingdom of Bahrain. They elicited the opinions of auditors on how to enhance that cooperation and conclude that the most important strategies are: (a) to request audit practitioners to teach accounting and auditing courses in their University; (b) to exchange visits; and (c) to conduct joint research and consultancy projects. The last chapter in this part, by Al-Khater and Innes, provides the results of an exploratory study of the management accounting practices in petrochemical firms in the GCC. This chapter provides a lot of insights, especially as there is little or no information on management accounting practices in this region,

Part II addresses accounting problems in Africa. The first chapter, by Anyanwu, seeks to define the problems confronting Sub-Saharan African countries as they adopt the historical accounting model. The theme of the chapter is the futility of the adoption of Western financial accounting and reporting models slavishly, without addressing the peculiar needs of their countries. In the next chapter, Uche, provides an eloquent history of how the need for banks to render accounts was ignored during the Colonial period in Nigeria. In Chapter 9, Taylor and Simon examine the audit services market in Nigeria and report that audit fee premium for services rendered by audit firms affiliated to the Big-5 independent international audit firms also exists in Nigeria. Brierley et al., examine, in the next chapter, the internal audit function in the Sudanese public sector. They reveal that many public sector organizations in the Sudan do not have internal audit departments, and those that have, do not have trained personnel. The last chapter in this part, by Mahmud and Russell, reports on the results of an investigation of the development and strategies of accounting education and practice in Libya. It is a survey study that elicited the opinions of Libyan accounting academics and professionals on: (a) the major problems likely to obstruct accounting education and practice in Libya; and (b) the usefulness of certain strategies for enhancing accounting education and accounting practice in that country.

There are two chapters in the last part of this volume that dwell on South East Asian Nations. The first chapter, by Saudagaran and Diga, examines alternative accounting harmonization options available to the five original members of the Association of South East Asian Nations (ASEAN), in the context of their economic integration. This chapter provides an object lesson for other emerging economies. The last chapter, by Yapa, looks at accounting education and training of the member-countries in ASEAN and describes the varying quality and experience in the region.

Once again, I reiterate the point I made in Volume 4 (p. xviii). It is not easy to publish an annual on accounting in emerging economies which carries quality chapters that are evaluated and accepted after a double-blind review. Such a task is more difficult in a world in which standards of research are rising and several specialist journals are emerging. I faced similar difficulty of getting sufficient quality articles for the volume, consequently, some chapters accepted several months ago have had to wait for other quality articles to join them before publication. I am grateful for the patience of the authors of the affected articles.

I very much appreciate the work done by all of the reviewers of the manuscripts in their incipient and later stages. The reviewers have all offered suggestions to improve the scope, focus and clarity of all the manuscripts in this volume. I am deeply grateful to Rosemary I. Wallace, for her careful reading and most helpful suggestions and whose formidable editorial skills have done so much to polish the text. Finally, I acknowledge the generous sponsorship of the editorial office of *Research in Accounting in Emerging Economies* by King Fahd University of Petroleum and Minerals, Dhahran, Saudi Arabia.

R. S. Olusegun Wallace
Managing Editor

INTRODUCTION TO THE SERIES

This *Annual* arose out of the belief that the international accounting literature should devote more attention to the study of the accounting problems and issues of emerging economies (developing and newly industrialized countries). The *Annual* continues to serve as a forum for new research into accounting in developing countries as well as to publish traditional work relevant to this area.

The task of the Joint Editors is to continue to justify a series of publications on accounting in emerging economies. Many readers might ask why the subject of accounting in emerging economies needs to be differentiated from accounting in developed countries. Why cannot, or should not, emerging economies just adopt the same practices, the same accounting concepts and techniques as those economies that have already industrialized with either market economies or planned economies?

Some readers might point to the growing literature on international accounting, suggesting that a certain amount of this is concerned with emerging economies. This is undoubtedly true. *The International Journal of Accounting* has over the last quarter of a century published numerous articles on the accounting practices in individual countries that populate the group describable as emerging economies. Most of the international accounting literature is not, however, concerned with the particular problems of accounting in these countries, and when it is, it is not always sensitive to their special needs. Often, the normative type articles tend to imply that all that emerging economies need to do is adopt the accounting techniques of, say, either the USA or the U.K., and this will satisfy their needs. Such literature assumes that capital markets in emerging economies are based predominantly on a stock exchange and that this stock exchange is efficient. The accounting techniques suggested for emerging economies are those that are believed will improve the efficient allocation of scarce resources through such capital markets. This is of course desirable, but often this 'international' literature ignores the particular problems of emerging economies, because the main objective of the accounting reports based on the U.K./USA model is to satisfy the needs of shareholders, whereas in many emerging economies few enterprises have private shareholders. Investment decisions are often not made on financial grounds, and the market for information is imperfect.

The *Annual* concerns itself with theoretical, empirical and applied research into the macro and micro accounting issues of emerging economies. It is

xix

concerned with the relevance of international accounting standards to emerging economies.

Undoubtedly, there is a need for such international accounting standards. With global capital markets, there is a need for a company quoted on more than one stock exchange to produce accounts that are similar in substance from one country to the next. Such harmonized accounting standards are needed by users, and are also helpful to preparers of accounts. But, the current over-emphasis on external reporting means that scant attention is paid to the areas of accounting which are considerably more important to emerging economies.

Further problems that many emerging economies face include:

- the need to increase the number of trained accountants;
- the question of the level of training required: technician level or full professional level;
- the organization of a profession: should it cover public as well as private sector accounting?;
- the lack of accountability: does anybody take any notice of the accounting and audit reports produced?;
- inadequate management accounting: too little attention is paid to the development of effective managerial accounting systems;
- inadequate internal and external reporting/auditing.

Some of the accounting needs in emerging economies are the same as those in industrialized countries and some are different. The *Annual* encourages debate on such issues and assists in the development of accounting as a subject in emerging economies.

The desire of the *Annual* is to raise the level of interest in the specific problems of accounting in emerging economies and raise the awareness of the real issues, so that accounting in these countries will not just be seen as a matter of copying what is done in the industrialized countries. Through an increasing awareness of the real issues and the accounting practices advocated in it, the *Annual* has become relevant to actual needs, and is making a real contribution to the accounting development process of emerging economies.

The editorial policy is to publish in the *Annual*, articles that comply with the foregoing.

R. S. Olusegun Wallace
Richard J. Briston
John M. Samuels
and Shahrokh Saudagaran

PART I:
ACCOUNTING AND CONTROL
IN GULF COUNTRIES

1. INFORMATION ETHICS: THE ROLE OF MORAL INTENSITY

Ajay Adhikari and Abdulridha Al-Shawaf

ABSTRACT

While there has been considerable research in the area of business ethics, researchers have only recently started focusing on the ethical issues surrounding the use of information technology, i.e. information ethics. Using Jones' (1991) construct of moral intensity, we examine the influence of magnitude of consequences and personal and situational factors on decision making in the information ethics area. The study is operationalized using a vignette and questionnaire-based research instrument administered to a sample of upper-level undergraduate business students at Kuwait University. The results of the study provide limited support that in the context of information ethics, decision making is contingent on magnitude of consequences and its interaction with gender effects. These findings have implications for academic research and public policy as discussed in the study.

1. INTRODUCTION

Information technology (IT) has pervaded all facets of modern society. The proliferation of IT is raising numerous ethical challenges for both individuals and societies. Advances in data storage, data mining techniques, and networking, including the Internet, have heightened ethical concerns and have put stress on

Research in Accounting in Emerging Economies, Volume 5, pages 3–18.
© 2003 Published by Elsevier Science Ltd.
ISBN: 0-7623-0901-6

existing social laws. A case in point is the issue of protecting individuals' privacy that is becoming a serious ethical concern in many countries. Accordingly, the relatively new area of information ethics is drawing increasing attention in the press as well as in the academic literature.

The term "information ethics" refers to the ethical issues that surround the development and use of information, information technologies, and information systems (Smith, 1997). Mason (1986) has identified four dimensions of information ethics (privacy, property, accuracy, and access) facing people in the information age. A stream of literature has developed that has examined the attitudes of subjects with respect to Mason's information ethics dimensions (Eining & Lee, 1997; Lally, 1996; Christensen & Eining, 1991).

On the public policy side, there is a growing awareness of the need to forcefully address the ethical issues that surround the increasing use of IT. Protection of intellectual property rights and issues surrounding software piracy have been at the center of several cross-border agreements including the mandate of the world trade organization (WTO). With the internet becoming an integral part of our daily lives, privacy concerns have surfaced, leading to proposed legislation in the U.S. congress and other countries. Accessibility concerns, the power of IT to splinter society into those who have access to IT and internet and those who do not, the so called 'digital divide' are also gaining currency.

A key component in enforcing agreements and forcing the debate on information ethics issues is educating the public and influencing public perceptions. For example, it has been very difficult to enforce software piracy laws in a number of Asian countries because of the general belief that intellectual works belong in the public domain and are, hence, a public good (Swinyard et al., 1990). In educating the public, therefore, it becomes very important that the communication/type and message/type of story or case being used be framed very carefully so that it elicits the desired response.

Research has shown that a key complicating factor in examining ethical decision making is the nature of the moral issue itself. Moral issues often contain ambiguous features. Jones (1991) has proposed a construct to encompass the characteristics of the moral issue itself into the study of ethical decision making. Jones argues forcefully that moral issues vary in terms of their level of "moral intensity". Thus, ethical decision making is contingent upon the nature of the ethical issue itself. Jones further argues that the overall intensity of a moral issue can influence the recognition of a moral issue and the intention plus the engagement of a moral act.

The objective of this study is to examine the impact of moral intensity on ethical decision making in the context of information ethics. We also expand the study to include the influence of gender on ethical decision choice with reference to moral intensity. The results of the study should be useful to both academics and public policy makers. The study extends the literature by examining the influence of moral intensity to a new area, that of information ethics. From a public policy perspective, the results of the study provide some insights into the potential impact of moral intensity cues on public perceptions in the context of information ethics.

2. MORAL INTENSITY

Jones (1991) asserts that the intensity of a moral issue is determined collectively by six components: (1) the magnitude or seriousness of potential consequences; (2) social consensus, the degree to which other people agree that an action is ethically questionable; (3) likelihood of effect, the probability that an act actually results in a negative outcome; (4) temporal immediacy, the length of time between an act and its consequences; (5) proximity, the feeling of nearness to the affected individual; and (6) concentration of effect, the number of affected people by the act. Jones combines these six components in an issue contingent model of moral intensity.

Several studies have been carried out to empirically validate Jones' theory. Some studies have selectively manipulated some components of the issue contingent model (Dukerich et al., 2000; Davis et al., 1998; Singer & Singer, 1997; Singer, 1996; Weber, 1996; Dukerich et al., 1993; Jones & Huber, 1992), while others have investigated all six components of the model simultaneously (Frey, 2000; Singhapakdi et al., 1996; Morris & McDonald, 1995). The results are not conclusive across the different studies for the six components of the moral intensity model. Part of the inconsistencies in the results of earlier studies may stem from different research designs, sampling differences, and choice of research instrument.

Given the exploratory nature of the present study, we choose to focus only on one component of the Jones' model, i.e. magnitude of consequences. Consideration of all six components could lead to an entangled data analysis where it may be difficult to draw insights about the impact of any one of the components on ethical decision making in the information ethics area. The magnitude of consequences component is chosen because it is the most often implicated factor in studies examining moral intensity and its impact on ethical decision making (Dukerich et al., 2000; Frey, 2000; Harrington, 1997; Singer & Singer, 1997; Singer, 1996; Weber, 1996; Morris & McDonald, 1995).

Jones defines magnitude of consequences as the "sum of the harms (or benefits) done to victims (or beneficiaries) of the moral act in question" (1991, p. 374). The response to a moral situation is partly contingent on the magnitude of consequences. Different moral reasoning will be demanded depending on the magnitude of consequences. A situation with trivial consequences may evoke a much weaker moral response than one with dire consequences. Moral dilemmas with serious consequences encourage ethical behavior (Fritzsche & Becker, 1983).

Additionally, a growing body of research seeks to assess the role gender plays in shaping perceptions of ethical decision making. "The sex-role system is at the core of our cultural norm", so stated (Chetwynd & Hartnett, 1978, p. 3). In every society, cultural norms and traditions stipulate that certain behaviors are more suitable for men while other behaviors are more suitable for women. These sex role patterns are perpetuated through a socialization process that is embedded in society. Jones (1991) also notes that the relative importance of personal and situational factors might vary considerably from issue to issue. Therefore, there might be an interaction between gender effects and the type of moral situation being examined.

In this paper, we seek to extend the literature by examining the impact of magnitude of consequences on ethical decision making with reference to information ethics. This study is exploratory in nature since the area of information ethics is still at an emergent state and the information ethics constructs proposed by Mason (1996) are complex and could be perceived as abstract notions. We also examine the influence of gender on ethical decision choice with reference to magnitude of consequences. More specifically, we seek to answer the following two questions:

- Does varying the level of magnitude of consequence affect the ethical decision of subjects with reference to information ethics?
- Does gender difference influence the ethical decision of subjects in situations with varying levels of magnitude of consequences?

We operationalized the study by surveying a sample of upper-level undergraduate business students at Kuwait University, using a vignette and questionnaire-based research instrument. The next section discusses the methodology of the study.

3. METHODOLOGY

Research Instrument

The research instrument for the study is adapted from Eining and Lee (1997) and consists of four dilemmas dealing with information ethics issues. The issues examined are privacy, property, accuracy, and access. Mason (1986) has suggested these as four important ethical issues of the information age.

Privacy refers to "the ability of the individual to personally control information about oneself" (Stone, et al., 1983). With the growth of IT, it has become much easier for organizations to collect, retrieve, and disseminate information about individuals, raising serious concerns about information privacy. Property refers to the intellectual property rights associated with software development. Software piracy is considered a serious threat to the continued and vigorous growth of the software industry. Accuracy refers to responsibility and accountability for failures in information systems. Many parties are involved in the design, development, sale, and use of information systems. Therefore, if something goes wrong it is oftentimes difficult to pinpoint which party is accountable and should be held liable for damages. Access refers to the ability of individuals to receive information that is available. Access depends on both the availability of technology as well as the skills to use it. There are concerns that, because some individuals may not be able to either afford technology or have the necessary skills required, an inequality in terms of information access may be created.[1]

The research instrument consisted of four case scenarios that encapsulate the above four dimensions of information ethics. Each case scenario contains a moral dilemma faced by a principal actor in the case. For the purpose of the study, two versions of the research instrument were constructed. The first version is labeled the "regular version" and the second version is labeled the "sensitive version". In the "sensitive version" for two case scenarios (privacy and accuracy), the level of magnitude of consequences was manipulated and these two cases are labeled the experimental cases. The manipulated level of magnitude of consequences in the privacy case was increased from drug trafficking in the regular version to rape in the sensitive version. The manipulated level of magnitude of consequences in the accuracy case was increased from an injury in the regular version to death in the sensitive version. The levels of magnitude of consequences in the property and access cases are kept constant in both versions of the instrument and, hence, are labeled as the control cases.

Participants in the study were asked to express their degree of disagreement or agreement with the action contemplated in each case. Responses were measured using a six-point Likert scale ranging from "1" = strongly disagree to "6" = strongly agree. A summary of the case scenarios in the two versions of the instrument is provided in Appendix A. Both versions of the research instrument were translated into Arabic and translated back into English to guard against bias introduced during the translation process. The two versions of the instrument were thoroughly pre-tested prior to their administration.

Sample

The study used an upper-level business student sample from Kuwait University. The sample was divided into two groups. The regular version of the instrument was administered to group 1 (the control group ($n = 139$). The sensitive version of instrument was administered to group 2 (the experimental group ($n = 129$). The research instrument was administered in classes with prior consent of instructors. Due to the sensitive nature of the study, participants were assured of strict confidentiality and participation in the study was optional.

The profile of the two responding groups is presented in Table 1. The sample consisted of significantly more females than males. This is reflective of the general demographic trend in Kuwait. Both the control and experimental groups have similar profiles with regards to gender, age, and computer experience distributions.

Table 1. Demographics – Profile of Respondents.

The Control Group: No. of cases 130	
Gender:	
Male	30.8%
Female	69.2%
Age:	
18–20	10.8%
21–23	73.1%
24–26	11.5%
> 27	4.6%
Frequency of use of computer: 3.81[a]	
The Experimental Group: No. of cases 126	
Gender:	
Male	29.4%
Female	70.6%
Age:	
18–20	14.3%
21–23	73.0%
24–26	8.7%
> 27	4.0%
Frequency of use of computer: 3.50[a]	

[a] Frequency of use of computer was measured on a Likert scale ranging from "1" = never to "6" = daily use.

4. RESULTS

The two-tailed test was used to test whether the responses of the student experimental group differed from those of the student control group.[2] The overall results for the four cases are presented in Table 2. For the experimental cases, the decision of subjects was probed further by examining the importance that subjects attached to a set of considerations that might have influenced their decision. Tables 3a and 3b report the results for the importance attached to considerations for the privacy case (experimental case 1) and the accuracy case (experimental case 2).

The privacy case (experimental case 1) involved a parent, Hamed, accidentally coming upon confidential information about a respected professor in his daughter's college suspected but not convicted of a drug trafficking (regular version)/rape (sensitive version) crime many years ago. Neither the control group (mean = 2.66) nor the experimental group (mean = 3.06) in this study felt very strongly that Hamed should report this matter, indicating a concern and respect for the professor's privacy. However, the experimental group was more inclined than the control group to report the matter and the difference between the two groups was significant. This suggests that the stronger stimulus (rape vs. drug trafficking) had an impact on the decision making of subjects with respect to this privacy case. This provides limited evidence that magnitude of consequences impacts ethical decision making in the information ethics area.

Table 3a presents the importance that subjects attached to a set of considerations that might have influenced their decision. In examining Table 3a, a pattern emerges, as magnitude of consequences increases (rape vs. drug-trafficking) subjects become less sympathetic with legalistic and privacy considerations in making a decision in the case. For example, the experimental group is less

Table 2. Results for Total Sample.

Case	Control Group[a] (n = 130)	Experimental Group (n = 126)
Experimental Case 1: Privacy	2.66	3.06*
Experimental Case 2: Accuracy	4.33	4.06
Control Case 1 Property	4.76	4.90
Control Case 2: Access	2.93	3.00

[a] Measured on a Likert scale ranging from "1" = strongly disagree to "6" = strongly agree.
* significant at 0.05 level.

Table 3a.   Considerations for Experimental Case 1 (Privacy).

Consideration	Control Group[a] (n = 130)	Experimental Group[a] (n = 126)
The professor could lose his job	4.01	3.43*
The professor was not convicted of any crime	4.36	4.08
The university's reputation could be affected	4.30	4.01
The information is confidential and personal in nature	5.00	4.59*
Hamed is concerned for his daughter	4.56	4.90**
The professor's relationship with his students could be affected	4.62	4.37
The professor has not committed any current crime	4.31	3.44*
Hamed had no authority to access the information	4.66	4.34
The professor could bring a lawsuit against Hamed and the University	3.85	3.80
The professor is highly respected	3.57	3.23
The professor could be negatively influencing his students	4.43	4.17

[a] Measured on a Likert scale ranging from "1" = strongly disagree to "6" = strongly agree.
* significant at 0.05 level; ** significant at 0.10 level.

concerned than the control group that the professor may lose his job, that the professor has not committed any current crime, or that the information is confidential. This provides additional evidence that magnitude of consequences may influence individuals' resolution of an ethical dilemma concerning information ethics.

The accuracy case (experimental case 2) involved a scenario where a patient's illness worsened (regular version)/patient died (sensitive version) after she was given a certain line of treatment based on the incorrect diagnosis of a medical diagnosis expert system. Both the experimental and control groups leaned more towards holding the software developer accountable for the patient's condition with no significant difference in the positions of the two groups. An examination of the considerations guiding the decisions of the respective groups (Table 3b) did not reveal any significant patterns.

The control cases dealt with property (control case 1) and access (control case 2). The property case dealt with copying of software for classroom purposes, while the access case dealt with a situation where a worker wanted to use his company's internet access to develop his own business to support his children's future college education. As expected, there were no significant differences between the control and experimental groups for the two control cases.

The above results provide limited support for the assertion that magnitude of consequences impact decision making in the area of information ethics.

Table 3b. Considerations for experimental Case 2 (Accuracy).

Consideration	Control Group[a] ($n = 130$)	Experimental Group[a] ($n = 126$)
Accuracy of information becomes more important in matters of life and death	5.65	5.56
The doctor is responsible for the proper use of the system	5.28	4.85*
Gulf Tech followed proper development guidelines in developing the software	4.10	3.92
Gulf Tech's image could be tarnished leading to loss of sales	3.82	3.99
The doctor should verify the diagnosis provided by the system	5.67	5.68
Gulf Tech should be responsible for the accuracy of the system	4.78	4.84
There is a possibility of the doctor or hospital suing Gulf Tech	4.16	4.15
The hospital had thoroughly tested the system before purchasing it	4.64	4.26**
The patient and her family suffered both emotionally and financially	5.53	5.50
No guarantee was provided on the software that it was 100% accurate	5.19	5.10

[a] Measured on a Likert scale ranging from "1" = strongly disagree to "6" = strongly agree.
* significant level at 0.05 level; ** significant at 0.10 level.

Significant differences among the experimental and control groups were found for one (privacy case) of the two experimental cases. An examination of the considerations that influenced the decision making of respondents for the privacy case also suggested that as the magnitude of consequences increased, subjects' attitudes hardened accordingly.

Gender Effects

To investigate possible gender effects, we segregated the sample groups by gender. The results of this analysis are provided in Panels *a* and *b* of Table 4. Panel *a* shows that for experimental case 1 (privacy), differences among the female control and experimental groups are highly significant. Differences are not detected in the remaining cases between the female control and experimental groups. The result is consistent with the results for the pooled sample. For the male sub-samples, however, no significant differences are detected for any of the four cases.

The greater responsiveness of the female subjects to manipulation of magnitude of consequences in the privacy case (experimental case 1) may also be due to the particulars of the case. The manipulated stimuli are drug trafficking (control case) and rape case (experimental case). The suspected crime in the case moves from a gender neutral crime (drug trafficking) to a gender specific

Table 4a.   Gender Results – Female.

Case	Control Group[a] (n = 90)	Experimental Group[a] (n = 89)
Experimental Case 1: Privacy	2.71	3.44*
Experimental Case 2: Accuracy	4.41	4.21
Control Case 1 Property	4.79	5.10
Control Case 2: Access	2.79	3.12

[a] Measured on a Likert scale ranging from "1" = strongly disagree to "6" = strongly agree.
* Highly significant at 0.05 level.

Table 4b.   Gender Results – Male.

Case	Control Group[a] (n = 40)	Experimental Group[a] (n = 37)
Experimental Case 1: Privacy	2.55	2.16
Experimental Case 2: Accuracy	4.15	3.68
Control Case 1 Property	4.80	4.38
Control Case 2: Access	3.25	2.70

[a] Measured on a Likert scale ranging from "1" = strongly disagree to "6" = strongly agree.

crime (rape). Social identity theory would suggest that issues involving an individual's own gender are likely to be more proximate and important than those affecting the opposite gender (Franke, et al., 1997). Individuals display greater empathy when confronted with issues that affect their own sex than with issues that are gender neutral or affect the opposite sex. This would explain the relatively greater responsiveness of the women subjects to the privacy case.

We also tested for differences between the female and male sub-samples for the control group. No significant differences were observed for any of the cases. Significant differences were, however, detected for experimental case 1 (privacy) and control case 1 (property) between the female and male sub-samples for the experimental group. The overall results in this section suggest that while gender effects by themselves may not be as important, they become much more significant when they interact with changes in magnitude of conse-quences in influencing subjects' attitudes towards information ethics.

5. CONCLUSION

The results of the study provide limited support for Jones' (1991) assertion that the magnitude of consequences impact ethical decision making. This study extended the examination of the influence of magnitude of consequences on decision making to the information ethics area. A large part of the effect documented in the study, however, emanates from the interaction of gender and magnitude of consequences. This is consistent with earlier studies reporting a greater magnitude and likelihood of consequence for female respondents than male respondents (Singer & Singer, 1997).

The results of the study have implications for both academic research and public policy. This study extends the literature to examine the impact of moral intensity in the context of ethical decision making in the newly emerging area of information ethics. The present study only examined one component of moral intensity, i.e. magnitude of consequences. A natural extension would be to examine the impact of other components of moral intensity on ethical decision making in the area of information ethics. Issues surrounding information ethics are still emerging and are still quite abstract. It may be interesting to replicate the study when information ethics issues become more crystallized and ingrained in the mainstream.

From a public policy standpoint, the framing of the information ethics issues, regarding its magnitude of consequences, may influence ethical behavior. A number of countries have launched publicity campaigns to promote greater public awareness of issues surrounding intellectual property rights, in particular software piracy. The results of the study suggest that the moral intensity of the message/case/story used in these campaigns will partly determine the effectiveness of such publicity campaigns in evoking desired behaviors. For example, a message that software piracy will seriously harm the emerging software industry that is vital to the national interests of a country will be more powerful than a message that focuses on the harm faced by one software company. Additionally, policymakers have to be aware that different messages might resonate differently among different sex groups.

The study used a Kuwaiti sample and, therefore, caution needs to be exercised in generalizing the results of the study. As the Middle East region, especially the Gulf States, share a similar cultural heritage and are at the same level of IT development, the results of the study could be extrapolated to this area. Future research should be extended to include countries from other regions to provide for a richer analysis. The study was exploratory, and therefore, we confined our analysis to only one component of moral intensity. The area of information ethics is still at a nascent stage, so issues such as accessibility, and accuracy in particular, may still be abstract notions to a lot of the students surveyed for this study. This may help explain some of the non-results in the study. More robust research design, growing familiarity with information ethics issues, and replication in other countries should increase our understanding of this important area.

NOTES

1. For a more detailed discussion of the four dimensions of information ethics, see Mason (1986) and Eining and Lee (1997).

2. We also used the non-parametric procedure, Mann-Whitney, to test our hypotheses. The results obtained from the Mann-Whitney test are similar and consistent with the T-test results that are reported in the paper.

ACKNOWLEDGMENTS

Professor Adhikari acknowledges the support of the Fulbright foundation. Professor Alshawaf acknowledges financial support from Kuwait University.

REFERENCES

Christensen, A., & Eining, M. M. (1991). Factors influencing software piracy: Implications for accountants. *Journal of Information Systems*, (Spring), 67–80.

Chetwynd, J., & Hartnett, O. (Eds) (1978). *The Sex-Role System: Psychological and Sociological Perspectives*. London: Routledge and Kegan Paul.

Davis, M. A., Johnson, N. B., & Ohmer, D. C. (1998). Issue-contingent Effects on Ethical Decision Making: A Cross-cultural Comparison. *Journal of Business Ethics*, *17*, 373–389.

Dukerich, J. M., Waller, M. J., George, E., & Huber, G. P. (1993). Moral Intensity in Group Problem Solving. Paper presented at the National Academy of Management Meetings, Atlanta, GA.

Dukerich, J. M., Waller, M. J., George, E., & Huber, G. P. (2000). Moral Intensity and Managerial Problem Solving. *Journal of Business Ethics*, (March), 29–38.

Eining, M. M., & Lee, G. M. (1997). Information Ethics: An Exploratory Study from an International Perspective. *Journal of Information Systems*, *11*(1), 1–17.

Forsyth, D. R. (1985). Individual Differences in Information Integration during Moral Judgment. *Journal of Personality and Social Psychology*, *49*, 264–272.

Forsyth, D. R., & Pope, W. R. (1984). Ethical Ideology and Judgments of Social Psychological Research: Multidimensional Analysis. *Journal of Personality and Social Psychology*, *46*, 1365–1375.

Franke, G. R., Crown, D. F., & Spake, D. F. (1997). Gender Differences in Ethical Perceptions of Business Practices: A social role theory perspective. *Journal of Applied Psychology*, *82*(6), 920–934.

Frey, B. F. (2000). The Impact of Moral Intensity on Decision Making in a Business Context. *Journal of Business Ethics*, (August), 181–195.

Fritzche, D. J., & Baker, H. (1983). Ethical Behavior and Marketing Managers. *Journal of Business Ethics, 2*, 291–299.

Harrington, S. J. (1997). A Test of a Person-issue Contingent Model of Ethical Decision Making in Organizations. *Journal of Business Ethics, 16*, 363–375.

Jones, T. M. (1991). Ethical Decision Making by Individuals in Organizations: An Issue-Contingent Model. *Academy of Management Review, 16*, 366–395.

Jones, T. M., & Huber, V. L. (1992). Issue Contingency in Ethical Decision Making. Paper presented at the 3rd annual conference of the International Association for Business and Society, Leuven, Belgium.

Lally, L. (1996). Privacy vs. Accessibility: The Impact of Situationally Conditioned Belief. *Journal of Business Ethics, 15*, 1221–1226.

Mason, R. O. (1986). Four Ethical Issues of the Information Age. *MIS Quarterly, 10*(1), 5–12.

Marshall, B., & Dewe, P. (1997). An Investigation of the Components of Moral Intensity. *Journal of Business Ethics, 16*(April), 521–529.

Morris, S. A., & McDonald, R. A. (1995). The Role of Moral Intensity in Moral Judgements: An Empirical Investigation. *Journal of Business Ethics, 14*(September), 715–726.

Singer, M. S. (1996). The Role of Moral Intensity and Fairness Perception in Judgments of Ethicality: A Comparison of Management Professionals and the General Public. *Journal of Business Ethics, 15*, 469–474.

Singer, M. S., & Singer, A. E. (1997). Observer Judgments about Moral Agent's Ethical Decisions: The Role of Scope of Justice and Moral Intensity. *Journal of Business Ethics, 16*, 473–484.

Singhapakdi, A., Vitell, S. J., & Kraft, K. L. (1996). Moral Intensity and Ethical Decision making of Marketing Professionals. *Journal of Business Research, 36*, 245–255.

Smith, M. M. (1997). Information Ethics. *Annual Review of Information Science and Technology, 32*, 339–366.

Stone, E. F., Gardner, D. G., Gueutal, H. G., & McClure, S. (1983). A Field Experiment Comparing Information-Privacy Values, Beliefs, and Attitudes Across Several Types of Organizations. *Journal of Applied Psychology*, (August), 459–468.

Swinyard, R. R., Deloong, T. L., & Cheng, P. S. (1990). The Morality of Software Piracy: A Cross-Cultural Analysis. *Journal of Business Ethics*, (August), 655–664.

Weber, J. (1996). Influences upon Managerial Moral Decision Making: Nature of the Harm and Magnitude of Consequences, *Human Relations, 49*, 1–22.

APPENDIX A1:

INFORMATION ETHICS SCENARIOS FOR THE REGULAR VERSION

Case 1: Privacy

Hamed works in the Data Processing Unit of the Police Department at the Ministry of Interior. The department's computer system is linked to a centralized data bank that contains criminal information for the entire country. One day, while working on the computer, Hamed accidentally entered the highly classified "drug crime suspect profiles" which he is not authorized to access. He was horrified to discover that one of the highly respected professors in his daughter's college was on the list. According to the record, the professor was suspected in a drug trafficking case twelve years ago. However, he was not convicted because of lack of evidence. The first thing that came to Hamed's mind was whether he should contact the dean of the college.

Case 2: Property

Adil is a senior student at the local college. Most of his class projects require the use of a computer. Although the college provides all of the software necessary to meet class requirements, the number of computers available is insufficient to meet students' needs. As a result, Adil has turned in his homework late twice because of this problem. He decided to buy his own computer so that he can do the projects at home any time he wants. However, after spending all his savings on a used computer, there was no money left for software. His best friend Mehdi comes from an affluent family. He not only owns a state-of-the-art computer but also has an impressive collection of software. Mehdi found out about Adil's problem and generously offered to let Adil copy his software.

Case 3: Accuracy

Gulf Tech Corporation has spent many years in research and finally developed a medical diagnosis expert system which allows doctors to feed a patient's symptoms and lab test results into the computer and receive a diagnosis. The local Hospital was satisfied with the reliability of the software after thorough testing and purchased the system from Gulf Tech. However, on the sales contract, Gulf Tech explicitly indicated that although they have considered all possible situations and have followed proper design guidelines, they do not guarantee 100% accuracy simply because there are always unknown medical cases that are yet to be discovered. A year after the purchase, a patient's illness worsened and she developed an infection after her doctor treated her according to the computer's diagnosis. Further testing indicated that the computer diagnosis was incorrect. The patient suffered both physically and financially because of the error and she later filed suit against the doctor for malpractice.

Case 4: Access

Khalid works full time during the day in a large corporation. His children will be going to college in a few years. In order to prepare for their education, he wanted to earn extra income by building and selling computer systems for small local businesses at home in his spare time. Khalid realizes that in today's world, quick access to information is power. He must stay ahead of other competitors in order to succeed in the volatile computer business. He decided that he should hook up to a 24-hour commercial on-line market information company. Besides the long-distance telephone charges, such service normally involves a small hourly usage charge plus an expensive monthly flat charge. Khalid can handle the telephone charges and the hourly charge because he will only be using it for a short time every evening. However, his current sales volume simply did not justify paying a large monthly fee at this point in time. The company Khalid works for has already connected to a similar service. Khalid decided to dial the service from his home computer in the evening using the company's user ID number. He figured the company is paying for the flat fee anyway. Therefore, the cost to the company is minimal.

APPENDIX A2:

INFORMATION ETHICS SCENARIOS FOR THE SENSITIVE VERSION

Case 1: Privacy

Hamed works in the Data Processing Unit of the Police Department at the Ministry of Interior. The department's computer system is linked to a centralized data bank that contains criminal information for the entire country. One day, while working on the computer, Hamed accidentally entered the highly classified "drug crime suspect profiles" which he is not authorized to access. He was horrified to discover that one of the highly respected professors in his daughter's college was on the list. According to the record, the professor was suspected in a rape case twelve years ago. However, he was not convicted because of lack of evidence. The first thing that came to Hamed's mind was whether he should contact the dean of the college.

Case 4: Access

Khalid works full time during the day in a large corporation. His children will be going to college in a few years. In order to prepare for their education, he wanted to earn extra income by building and selling computer systems for small local businesses at home in his spare time. Khalid realizes that in today's world, quick access to information is power. He must stay ahead of other competitors in order to succeed in the volatile computer business. He decided that he should hook up to a 24-hour commercial on-line market information company. Besides the long-distance telephone charges, such service normally involves a small hourly usage charge plus an expensive monthly flat charge. Khalid can handle the telephone charges and the hourly charge because he will only be using it for a short time every evening. However, his current sales volume simply did not justify paying a large monthly fee at this point in time. The company Khalid works for has already connected to a similar service. Khalid decided to dial the service from his home computer in the evening using the company's user ID number. He figured the company is paying for the flat fee anyway. Therefore, the cost to the company is minimal.

2. PERCEPTIONS OF AUDITORS' INDEPENDENCE: A REGIONAL STUDY INVOLVING SAUDI ARABIA, KUWAIT AND UNITED ARAB EMIRATES

Robert W. Rutledge, Ahmad Adbullah Al-Meghanes and Gilda M Agacer

ABSTRACT

There are incentives for increasing uniformity or harmonization of auditing standards. These incentives are partially derived from the increasing maturity of capital markets throughout the world. Participants in the markets require increased consistency in order to make informed financial decisions. However, many regional differences in standards need to be sorted out before global standards can be established (Ward, 1998).

The purpose of this study is to examine the issue of auditor independence. We use a "regional approach" to determine if countries within a single region (i.e. Arabic Gulf countries) have similar views on the issue of auditor independence. The study examines the responses of auditors and financial analysts as to their perception of auditor independence subject to four independent variables (client size, provision of MAS services, unpaid client fees, and employment of a family member by the audit client).

Research in Accounting in Emerging Economies, Volume 5, pages 19–42.
Copyright © 2003 by Elsevier Science Ltd.
All rights of reproduction in any form reserved.
ISBN: 0-7623-0901-6

The results of the study indicate that both auditors (H1) and financial analysts (H2) have no significant differences in their perceptions of auditor independence. Implications for global harmonization of auditing standards and related issues are discussed.

1. INTRODUCTION

On July 13, 2000, the United States Securities and Exchange Commission issued a proposed new rule that would cause major restructuring of the accounting profession and principles regarding auditor independence (Securities and Exchange Commission, 2000). The proposal would establish a basic test whereby an auditor would not be considered independent if s/he 'is not, or would not be perceived by reasonable investors . . . knowing all the relevant circumstances . . . to be independent" (p. 17).

The American Institute of Certified Public Accountants (AICPA) fired back its stance on the issue. They stated that this rule, if enacted, would significantly reduce the ability of accounting firms to provide most non-audit and tax services to their SEC audit clients. Further, they suggest that the SEC has proposed the new rule without supporting facts or evidence, and the proposal is "draconian and unwarranted" (AICPA, 2000a). Although various independence-related battles have been brewing since the 1970s, now the war is on. However, having the issue of auditor independence resolved on a U.S. basis is just a small part of the resolution of the larger issue; that of harmonization of accounting and auditing standard on a global basis.

Several factors in the world's economy exist today that provide incentives for more uniformity or harmonization among auditing standards. For example, the nature of industry and capital markets has become increasingly international over the last decade. Paralleling the increased activity in international financial markets, Multinational Corporations (MNCs) also reflect the globalization of business during the 1980s and 1990s. A parent company in one country may have operations around the world. The company may control hundreds of subsidiaries and have investments in hundreds of other associated companies in many different countries. Other important international capital markets (e.g. Europe) were regulated in the past, but are now deregulated to improve efficiency. Some markets which have traditionally prohibited or restricted ownership of securities (e.g. Korea) are opening up to foreign investment. The surges in international trading have increased the use of, and demand for, reliable financial information. When the financial information is used internationally, there is a need to ensure that the applied auditing standards and procedures are of high quality regardless of the information source or audit location. Further, when auditing standards are determined and set on a country-by-country basis, financial statement users are more likely to be unsure of the reliability of information in the financial statements.

The objective of harmonizing auditing standards is to reduce the differences in auditing practices among countries. This, in turn, should promote increased efficiency and consistency in decisions made by participants in the global financial markets (Ward, 1998). The efforts to harmonize auditing standards have met with limited success in their implementation (Rivera, 1989; Mueller et al., 1991; Choi & Mueller, 1992). Reasons for this limited success are lack of enforcement by the international auditing standards' bodies, such as the International Federation of Accountants (IFAC) and lack of adequate representation of developing nations' interests on councils developing those standards (Abu-Ghazaleh, 1989). A more fundamental reason, which may be responsible for this lack of progress toward harmonization, is differences in each nation's cultural, social and political environments. These differences may prevent or severely limit the extent of audit harmonization across nations (Puxty, 1987; Beresford, 1990; Choi & Mueller, 1992; Ward, 1998).

There must be agreement on fundamental international auditing concepts in order to establish acceptable international auditing standards (Beresford, 1990). One fundamental international auditing standard is independence. Independence is an essential auditing standard for the independent accountant in order to add creditability to financial statements (Carmichael, 1999). If the concept of independence differs between countries, then the credibility that financial statement users place in the audit process will differ between countries. Further, there is little chance for having universal standards if different countries have a different understanding of the concept of independence. Comparative research across various regimes is needed to improve the understanding of auditor independence and regulations regarding auditor independence (Kinney, 1999).

The purpose of this study is to examine an alternative to establishing worldwide international standards. This alternative is a "regional approach" to establishing standards (Rivera, 1989; Wood, 1993; Ward, 1998). Rivera (1989) suggests that achieving harmonization could be more successfully done on a regional level, involving homogeneous countries, than on a global level. The regional approach looks at clustering countries by regions according to similar cultural and environmental factors and narrowing differences in auditing standards among member nations. Worldwide economic growth and increasing competition in the capital and money markets have made it difficult for a country to survive economically on its own. Therefore, throughout the world, there is a movement for many countries in a single region with similar culture and common political and economic goals to cluster themselves and establish a unified economic system. This clustering is called Regional Economic Integration, which reduces the economic significance of national political boundaries within a geographical area.

One example is the Arabic Gulf countries – Saudi Arabia, Kuwait, Qatar, Oman, Bahrain, and United Arab Emirates. Because of economic integration, countries belonging to a region will compromise and remove barriers that hinder harmonization among member countries. Other regional groupings are the European Community (EC), the Association of Southeast Asian Nations (ASEAN), and the North America Free Trade Agreement (NAFTA). Therefore, a study of perception of auditor independence by regions is needed to answer the research question, "Is the concept of independence similar among countries within one region that share similar cultural and environmental factors?"

Specifically, the study examines the effects of four variables on the perception of two subject groups (auditors and financial analysts) with respect to auditor independence in three countries (Saudi Arabia, the State of Kuwait, and the United Arab Emirates). The four variables are: (1) the percentage of total office revenues generated from the client; (2) whether management advisory services (MAS) are provided in addition to the external audit; (3) the number of months client fees remain unpaid; and (4) whether a relative of a member of the audit staff is employed by the client.

The remainder of this paper is organized as follows: Section 2 presents a discussion of the relevant issues and the development of testable hypotheses; Section 3 describes the experimental design. This is followed by data analyses and the results of the study in Section 4; Section 5 provides limitations and conclusions of the study.

2. RELEVANT LITERATURE AND DEVELOPMENT OF HYPOTHESES

Cross-Cultural Studies

Several studies have examined the impact of culture on accounting and financial reporting (Bloom & Naciri, 1989; Agacer & Doupnik, 1991; Riahi-Belkaoui & Picur, 1991; Merchant et al., 1995; Chow et al., 1996; Ralston et al., 1997; Harrison et al., 1999). Bloom and Naciri (1989) concluded that significant differences in the standard-setting process of nine countries are due to cultural differences. Agacer and Doupnik (1991) found that differences in the perception of auditor independence were significantly related to the differences in culture among countries and concluded that harmonization of auditing standards would be difficult to achieve. Riahi-Belkaoui and Picur

(1991) found that the meaning of accounting concepts varies in the manner with which they can be recognized, grasped or understood by users from different cultural groups working for the same global organization. Harrison et al. (1999) found Chinese culture affects managers' decision as to the continuance of unprofitable projects (when compared to their U.S. counterparts).

Many studies have focused on country groupings based on accounting and economic variables (Nair & Frank, 1980; Nobes, 1983; Doupnik, 1987; Doupnik & Salter, 1993). Each of these studies based their classifications on accounting aspects such as measurement and disclosure practices, accounting practices or judgmental aspects. Alternatively, other studies utilized auditing characteristics to focus on country characteristics (e.g. Hussein et al., 1986; Wood, 1993).

A number of studies have investigated the professional and work characteristics of accountants across cultures. In a study of American CPAs and British Chartered Accountants, Shoenthal (1987) attributed the differences between the two groups to auditing procedures, professional ethics, educational preparation, training and culture. Other studies have examined the effects of national culture on accounting and harmonization (e.g. Nair & Frank, 1980; Choi & Mueller, 1992; Ueno & Wu, 1993).

Studies of Auditor Independence

Various aspects of independence have been studied on a within-country basis, in the United States, the U.K., Canada, West Germany, and Malaysia. Most of the empirical studies, however, have been conducted in the U.S. Ward (1998) suggests that the significant international differences that exist in independence rules may be due to differences in cultures' view on what is seen as ethical behavior. He suggests that, "we should get state-by-state differences sorted out before we tackle the world" (Ward, 1998, p. 34).

However, a review of the existing literature on auditor independence shows that there are currently no studies that examine the regional perception of auditor independence.

Since differences in the perception of auditor independence have been found between countries, examinations of smaller units are needed. Examining perception of countries in the same region is a logical next step in the search for consensus of perception. Many studies have suggested that harmonization of accounting or auditing may be enhanced with less opposition if standards are constructed for an individual grouping of countries that share homogeneous factors (Doupnik, 1987; Rivera, 1989; Wood, 1993; Ward, 1998). It is assumed that the inhabitants of these countries share similar factors that affect their perception and understanding of concepts. However, there is no empirical research examining whether countries with homogeneous factors have a similar understanding of concepts. A review of the literature further suggests that regional harmonization should be first undertaken prior to global harmonization. Regional harmonization of auditing standards should face less opposition than that of global harmonization.

Hypothesis Development

Two primary null hypotheses and eight null sub-hypotheses were developed to test the independent variables. The main justification of these hypotheses is that culture has been shown to be a major obstacle to harmonization. The inhabitants of different countries may have different perceptions of the concept of independence, notably that of "independence in appearance." Alternatively, countries with similar cultures that possess homogeneous factors should have similar perceptions of auditor independence. Determining if regional differences exist is a necessary prerequisite to "sorting out" global differences (Ward, 1998). Thus, the following null hypotheses are suggested:

H1: There is no difference between auditors in Saudi Arabia, the State of Kuwait, and the United Arab Emirates in their perception of the risk of losing independence.

H2: There is no difference between financial analysts in Saudi Arabia, the State of Kuwait, and the United Arab Emirates in their perception of the risk of losing independence.

Official pronouncements and prior research suggest there are specific factors that may affect the perception of the risk of losing independence. Such factors include: (1) one client providing a large portion of the auditor's revenues; (2) the auditor providing management advisory services (MAS) to the client; (3) the audit firm having a financial interest (e.g. past due fees) in the client; and (4) the client's employment of a relative of a member of the audit staff.

Client Size

When one client is the source of a large portion of an accounting firm's revenue, an independence problem could exist or be perceived to exist (Lowe and Pany 1996). This issue is frequently raised and discussed in the accounting literature. Some researchers found that to have a client that is the source of a large portion of a firm's revenue can affect the perception of independence vis-à-vis that client. However other researchers found the perception of independence was not affected by such a relationship.

Pany and Reckers (1980) asked a sample of shareholders to examine the ability of the auditor to resist pressures under various conditions. These conditions included the issue of client size in combination with gift size and discount size. They chose 1% and 10% of office revenue respectively to approximate a small-to-average-size client and a large client. They found that client size did not appear to have a significant effect, but it was noted that in all cells the mean score of the larger client level of the size of a client factor exceeded the mean score of the smaller client level. This meant that less confidence was expressed for audits of large clients.

Lindsay et al. (1987) examined the effect of fifteen auditor-client relationships. There are a number of relationships which significant numbers of users (financial analysts and bankers) saw as impairing independence, which include the issue of client size.

Mutchler et al. (1997) investigated why auditors often fail to give "soon-to-be-bankrupt" companies a modified opinion. They found that larger clients were less likely to receive modified opinions than smaller companies (even after controlling for the probability of bankruptcy, default status, and other factors). The reduced likelihood of giving modified opinions to the large clients may indicate a lack of independence by auditors toward their largest revenue sources.

From the above discussion, additional empirical investigation is warranted to see whether the auditors and financial analysts of three developing countries in one region will perceive client size as an important factor that may impair the independence of the external auditor. This suggests the following sub-hypotheses (in the null form):

H1.1: There is no difference between auditors in Saudi Arabia, the State of Kuwait, and the United Arab Emirates in their perception of risk of losing independence when an audit firm has a relatively large percentage of its revenue derived from a particular client.

H2.1: There is no difference between financial analysts in Saudi Arabia, the State of Kuwait, and the United Arab Emirates in their perception of risk of losing independence when an audit firm has a relatively large percentage of its revenue derived from a particular client.

Management Advisory Services (MAS)

Providing MAS raises questions of auditor objectivity and independence. For example, providing such services may force the auditors to audit their own work (Clikeman, 1998). The question of whether providing MAS would harm independence has been extensively debated and is the most prevalent topic for independence-related research. The effect of MAS on independence has been examined extensively in the U.S. Researchers from other parts of the world that have examined the effect of MAS on independence include Lindsay et al. (1987) in Canada; Gul (1987) in Australia; and Gul and Yap (1984) in Malaysia.

A number of studies support the argument that MAS increases an audit firm's independence or that providing MAS does not significantly affect perceptions of financial statement reliability (Hartley & Ross, 1972; McKinley et al., 1985; Pany & Reckers, 1988). However, several studies found that auditor independence was perceived to be impaired when MAS services are provided (Pany & Reckers, 1980; Shockley, 1981; Brody et al., 1998).

Because of the conflicting results of previous research and because of requirements of the rules of conduct in Saudi Arabia and Kuwait which prohibit a CPA from rendering MAS to external audit clients, the MAS-independence issue requires additional research, and therefore represents an important variable in this study. Therefore, the following sub-hypotheses (in the null form) are suggested:

H1.2: There is no difference between auditors in Saudi Arabia, the State of Kuwait, and the United Arab Emirates in their perception of risk of losing independence when an audit firm provides MAS to a client.

H2.2: There is no difference between financial analysts in Saudi Arabia, the State of Kuwait, and the United Arab Emirates in their perception of the risk of losing independence when an audit firm provides MAS to a client.

Past Due Fee

Section 101.02 (a) of the Professional Standards (2000) states that "Independence will be considered impaired if, during professional engagement, or at the time of expressing an opinion, the firm had or was committed to acquire any direct or material indirect financial interest in the enterprise . . ." Past due fees are considered loans which imply a financial interest in the company (Bailey, 1992). Unless audit fees are paid in advance, auditors risk losing fees if their audit decisions conflict with the wishes of their client. Unpaid fees, therefore, may provide audit clients an opportunity to exert pressure on auditors to revise their opinion. On the same question of whether an audit firm's independence would be considered impaired with respect to a client whose fees for the preceding year are unpaid and past due, the AICPA Ethics Committee ruled (ET 191.103):

> Independence of the member's firm is considered impaired if when the report on the client's current year is issued, billed or unbilled fees, or a note receivable arising from such fees,

remain unpaid for any professional services provided more than one year prior to the date of the report (AICPA Professional Standards, 2000b ¶ 4459).

Thus, the variable "past due fee" is selected to operationalize "financial interest in the enterprise," and the following sub-hypotheses (in the null form) are provided:

H1.3: There is no difference between auditors in Saudi Arabia, the State of Kuwait, and the United Arab Emirates in their perception of risk of losing independence when an audit firm has fees remaining unpaid by a particular client for a relatively long period of time.

H2.3: There is no difference between financial analysts in Saudi Arabia, the State of Kuwait, and the United Arab Emirates in their perception of risk of losing independence when an audit firm has fees remaining unpaid by a particular client for a relatively long period of time.

Family Member of the Audit Staff Employed by Client

Personal relationships such as those arising from family bloodlines and marriage give rise to circumstances that may impair a CPA's independence (AICPA Professional Standards, 2000b). This becomes more relevant in countries known to value close family ties. Rule of Conduct 101 prohibits relationships that impair a CPA's independence through direct financial interests, material indirect financial interests, or other involvement. The employment of a relative of a member of the audit staff by the client is selected to represent and operationalize "personal relationship and protection of someone else's interest."

To avoid ambiguity for subjects, a specific type of employment for the relative of a member of the audit staff had to be selected. The employment must include job activities that are somewhere between bookkeeping and management level. The position of computer programmer was selected because this is a type of employment whose activities are not obviously management level or obviously bookkeeping. The use of "a relative" of a member of the audit staff instead of "the spouse" is motivated by the type of countries included in the study. These countries are family oriented and described as possessing collectivism cultural value, which means that an individual is not isolated from relatives and will work for their interests. The above discussion suggests the following sub-hypotheses (in the null form):

H1.4: There is no difference between auditors in Saudi Arabia, the State of Kuwait, and the United Arab Emirates in their perception of risk of losing independence for an audit firm where a family member of the audit staff is employed by the client.

H2.4: There is no difference between financial analysts in Saudi Arabia, the State of Kuwait, and the United Arab Emirates in their perception of risk of losing independence for an audit firm where a family member of the audit staff is employed by the client.

3. METHODOLOGY

Independent Variables

As discussed in the previous section, four treatment variables were selected in this study of the perception of auditor independence. These include: (1) the percentage of total office revenues generated from the client; (2) whether management advisory services (MAS) are provided in addition to the external audit; (3) the number of months client fees remain unpaid; and (4) whether a relative of a member of the audit staff is employed by the client.

Countries with similar cultural and environmental factors should have similar perceptions of independence since differences in cultural factors have shown to be the cause of the differences in the perception of auditor independence (Agacer & Doupnik, 1991). For this study, data was gathered in three countries with similar culture and possessing homogeneous environmental factors. Therefore, in addition to the four treatment variables, "homogeneous cultural and environmental factors" was employed as a non-repeated grouping variable. This construct was operationalized by a grouping variable with three levels (the three countries involved in the study: Saudi Arabia, the State of Kuwait, and the United Arab Emirates).

Countries Selected

The purpose of this study was to examine the regional perception of auditor independence. The three countries of Saudi Arabia, the State of Kuwait, and the United Arab Emirates were selected based on the following criteria: (1) they share similar cultural and environmental factors; (2) all three countries follow auditing standards and/or accounting laws that directly or indirectly stress both the appearance and fact of independence; and (3) they belong to the same regional organization.

The primary criterion in the selection of countries was that these countries share similar cultural and environmental factors. The international accounting literature has suggested that accounting practices are shaped and formed by their environments (Nobes, 1983, 1984; Arpan & Radebaugh, 1985; Hofstede, 1987; Schreuder, 1987; Perera, 1989; Riahi-Belkaoui & Picur, 1991). Hofstede (1983) grouped the three countries in one cluster because they have similar indexes of cultural values – high Power Distance, high Uncertainty Avoidance, lower Individualism, and high Masculinity. Ronen and Shenkar (1985) classified Saudi Arabia, the State of Kuwait, and the United Arab Emirates in one cluster based on four attitudinal variables – work goals, values, needs, and job attitudes.

Muller et al. (1991) and Hussein et al. (1986) identified type of economy as one of the major environmental factors that affects the development of accounting and auditing. According to Choi and Mueller (1992), inventory methods, accounting for accretion or discovery of natural resources, audit function, and other accounting and auditing procedures all have some relevance to the type of economy involved. The economies of the three countries in the study depend on exploitation of a natural resource – oil. As to the type of economic system, the three countries fall into a category known as "capitalist-statist" (Belkaoui, 1985, p.46).

Additionally, these countries share the following: (1) they are at a similar stage of economic development; (2) they have similar ruling bodies (ruled by families); (3) they share the same primary language (Arabic) and English is often used in each country as the language of business; (4) they share the same primary religion (Moslem); (5) their legal systems are mainly based on Islamic law; and (6) they have similar educational levels. In summary, these countries can be grouped together according to the above environmental and cultural factors. Therefore, the first criterion that the three countries share similar cultural and environmental factors was met.

The second criterion required that countries have similar auditing standards and/or accounting laws that stress both the appearance and the fact of independence for the external auditor. Needles (1985, p. 26) defines concepts of independence as "independence in fact and in appearance." All three countries follow auditing standards and/or accounting laws that directly or indirectly stress both the appearance and the fact of independence. The reason for including this criterion is to show that the results of this study would be free from the confounding effect of different laws concerning the concepts of independence.

The third criterion required that countries be members of a regional organization. Currently, countries in all parts of the world are grouping themselves primarily for economic and political reasons. As a consequence, different areas of endeavors, of which the accounting profession is an example, are being integrated into a harmonized system. The willingness to belong and then to compromise is an important criterion because enforcement power is one of the success tools for any harmonization process. One example is the European Community (EC). In 1981, similar economic, social, and political goals drove Bahrain, Kuwait, Oman, Qatar, Saudi Arabia, and the United Arab Emirates to establish the Gulf Cooperation Council (GCC). One of the results of the efforts of GCC is the proposal for regional auditing regulations to regulate the auditing profession across these countries. When finalized, member states are required to adopt and follow the regulations. Therefore, the criterion of belonging to a regional organization is met because the three countries are members of the same regional organization.

Subjects

This study examines the perception of two respondent groups. It compares the perceptions of auditors and financial analysts. Financial analysts were chosen as a surrogate group for investors or creditors. The selection of these groups of subjects was motivated by the need to obtain a general perception of two groups whose opinions are valued when establishing or setting new standards. Financial analysts are sophisticated users of financial statements. Most (1994, p. 5) suggests that "financial analysts have become important influencers on accounting standard-setting and harmonization, both directly and through their professional associations." Auditors' opinions are important in this study because of their familiarity with the concept of independence and for their role in implementing the auditing standards.

In this study, the financial analysts of national commercial bank institutions in Saudi Arabia, the State of Kuwait, and the United Arab Emirates were chosen to represent financial statements' users. Financial analysts of loan departments and investment departments were selected to be included in this study. Financial analysts from the commercial national banks were selected because of the lack of national organizations representing this group in these countries. Another reason for selecting this group of financial analysts was because they represent a well-informed and important segment of financial statement users in these countries. The reason for choosing national banks in Saudi Arabia and the State of Kuwait is because only banks with more than 50% of the capital owned by local shareholders are permitted to do business within their borders. To be consistent with respect to the remaining country, United Arab Emirates, this study limited the subjects of user groups to include only those who are working with national commercial banks.

Data Collection

Due to the physical distance of the countries included in this study, data necessary for this study was obtained using the medium of a mail survey. The questionnaire was initially reviewed and tested in a pilot study involving Saudi Arabian academicians and auditors. A number of steps were taken to increase responses. The questionnaire included a cover letter requesting cooperation in responding to the survey and guaranteeing the anonymity of the individual and the firm. An official letter from King Saud University requesting that the respondent cooperate and answer the questionnaire was included. A space was provided for the respondent to write his or her address for a copy of the study's results. For the auditor subject group in the three countries, a follow-up letter with a copy of the questionnaire was sent four weeks after the first attempt. The purpose of this letter was to thank them if they had already sent the questionnaire back and to ask them to ignore the attached questionnaire, or to remind the respondent to answer and send the attached questionnaire. Each questionnaire included a postage-paid return envelope.

Trips were made to the three countries to collect the data for the two subject groups. Since the number of auditors allowed to practice in each country is relatively small, this study solicited the opinion of all auditors actively involved in external audits. For Saudi Arabia, the list of auditors came from the Saudi Organization for Certified Public Accountants (SOCPA). The list indicated that 216 auditors practiced (with permission) in the area of external audits. For the State of Kuwait, the list was obtained from the Kuwaiti Accountants and Auditors Association (KAAA). The list showed 52 auditors were permitted to practice and were actually practicing in external audits. For United Arab Emirates the list was obtained from the Commercial Directory of United Arab Emirates. The list showed 102 auditors were allowed to conduct the external audit throughout the seven Emirates.

For the user groups (financial analysts) the survey instrument was carried to the targeted bank and distributed to the bank's financial analysts including the directors of the loan departments and investment departments. The respondents had the choice of filling the questionnaire and submitting it in person or mailing it back using the postage-paid envelope provided. The goal of the visits was to see how many respondents could understand and were willing to answer the questionnaire. Because of the difficulty in accessing individual financial analyst in each bank in the three countries, the heads of the investment and credit department in each contacted bank were given a number of questionnaires to distribute among the financial analysts in their departments. In Saudi Arabia, 110 questionnaires were distributed; in the State of Kuwait, 75 questionnaires were distributed; and in United Arab Emirates, 84 questionnaires were distributed.

Research Instrument

The research instrument used in this study was developed by Agacer and Doupnik (1991). The instrument involved a scaling task. Each subject was presented with seventeen scenarios, one of which was a repeated scenario. Figure 1 shows an example of a scenario.

Scenario 1:	
Client size (as a percentage of office revenues)	3%
MAS rendered	Yes
Number of months client's fees remain unpaid	12 months
Relative of a member of the audit staff of the CPA firm is employed as a computer Programmer by client	Yes
Risk that external auditor's independence may become impaired: very low risk 1 2 3 4 5 6 7 8 9 very high risk	

Fig. 1.   Example of Scenario Used in the Study.

Each scenario represented one of the 16 possible combinations of two levels of the four treatment variables: client size; provision of MAS; number of months client's fees remained unpaid; and employment by the client of a family member of a member of the audit staff. Each subject was asked to indicate the level of risk that the auditor independence may become impaired along a numerical scale from one (very low) to nine (very high risk). Thus, the dependent variable in this study was the risk that an audit firm's independence may become impaired. The sixteen scenarios were randomly ordered to minimize any possible bias due to order and learning effects. Figure 2 shows the two levels for each treatment.

Independent Variables	Treatment Levels	
	(Low)	(High)
Client Size (as a percentage of office revenues)	3%	10%
MAS rendered	No	Yes
Number of months client fees remain unpaid	3 months	12 months
Relative of a member of the audit staff of the CPA firm is employed as a computer programmer by client	No	Yes

Fig. 2.   Treatment Levels of the Independent Variables.

The choice of the high and low level of the treatment is based on Agacer and Doupnik (1991) which states:

> The choice of the 10% to indicate high level for the variable client size was based on the Accountants International Study Group's 1976 recommendation that the auditor should refrain from accepting engagement for which the fee constitutes 10% or more of the total fee income. Choosing the low treatment level for the same variable presented a problem in that the difference should not be too obvious as to direct the subjects into a no choice position, e.g. the choice of 1% vs. 10%. The selection of 3% appeared to offer more of a choice vis-à-vis 10% than 1%. The selection of 12 months to represent the high treatment level for the variable "number of months fees remaining unpaid" was based on the AICPA Ethics Ruling that independence may be impaired if more than one year's fees due from a client remain unpaid (ET 191.03). Again, the choice for the low level of three months was arbitrary to provide a less clear choice than one month as against 12 months. For the variables "MAS provided" and "member of family employed by client" the use of "yes" to represent the high treatment level and "no" for the low level are obvious.

The instrument contained full instructions. Additional information includes a hypothetical audit firm described as a national firm and a hypothetical audit firm described as having shares of stock that are publicly traded. Based on this information, each subject was asked to indicate the risk of impairment of independence in each scenario. Additional questions were included at the end of the instrument to collect demographic data about the respondents.

Before using this instrument, a pilot study was conducted involving Saudi academicians and CPAs to make sure that Agacer and Doupnik's instrument is valid in obtaining perceptions of independence from inhabitants of that part of the world. The result showed that this instrument could be used for its purpose. Scenarios were translated into Arabic by a competent person and then translated back to English by a different person to insure that the translated measurement carried the same meaning as the English original. The questionnaire was available in two languages, Arabic and English, and the respondent had the choice of using either the English or the Arabic version of the questionnaire.

4. DATA ANALYSIS

The experimental design called for repeated judgment by individual subjects across the sixteen scenarios (scenario seventeen is a duplicate). The experimental design is a repeated-measure block design with one grouping factor and four trial factors (Winer, 1971). The grouping factor, which is defined as "homogeneous cultural and environmental factors," has three levels corresponding to the three countries. The four trial factors correspond to the four treatment variables – each has two treatment levels.

Responses

Of the 370 questionnaires mailed to the auditor group, 148 were completed and returned (40%). Out of 216 questionnaires sent to Saudi auditors, 93, or 43%, were returned and used in the analysis, and nine questionnaires were undelivered or returned blank. In the State of Kuwait, out of the 52 questionnaires mailed, 21 were completed and returned (40%), and three were either undelivered or returned blank. For the United Arab Emirates (U.A.E.), 102 questionnaires were mailed. Thirty-four (34) were completed and returned for a response rate of 33%, and seven (7) were either undelivered or returned blank.

For the financial analysts group, questionnaires were distributed through the heads of either the credit or investment departments of the national commercial banks. Out of 110 questionnaires distributed in Saudi Arabia, 42 were returned completed and usable (response rate of 38%). In the State of Kuwait, 75 questionnaires were distributed, and 20 were used in the analysis (a response rate of 26%). In the United Arab Emirates, 84 questionnaires were distributed and 21 were returned completed for a response rate of 25%. Many of the questionnaires provided to department heads were not subsequently distributed to financial analyst employees. One justification given by some of the department heads was that those returned questionnaires represented the views of the more experienced financial analysts in the bank.

A summary of the demographic data collected from the auditor respondents is shown in Table 1. The auditor-respondents from the three countries exhibited similarities among the demographic characteristics. A majority of these respondents across the three countries had either U.S. or European certification, held bachelor's degrees, had more than 10 years of experience, and were between 36–45 years of age.

For the financial analysts, the three countries also possessed similar demographic characteristics. A majority of respondents did not hold any certificate, and had bachelor's degrees. Most respondents from Saudi Arabia and the United Arab Emirates were between the ages of 36–45 years of age, and had more than ten years' experience. The respondents from the State of Kuwait were younger and less experienced.

Test of the Reliability of the Instrument

The reliability of the instrument used in this study was tested using Cronbach's alpha. The test was applied to all auditors and financial analysts, and resulted

Table 1. Demographic Information for Auditor and Financial Analyst Groups.

Demographic Data	Auditor Group				Financial Analyst Group			
	Total	Saudi Arabia	Kuwait	U.A.E	Total	Saudi Arabia	Kuwait	U.A.E
Type Of Firm:								
Local	35.0%	39.1%	41.2%	6.2%				
National	30.0%	33.3%	17.6%	25.0%				
International	35.0%	27.6%	41.2%	68.8%				
Professional Certificate:								
No Certification	29.5%	31.4%	35.3%	12.5%	72.6%	66.7%	84.6%	85.7%
Arabic Certificate	23.5%	31.4%	0.0%	6.2%	3.2%	4.8%	0.0%	0.0%
Asian Certificate	5.0%	3.5%	0.0%	18.8%	22.6%	26.1%	15.4%	14.3%
USA/European Cert.	42.0%	33.7%	64.7%	62.5%	1.6%	2.4%	0.0%	0.0%
Level Of Education:								
Less than College	1.7%	1.2%	0.0%	6.3%	6.4%	2.4%	23.1%	0.0%
Bachelor's Degree	69.75	72.0%	70.6%	56.2%	62.9%	61.9%	76.9%	42.9%
Master's Degree	21.0%	22.1%	11.8%	25.0%	27.5%	33.3%	0.0%	42.9%
Ph.D. Degree	7.6%	4.7%	17.6%	12.5%	3.2%	2.4%	0.0%	14.2%
Experience:								
Less than a Year	0.8%	1.2%	0.0%	0.0%	6.4%	0.0%	30.8%	0.0%
1–4 Years	6.7%	7.0%	11.8%	0.0%	9.7%	7.2%	23.1%	0.0%
5–10 Years	16.8%	18.6%	5.9%	18.8%	24.2%	23.8%	30.8%	14.3%
More than 10 Years	75.7%	73.2%	82.3%	81.2%	59.9%	69.0%	15.3%	85.7%
Age:								
Between 20–35 Years	20.2%	20.9%	11.8%	25.0%	37.1%	40.4%	46.2%	0.0%
Between 36–45 Years	50.4%	51.2%	47.0%	50.0%	50.0%	54.8%	30.7%	57.1%
More than 45 Years	29.4%	27.9%	41.2%	25.0%	12.9%	4.8%	23.1%	42.9%

in alpha coefficients of 0.93 and 0.92, respectively. This indicates how well the treatment variables were captured in the construct of "impairment of independence." Additionally, the reliability of the instrument was tested for each country. The alpha coefficients for Saudi Arabia, the State of Kuwait, and the United Arab Emirates ranged from 0.92 to 0.95 for auditors and from 0.86 to 0.93 for financial analysts.

Test of Consistency within Subjects

To test the subjects' response consistency, an additional scenario was included (scenario #17) in the research instrument which was the exact replication of scenario #4. To test the null hypothesis that there is no significant difference between the means of the two identical scenarios, a paired comparison t-test was performed with each country and across countries for the two subject groups. Results of the t-tests for both groups (auditors and financial analysts) and for within each country failed to reject the null hypotheses of no group differences between means of the identical scenarios. Thus, subjects appear to have responded consistently to the various scenarios.

Results of Hypotheses Testing

The objective of this study was to test whether two subject groups of three countries, which were located in one region and shared similar environmental, economic, political, and cultural factors, had similar perceptions of auditor independence. The two primary hypotheses of no group differences were examined by testing for between subject effects of the grouping variable, similar cultures.

The results presented in Table 2, Panel A, failed to reject the two primary null hypotheses (H1 and H2) of no group differences for the auditors' group, and the financial analysts' group as it was expected that the inhabitants of similar cultures would have similar perceptions.

Thus, no significant differences between groups of countries for the two subject groups, and across the four treatment variables were found. This is confirmed by looking at the results for the eight sub-hypotheses (H1.1 through H2.4) which were tested by examining the interactions between the grouping variable and each of the four treatment variables. The results of these tests are shown in Table 2, Panel B.

In summary, the results of tests conducted did not indicate any significant differences among groups for two subject groups or significant differences among the treatment variables.

Table 2. Anova Results for Tests of Hypotheses.

Panel A: Tests Of The Two Primary Hypotheses For Between Group Effect:

Source:	Anova SS	Mean Square	F Value	Pr > F
Auditor Group . . . . . . (H1)	35.77	17.88	0.55	0.575
Financial Analyst Group . . . . (H2)	23.96	11.80	0.36	0.700

Panel B: Tests Of The Sub-Hypotheses For Wtihin Subject Effects For Two Sub-Groups:

Source:	Anova SS	Mean Square	F Value	Pr > F
Auditor Group:				
Hypothesis 1-1[a]	11.52	5.76	1.09	0.3400
Hypothesis 1-2[b]	3.70	1.85	0.57	0.5677
Hypothesis 1-3[c]	26.67	13.34	1.79	0.1707
Hypothesis 1-4[d]	6.78	3.39	0.33	0.7207
Financial Analyst Group:				
Hypothesis 2-1[a]	14.69	7.35	0.75	0.4745
Hypothesis 2-2[b]	5.64	2.82	0.50	0.6055
Hypothesis 2-3[c]	3.04	1.52	0.24	0.7837
Hypothesis 2-4[d]	1.17	0.58	0.07	0.9295

[a] No Group – Client Size Interaction Effect.
[b] No Group – MAS Interaction Effect.
[c] No Group – Fee Interaction Effect.
[d] No Group – Relative Interaction Effect.

5. SUMMARY AND CONCLUSIONS

Limitations

The contributions of any study must be evaluated within the context of its limitations. One of the limitations of this study is commonly attributed to survey research methods. There is always the possibility that sample subjects misunderstood the purpose of the research or misunderstood the questionnaire. However, the purpose of the research was explained and detailed instructions were provided to each subject so as to avoid any ambiguity which could have altered the results. Second, the results may not be generalized beyond the three countries under examination. Lastly, data gathered from banks (financial analysts) limits the generalizability of the results of the data to financial analysts working for national commercial banks only.

Discussion of Findings and Implications

The two primary null hypotheses tested in this study were that no difference in the perceptions of the risk of losing independence exists among auditors (H1) and financial analysts (H2) in Saudi Arabia, the State of Kuwait, and the United Arab Emirates (U.A.E.). The results of the statistical tests conducted in this study have failed to reject the two primary null hypotheses as expected with respect to the four variables considered. The eight sub-null hypotheses related to the four treatment variables for the two subject groups all failed to be rejected at the 0.05 level. This indicates that no significant differences exist between auditors or financial analysts in Saudi Arabia, the State of Kuwait, and U.A.E. regarding the impact of each of the four variables on their perception of auditor independence.

Thus, this study supports the claim that the perception of auditor independence is sensitive to culture. The findings of this study suggest that the process of harmonization should be and could be achieved first on a regional basis. This could lead later to harmonization involving more regions until worldwide internationalization is achieved.

In conclusion, the results of this study showed that wide agreement on concepts can be achieved as a prerequisite for harmonizing auditing standards regionally. Moving the effort toward regional harmonization is needed to speed up the process of harmonization and to overcome some of the several obstacles standing in the face of harmonization. Among these are different cultural values, different political systems, different legal systems, different languages, different accounting objectives, different religions, different levels of education, different levels of economic development, and different levels of capital markets. Other major obstacles are the lack of enforcement power by the International Accounting Standards Committee (IASC), the lack of representation by smaller countries in both the drafting stage and the final decision stage, and the lack of recognition of different circumstances in different countries.

To overcome these obstacles, the plan for harmonizing auditing standards should focus first on regions rather than on a country-by-country basis before worldwide harmonization can be attained. This argument is supported by the movement of establishing regional economic integration among countries in one region having similar cultural, political, and economic goals. Thus, economic integration has given the governments of member countries the power to set standards in cooperation with professional accounting groups. Consequently, enforcing the standards is made more effective through the action of the governments of member countries. The European Community (EC) exemplifies this where any directive passed by the organization is automatically adopted by all member countries as law.

Thus, it had been shown that harmonization is easily achieved through a regional approach. The involvement of regional professional accounting organizations will make the acceptance of international standards easier in a number of ways. First, the regional professional accounting group represents a smaller number of countries. The task of promoting understanding among member countries and sensitizing them to differences in each other's needs is made easier because of the smaller number of countries involved. Second, the regional professional accounting group is able to formulate regional auditing standards that are either modified according to the needs of the member countries or are exactly similar to existing international auditing standards. Because of the involvement of the governments of member countries and the efforts of the regional professional accounting group, successful harmonization of auditing standards in the region becomes a certainty.

Since this study has shown that Saudi Arabia, the State of Kuwait, and U.A.E. have similar perceptions of auditor independence, international and regional audit firms can then develop a set of rules and procedures to be followed by their employees throughout the region without fear of impairing an auditor's independence. Potential cost savings could be realized by having one set of rules for more than one country.

The contributions of this study include the following: (1) it provides a framework within which factors should be used in grouping or clustering homogeneous countries; and (2) it adds knowledge to the international accounting and finance areas by providing evidence as to the similarity of perception of auditor independence within one region. Because of these contributions, this study is able to provide guidance to international bodies actively involved in the difficult task of harmonization.

REFERENCES

Abu-Ghazaleh, T. (1989). Policy Challenge to IFAC Council. *The Financial Times Limited: World Accounting Report*, (January), 64.

Agacer, G., & Doupnik, T. (1991). Perception of Auditor Independence: A Cross-Cultural Study. *The International Journal of Accounting, 26*, 220–237.

American Institute of Certified Public Accountants (2000a). SEC Proposes Sweeping Rules; Ripple Effect could Impact Firms that Audit Private Companies. *The CPA Letter, 80*(7), 1–8.

American Institute of Certified Public Accountants (2000b). *AICPA Professional Standards*. New York, NY: American Institute of CPAs, Inc.

Arpan, J., & Radebaugh, L. (1985). *International Accounting and Multinational Enterprises*. Boston and New York: Warren, Gorham, and Lamont.

Bailey, J. (1992). Audit Fee Effects on Auditor Independence: Prospect Theory. Unpublished Ph.D. Dissertation, The University of Nebraska-Lincoln.

Belkaoui, A. (1985). *International Accounting*. Westpot, CT: Quorum Book.

Beresford, D. (1990). Internationalization of Accounting Standards. *Accounting Horizons*, (March), 99–107.

Bloom, R., & Naciri, M. (1989). Accounting Standard Setting and Culture: A Comparative Analysis of the United States, Canada, England, West Germany, Australia, New Zealand, Sweden, Japan, and Switzerland. *The International Journal of Accounting*, *24*, 70–97.

Brody, R. G., Lowe, D. J., & Pany, K. (1998). CPA Business Relationships with Audit Clients: Effects on Loan Officer Judgments. *Commercial Lending Review*, *13*(2), 59–60.

Carmichael, D. R. (1999). In Search of Concepts of Auditor Independence. *The CPA Journal*, *69*(5), 31–43.

Choi, F., & Mueller, G. (1992). *International Accounting* (2nd ed.). Englewood Cliffs, NJ: Prentice-Hall, Inc.

Chow, C. M., Kato, Y., & Merchant, K. A. (1996). The Use of Organizational Controls and their Effects on Data Manipulation and Management Myopia: A Japan vs. U.S. Comparison, *Accounting, Organizations and Society*, *21*, 75–92.

Clikeman, P. M. (1998). Auditor Independence: Continuing Controversy. *Ohio CPA Journal*, *57*(2), 40–43.

Doupnik, T. (1987). Evidence of International Harmonization of Financial Reporting. *The Journal of Accounting Education and Research*, *23*(4)(Fall), 47–67.

Doupnik, T., & Salter, S. (1993). An Empirical Test of A Judgmental International Classification of Financial Reporting Practices. *Journal of Internationa Business Studies*, (First Quarter), 41–60.

Frank, W. (1979). An Empirical Analysis of International Accounting Principles. *Journal of Accounting Research*, *17*(Autumn), 593–605.

Gul, F. (1987). Field Dependence Cognitive Style as a Moderating Factor in Subjects' Perception of Auditor Independence. *Accounting and Finance*, *27*(May), 37–48.

Gul, F., & Yap, T. (1984). The Effects of Combined Audit and Management Services on Public Perception of Auditor Independence in Developing Countries: The Malaysian Case. *The International Journal of Accounting Education and Research*, *20*(Fall), 95–105.

Harrison, P. D., Chow, C. W., Wu, A., & Harrell, A. M. (1999). A Cross Cultural Investigation of Managers' Project Evaluation Decisions, *Behavioral Research in Accounting*, *11*, 143–160.

Hartley, R., & Ross, T. (1972). MAS and Audit Independence: An Image Problem. *Journal of Accountancy*, (November), 42–52.

Hofstede, G. (1983). Dimensions of National Cultures in Fifty Countries and Three Regions. In: J. Deregowski, S. Dziurawiec & R. Annis (Eds), *Explications in Cross-Cultural Psychology*. Lisse, Scotland: Swets and Zeitlinger B.V.

Hofstede, G. (1987). The Cultural Context of Accounting. In: B. Cushing (Ed.), *Accounting and Culture*. Sarasota, FL: American Accounting Association.

Hussein, M., Bavishi, V., & Gangolly, J. (1986). International Similarities and Differences in the Auditor's Report. *Auditing: Journal of Practice and Theory*, (Fall), 124–133.

Kinney, W. R., Jr. (1999). Auditor Independence: A Burdensome Constraint or Core Value. *Accounting Horizons*, *13*(1), 69–75.

Lindsay, D., Murphy, M., & Silvester, H. (1987). Independence of External Auditor: A Canadian Experience. *Advances in International Accounting*, *1*, 169–189.

Lowe, D. J., & Pany, K. (1996). An Examination of the Effects of Type of Engagement, Materiality and Structure on CPA Consulting Engagements with Audit Clients. *Accounting Horizons*, *10*(4), 32–51.

McKinley, S., Pany, K., & Reckers, P. (1985). An Examination of the Influence of CPA Firm Type, Size, and MAS Provision on Loan Officer Decisions and Perceptions. *Journal of Accounting Research*, *23*(Autumn), 887–910.

Merchant, K., Chow, C., & Wu., A. (1995). Measurement, Evaluation and Reward of Profit Center Managers: A Cross-Cultural Field Study. *Accounting, Organizations and Society*, *20*, 619–638.

Most, K. (1994). A Critique of International Accounting Theory. *Advances in International Accounting*, *6*, 3–14.

Mueller, G., Gernon, H., & Meek, G. (1991). *Accounting: An International Perspective*. Homewood, IL: Richard D. Irwin, Inc.

Mutchler, J. F., Hopwood, W., & McKeown, J. M. (1997). The Influence of Contrary Information and Mitigating Factors on Audit Opinion Decisions on Bankruptcy Companies. *Journal of Accounting Research*, *35*(2), 295–310.

Nair, R., & Frank, W. (1980). The Impact of Disclosure and Measurement Practices on International Accounting Classification. *The Accounting Review*, *40*(July), 426–450.

Needles, B., Jr. (Ed.) (1985). *Comparative International Auditing Standards*. Chicago, IL: American Accounting Association.

Nobes, C. (1983). A Judgmental International Classification of Financial Reporting Practices. *Journal of Business Finance and Accounting*, (Spring), 1–19.

Nobes, C. (1984). *International Classification of Financial Reporting*. London: Croom Helm.

Pany, K., & Reckers, P. (1980). The Effect of Gift, Discounts, and Client Size on Perceived Auditor Independence. *The Accounting Review*, (January), 50–61.

Pany, K., & Reckers, P. (1988). Auditor Performance of MAS: A Study of Its Effects on Decisions and Perceptions, *Accounting Horizons*, *2*(2), 31–38.

Perera, M. (1989). Towards a Framework to Analyze the Impact of Culture on Accounting. *International Journal of Accounting*, *24*, 42–56.

Puxty, A., Willmott, H., Cooper, D., & Lowe, T. (1987). Modes of Regulation in Advanced Capitalism: Locating Accounting in Four Countries. *Accounting, Organizations and Society*, *12*, 273–291.

Ralston, D. A., Holt, D., Terpstra, R. H., & Yu, K. (1997). The Impact of National Culture and Economic Ideology on Managerial Work Values: A Study of the United States, Russia, Japan, and China. *Journal of International Business Studies*, *28*(1), 177–207.

Riahi-Belkaoui, A., & Picur, R. (1991). Cultural Determinism and the Perception of Accounting Concepts. *The International Journal of Accounting*, *26*, 118–130.

Rivera, J. (1989). The Internationalization of Accounting Standards: Past Problems and Current Prospects. *International Journal of Accounting*, *24*, 320–341.

Ronen, S., & O. Shenkar. (1985). Clustering Countries on Attitudinal Dimensions: A Review and Synthesis. *Academy of Management Review*, *10*(3), 435–454.

Schreuder, H. (1987). Accounting Research, Practice, and Culture: A European Perspective. In: B. Cushing (Ed.), *Accounting and Culture*. Sarasota, FL: American Accounting Association.

Securities and Exchange Commission (2000). Revision of the Commission's Auditor Independence Requirements; Proposed Rule (File No. 57–13–00), Fed. Reg. 48, 148 (also: http://www.sec.gov/rules/proposed/34–42994.htm).

Shockley, R. (1981). Perception of Audit Independence: An Empirical Analysis. *The Accounting Review*, *4*(October), 785–800.

Shoenthal, E. (1987). Differences in the Characteristics of Certified Public Accountants And Chartered Accountants: An Obstacle to Harmonization. *The International Journal of Accounting*, *22*, 95–103.

Ueno, S., & Wu, F. (1993). The Comparative Influence of Culture on Budget Control Practices in the United States and Japan. *The International Journal of Accounting*, *28*, 17–39.

Ward, G. M. (1998). The Big-Five Battle: CPAs and Non-CPAs Square Off on Auditor Independence. *Financial Executive*, *14*(4), 32–36.

Winer, B. (1971). *Statistical Principles in Experimental Design*. New York: McGraw-Hill Book Company.

Wood, R. (1993). An Empirical Study of the Associations among Cross-National Audit Characteristics and Environmental Factors. Unpublished Ph.D. Dissertation, Saint Louis University.

3. THE RELATIONSHIP BETWEEN LARGE STOCK AND SMALL STOCK RETURNS IN A THIN EMERGING MARKET

Nabeel E. Al-Loughani

ABSTRACT

Various explanations have been suggested for the existence of a lead-lag price relationship between large and small company shares in many markets. The differential information hypothesis and the dynamic information environment hypothesis are two such explanations that has received some support. The present study examines the validity of these hypotheses in the Kuwaiti context. The study finds that large companies' stock prices lead small companies' stock prices in the short run during the bull phase. This finding is interpreted to be a result of industry differences, ownership structure, quality of information and the role of institutional investors.

INTRODUCTION

In a recent study, Hodgson, Masih and Masih (1999) examine the price movements of large and small stocks in Australia and find them to be linked by a lagged causal relationship. This type of investigation was previously undertaken by Connolly and Conrad (1991) and Martikainen, Perttunen and Puttonen (1995),

Research in Accounting in Emerging Economies, Volume 5, pages 43–51.
Copyright © 2003 by Elsevier Science Ltd.
All rights of reproduction in any form reserved.
ISBN: 0-7623-0901-6

but Hodgson et al.'s analysis shows that the direction of causality changes according to market trading conditions. Specifically, they show that small stocks provide the dominant price lead during the bull market phase but not in the bear phase, while large stock prices play an equally dominant role in both phases.

At the top of the list of factors that could induce a lead-lag relationship between large and small stocks returns is the notion of "differential information sets". The differential information hypothesis advanced by Atiase (1980 and 1985) postulates that information production increases with firm size. Moreover, if the costs of information search are fixed and constant across firm size, then it is more feasible to undertake research for mispricing in large firms than in small ones. Therefore, profits due to insider information trading are higher for large firms than for small firms.

Freeman (1987) rationalizes the assumption of constant information search cost across firms. He advances three elements that offset the higher search cost associated with large firms'complexity. First, large firms provide a greater variety of information than small firms. Second, large firms have a higher degree of coverage in the financial press. Third, large firms are more focused on by security analysts than small firms. Finally, if information production is dependent on costs that do not increase with size, then the effects of increasing search costs are less felt as firm size increases.

Another source of differential information is suggested by Grossman and Stiglitz (1976) who note that trading by informed investors partially reveals private information. And given that informed investor trading is more noticeable in small-firms, Atiase (1980) argues that partial signalling reduces the potential profit from small firm information more severely than profit from large firm information.

Finally, Anderson, Clarkson and Moran (1997) suggest that information risk plays a role in the pricing of small firms which suffer a significant information deficiency. The body of literature reviewed so far indicates that the costs of information search are fixed and constant and the incentive to undertake research for mispricing is greater for large firms than for small firms. This view can be interpreted to imply that larger firms will rationally provide a short term price lead for smaller firms.

An alternative view has been advanced by Hodgson, Masih and Masih (1999). They argue that the incentives to undertake information search about small firms are asymmetric, because, whilst the cost of information search may be constant, the potential payoff structure will change. Their argument is based on the observation that expectations about future returns are increased during periods of rising prices and optimistic sentiment. Furthermore, they note that, if prices are noisy, do not adjust instantaneously, and information search is a cost-benefit tradeoff between costs and expected returns, then the incentive to undertake information search will be related to the contemporaneons trading phase of the market. Accordingly, they postulate that, during optimistic periods in the stock market the high cost of information search for small firms may be outweighed by potential high profits for identifying and investing in small stocks. Therefore it is predicted that information flows from small stock prices to large stock prices during bull market periods.

Hodgson et al.'s (1999) hypothesis that investors will undertake information search on small stocks rather than large stocks during a bullish trading phase is based on: (1) the "leverage effect" associated with the high proportion of liabilities in the funding structure of small firms; (2) the high systematic risk of small firms; and (3) bullish periods' increased trading which reduces the probability that information mappers will observe private information trading.

This paper investigates the hypothesis that price movements of small stocks are always led by large stock prices versus the competing hypothesis that small stock prices lead large stock prices during bull phases, using Kuwait Stock Market data. Several reasons make this study particularly interesting. First, the Kuwait market is a small emerging market, dominated by trading in large stocks. Second, large Kuwaiti firms provide higher quality information than small firms. Third, small firms stock prices adjust slower than large firm stock prices as a result of thin trading in the market in general and the infrequent trading in small firms stocks in particular. Finally, prior studies indicate that the Kuwaiti market is inefficient (see for example, Al-Loughani, 1995, 2000; Al-Loughani & Chappell, 2000).

METHODOLOGY

Causality analysis will be used to examine the lead-lag relationship between large firms and small firms prices. The following autoregressive time series model is used to test for Granger-causality between the return of two groups of firms

$$\Delta S_t = \alpha_0 + \sum_{i=1}^{m} \alpha_i \Delta S_{t-i} + \sum_{i=1}^{m} \beta_i \Delta L_{t-i} + u_t \qquad (1)$$

where ΔS is the first difference of the logarithmic index of small firms, ΔL is the first difference of the logarithmic index of large firms, and u_t is a well behaved normally distributed error term. A common practice in causality testing is to arbitrarily set the lag length, m, for α_i and β_i in Eq. (1). However, results from Granger tests are sensitive to the selection of lag length. For that reason, results are obtained for lags ranging from one to six days in length. To carry out the causality test in Eq. (1), the F test statistics are calculated for the null hypothesis of no lagged causal influence by large firms prices on small firms prices. The null hypothesis is represented by $H_0: \beta_i = 0 \forall_i > 0$.

If the dependent and independent variables in Eq. (1) are reversed then the opposite hypothesis that small firms prices influence the prices of large firms can be examined in the same fashion.

A prerequisite for using Eq. (1) to carry out causality analysis in first differences is that the variables are both nonstationary and do not cointegrate. If, however, two variables have the same order of integration and a cointegration relationship exists between them, then Eq. (1) must be corrected by incorporating the lagged residuals from the cointegrating regression as an additional independent variable. In this case, evidence in favour of long-run causality is found if the coefficient on the error correcting term is significantly different from zero.

Therefore, it is necessary to determine the order of integration of the two variables and to test for cointegration between them prior to carrying out causality testing. The order of integration is determined by testing for unit root in the levels and first differences of the variables. This is carried out using the classical procedure of Dickey and Fuller (1979) which assumes an independent and identically distributed (iid) process.

As the ADF test relies on a parametric approach to deal with serial correlation and heterogeneity, its power is questionable. We therefore also test for unit roots using the Phillips-Perron (PP) test (Phillips, 1987; Phillips & Perron, 1988). The iid assumption of the ADF test is relaxed in the PP procedure, which imposes much weaker conditions on the error term. The PP is thus robust to a wide variety of serial correlation and time-dependent heteroskedasticity.

To test for cointegration the ADF and (PP) test statistics are applied to the residuals of the cointegrating regression

$$S_t = \beta_0 + \beta_1 L_t + \varepsilon_t \tag{2}$$

DATA AND RESULTS

The empirical results of this study are based on daily observations of the Large Cap and Small Cap indices prepared and published by Global Investment House. The Global Index is a market capitalization weighted index based on International Finance Corporation (IFC) formulas. The Large Cap and Small Cap Indices include, respectively, the largest and smallest ten companies in market capitalization.The sample data covers the period 3 January 1993–5 April 2000 and displays two distinct price phases. The bull phase coincides with the first part of the data set from 3 January 1993 to 22 November 1997 when the value of the Global Index soared by some 120 % from 44.72 to 99.01. The bear period coincides with the second part of the data set when the index declined by 37 % from 98.40 on 23 November 1997 to 62.24% on 5 April 2000. Daily returns are computed as first differences of logarithmic indices.

Table 1 reports the correlation coefficients between the returns of large and small stocks. The table shows that contemporaneous correlation between large stocks and small returns is positive and stronger during the bear phase than during the bull phase. The table also shows that the correlation between lagged large (small) stocks returns and small (large) stocks returns is positive but lower than the contemporaneous correlation. These results are different from those reported in previous studies (see, for example, Lo & Mackinlay, 1990).

Table 2 summarizes the basic statistical properties of large and small stocks returns. The average return of small stocks has clearly outperformed the returns of large stocks. This finding is consistent with evidence uncovering the small-firm effect in the majority of world stock markets. The stock returns are, however, more volatile for small firms than for large firms, a finding reported in earlier studies (see for example, Cohen et al., 1980). With the exception of large firms returns during the bear phase, the Ljung-Box statistics indicate significant autocorrelation in Kuwait stock market returns. The highest positive autocorrelation is observed for the return series of small firms during the bull market phase, with a first-order autocorrelation of 0.2895 indicating that about 8% of the daily return variation is predictable, using only the preceding day's returns. Interestingly, autocorrelation tends to be positive for small firms and negative for large ones, a finding inconsistent with previous studies (see Cohen et al., 1980). Thus, in general, it appears that the basic statistical characteristics of the Kuwaiti data are only partially similar to those used in earlier studies.

Tables 3 and 4 report the results of applying the ADF and PP tests of unit root and cointegration on the data set. The results in Table 3 indicate that the stock market indices are integrated of order one, while the stock returns are stationary. The results in Table 4 indicate that the null hypothesis of no-cointegration between

Table 1. Correlation Between Large Stock and Small Stock Returns.

	Full period	Bull market period	Bear market period
L, S	0.312	0.156	0.500
L_{t-1}, S	0.086	0.099	0.062
L, S_{t-1}	0.070	0.069	0.063

Table 2.   Summary Statistics of Stock Returns.

	Mean	SD	1	2	3	4	5
Full period							
L	0.00022	0.0086	0.0604	–0.0352	0.0018	–0.0435	–0.0003
			(6.567)*	(8.471)*	(8.476)*	(11.887)*	(11.888)*
S	0.00066	0.0096	0.2124	0.0542	0.0162	0.0264	0.0637
			(81.233)*	(86.524)*	(86.995)*	(88.257)*	(95.575)*
Bull market period							
L	0.00052	0.0084	0.0758	–0.0440	–0.0129	–0.0178	0.0028
			(6.800)*	(9.096)*	(9.293)*	(9.671)*	(9.680)
S	0.00159	0.0079	0.2895	0.0931	0.0438	0.0514	0.0540
			(99.290)*	(109.564)*	(111.845)*	(114.986)*	(118.449)*
Bear market period							
L	–0.0003	0.0089	0.0284	0.0185	0.0226	–0.0925	–0.0105
			(0.498)	(0.710)	(1.026)	(6.353)	(6.422)
S	–0.0011	0.0121	0.1218	–0.0075	–0.0484	–0.0425	0.0267
			(9.179)*	(9.214)*	(10.668)*	(11.791)*	(12.235)*

Figures in parenthesis are Ljung-Box statistics.
* Significant at the 5% level.

Table 3.   Unit Root Testing.

	Full period		Bull market period		Bear market period	
	ADF	PP	ADF	PP	ADF	PP
Stock Prices						
L	–1.412	–1.63	0.417	0.54	–2.173	–2.30
S	–2.521	–2.14	2.802	1.73	–0.011	–0.03
Stock Returns						
L	–39.869*	–36.124*	–31.826*	–29.850*	–24.068*	–25.921*
S	–34.162*	–35.318*	–25.354*	–26.845*	–21.972*	– 19.274*

* Significant at the 5% level.

large and small stock prices cannot be rejected. This finding does not indicate that large stocks and small stocks prices are bound together by a long run equilibrium relationship. Accordingly, the only valid relationship that can exist between them is in terms of an ordinary first-differenced VAR.

The results of testing for short-run causality between large firms and small firms prices are given in Table 5. From this table, results for the bull and bear

Table 4. Testing for Cointegration between Large Stock and Small Stock
Prices.

Full period		Bull market period		Bear market period	
ADF	PP	ADF	PP	ADF	PP
−2.60	−2.43	−2.94	−2.81	−0.49	−0.67

Table 5. Testing for Causality between Large Stock and Small Stock
Returns.

K	Full period		Bull market period		Bear market period	
	L → S	S → L	L → S	S → L	L → S	S → L
1	0.84	2.34	4.81*	2.76	0.01	1.93
2	1.56	2.62	3.63*	2.30	0.54	1.50
3	1.18	2.34	3.55*	1.85	0.36	1.08
4	0.96	1.58	3.16*	1.18	0.73	0.83
5	0.83	1.58	2.76*	1.21	0.75	1.24
6	0.69	1.43	2.33*	1.12	0.82	1.22

market periods reject neither that large firms prices do not cause small firms
prices, nor that small firms prices do not cause large firms prices. These results
suggest that the stock prices of large and small firms are independent during
the bear phase. The results of testing for causality during the bull phase however,
indicate that rising large stocks prices induce future variations in small stock
prices and not the other way around.

In summary, the information leadership exists only during the bull phase and
is constrained to the short term horizon and flows from large stocks towards small
stocks. This finding is partially consistent with the differential information
hypothesis and completely inconsistent with the competing hypothesis postulat-
ing that the incentive to undertake costly information search is outweighed by
the benefits derived from investing in small stocks during bull markets.

CONCLUSION

This paper examines whether the lead-lag relationship between large and small
Kuwaiti firms changes according to market trading conditions. A preliminary
analysis of the data set indicates that the basic statistical properties of the

Kuwaiti stock price series are only partially similar to the ones used in previous studies. In the short term, it was found that large stocks provide a lead in the bull phase. This finding constitutes further evidence on the informational inefficiency of the Kuwaiti market. The dominant role of large stock prices during the bull phase can be explained in light of industry differences, ownership structure, quality of information and the role of institutional investors. First, large firms are, largely, part of the more mature and less risky industries. Second, these firms are owned and controlled by prominent merchant family members who play the major role in setting the tone for stock trading. Third, large firms' information (i.e., financial reports) are more informative, timely and reliable than those of small firms which are usually released several months after the end of the operating year. Finally, stock trading has recently become largely dominated by institutional investors who prefer large firms stocks due to the liquidity constraints associated with small firms.

REFERENCES

Al-Loughani, N. E. (1995). Random Walk in Thinly Traded Stock Markets: The Case of Kuwait. *Arab Journal of Administrative Sciences, 3*, 189–209.

Al-Loughani, N. E. (2000). The Analysis of Causality Relationship between Share Prices and the Number of Shares Traded in the Kuwaiti Stock Market (In Arabic). *Journal of Economics and Administrative Sciences*.

Al-Loughani, N. E., & Chappell, D. (2000). Modeling the Day-of-theWeek Effect in the Kuwait Stock Exchange: A non-linear GARCH Representation. *Applied Financial Economics*.

Anderson, D., Clarkson, P., & Moran, S. (1997). The Association Between Information, Liquidity and Two Stock Market Anomalies: The Size Effect and Seasonalities in Equity Returns. *Accounting Research Journal, 10*, 6–19.

Atiase, R. K. (1980). Predisclosure Informational Asymmetries, Firm Capitalization, Earnings Reports and Security price Behavior. Unpublished Ph. D. Thesis, University of California, Berkeley, CA.

Atiase, R. K. (1985). Predisclosure Information, Firm Capitalization and Security price Behavior Around Earnings Announcements. *Journal of Accounting Research, 23*, 21–36.

Connolly, R. A., & Conrad, J. (1991). Cointegration and Lagged Security Price Adjustment. Working paper, Kenan-Flager Business School, Chapel Hill, University of North Carolina, October.

Dickey, D. A., & Fuller, W. A. (1979). Distribution of the Estimators for Autoregressive Time Series with a unit Root. *Journal of the American Statistical Association, 74*, 427–431.

Freeman, R. N. (1987). The Association between Accounting Earnings and Security Returns for Large and Small Firms. *Journal of Accounting and Economics*, (July), 195–228.

Gross, S. J., & Stiglitz, J. E. (1976). On the Impossibility of Informationally Efficient Markets. *American Economic Review, 70*, 393–407.

Hodgson, A., Masih, A., & Masih R. (1999). Dynamic price Relationships between Small and Large Stocks. *Accounting Research Journal, 12*(2), 151–162.

Lo, A., & Mackinlay, A. C. (1990). When are Contrarian Profits Due to Stock Market Over-reaction? *Review of Financial Studies*, *3*(2), 175–205.

Martikainen, T., Prettunen J., & Puttonen, V. (1995). The Lead-lag Effect Between Large and Small Firms: Evidence From Finland. *Journal of Business Finance and Accounting*, *22*(3), 449–453.

Phillips, P. C. B. (1987). Time Series Regression with a Unit Root. *Econometrica*, *55*, 277–301.

Phillips, P. C. B., & Perron, P. (1988). Testing for a Unit Root in Time Series Regressions. *Biometrika*, *75*, 335–346.

4.   PRICING THE INTERNAL TRANSFER OF FUNDS: EVIDENCE DRAWN FROM ISLAMIC BANKING

Taha Eltayeb Ahmed

ABSTRACT

Transfer pricing systems are needed to evaluate the performance of respon-sibility centres in decentralized organizations where resources are transferred internally. In a banking organization, the most important resource is the funds that business units mobilize. Previous studies of the subject in conventional banking have found that various alternative rates are used to price the internal transfer of funds including the market rate, the average cost of funds and the marginal cost of funds. In Islamic banking, where interest-bearing deposits do not exist, these rates may not be applicable.

This paper examines the transfer-pricing problem in Islamic banking organizations through an empirical study of three Islamic banks operating in the Middle East. It is found that Islamic banks use Murabaha or Mudaraba to price the internal transfer of excess liquidity between the responsibility centres. The Murabaha and Mudaraba are the most popular Islamic banking instruments used, respectively, to allocate resources and mobilize funds. It is also found that an Islamic bank's choice of an invest-ment strategy can have far reaching implications for transfer pricing systems, because the investment strategies determine the organization

Research in Accounting in Emerging Economies, Volume 5, pages 53–70.
© 2003 Published by Elsevier Science Ltd.
ISBN: 0-7623-0901-6

structure. An Islamic bank may either adopt the "pooling of funds" strategy or the "separation of funds" strategy.

1. TRANSFER PRICING

Business organizations have grown in size to a large extent in an unprecedented move to capture new markets. Central management had to adopt new structural and/or procedural arrangements, such as decentralization, so as to run these big organizations effectively. However, decentralization would necessitate the need for more advanced control systems, which would enable the center to monitor the autonomous units. The role of such systems is to help with the evaluation of the performance of the autonomous units and make sure that there is complete congruence between the overall goals of the organization and those of its divisions. Moreover, central management needs to coordinate the activities of the divisions so as to maximize the overall profit of the organization. However, in order to put in place a good performance evaluation system and maintain effective coordination, central management needs to measure the contribution of each unit to the profit of the organization. But how could central management evaluate the performance of decentralized units when resources are transferred internally? A common solution to this problem is what is known as transfer pricing.

Transfer pricing was first reported by Hirshleifer (1956) who described it as a maximization problem. According to him, the optimal solution is achieved when "the marginal cost of the selling division equals the marginal gross profit of the buying division." During the sixties, a large number of researchers looked at the problem in industrial firms using mathematical techniques. For an elaborate review of this part of the literature see Abdel-Khalik and Lusk (1974).

Although the transfer pricing problem was studied from strategic, behavioristic and accounting perspectives, the latter seemed to be the dominant to the extent that the issue is looked at as an exclusively accounting problem. Accountants suggest various methods to be used as alternative mechanisms to price transfers. These mechanisms include full cost, full cost plus, standard variable cost, dual-pricing and market price. A comprehensive coverage of accounting methods can be found in Kaplan (1977).

Commercial banks are geographically diversified so as to reach customers. The location of the branch plays a great role in deciding its business. Paik (1963) studied the branches of Chemical Bank and found that some branches were "deposit-heavy" while others were "loan-heavy." A central pool was created to receive the excess funds of the "deposit-heavy" branches and allocate them to "loan-heavy" branches so as to be lent. As branches were structured as profit centers, a transfer pricing mechanism was instituted to compensate "deposit-heavy" branches. This pricing mechanism was found to be very important for the effectiveness of the branch performance report.

Credit was given to Paik (1963) because his study was the first to examine the issue of the control of deposits and loans (transfer pricing) in commercial banks. Funds are a banks primary raw material. At any point total sources should equal total uses so that, overall, the bank is in balance. However, when a bank is divided into smaller units for which profitability has to be reported separately (products, markets, customer groups, responsibility centers) sources may not equal uses in each unit. Those units with excess funds trnasfer it to a central pool from which deficient units satisfy their loan requirements. In such circumstances, an appropriate transfer rate must be set to compensate suppliers and to charge borrowers.

The rate set for the internal transfer of funds, as a credit to suppliers and a charge to users, is the most critical variable in commercial banking. This rate should be set at a level that will ensure a profitable return on all products and customer relationships. It should also motivate or influence responsibility centers to improve reported profits while at the same time maximize, overall, the bank income (Jewes, 1976).

At least four major decision areas are greatly affected by the internal pricing policy a bank may use. Tyler and Fridholm (1975) summarized these decision areas as follows:

(1) Key strategic decisions: These include pricing and re-pricing corporate relationships, pricing services and adding or eliminating branches.
(2) Measurement of responsibility centers: Due to factors such as the branch location, its size and limits on branch managers, some branches are "deposit-heavy." In order to establish a fair and objective evaluation of each branch, an acceptable transfer price needs to be determined for transferable funds.
(3) Measurement of customers and products: Banks provide a variety of services to a large number of customers. Using the wrong rate can alter the reported contribution of specific customers or products from a level of high profitability to one of significant loss.
(4) Proper allocation of resources to competing uses: Establishing the correct internal rate is the key factor in determining whether certain liabilities should be incurred, or whether various categories of loans and securities should be acquired. Payne (1977) reported that: "profitability can be changed by as much as 500% merely by selecting a different funds transfer rate or even by computing the rate differently."

In theory there are various alternative rates to be used as internal transfer pricing mechanisms in order to reimburse a producing profit center and charge the user. The market rate, the average cost of funds and the marginal cost are among the most mentioned rates (Holden, 1972). Paik (1963) found that the Chemical Bank had been using the following three transfer pricing formulas:

(1) The rate of interest on excess funds equals: Net earnings from loans and investments of the entire bank divided by the average deposits of the entire bank less reserve requirements.
(2) The rate of interest on excess funds equals: Net earnings from investments of the entire bank divided by the average deposits of the entire bank less reserve requirements less average loans of the entire bank.
(3) One rate is established for demand deposits and another rate for time deposits. "Deposit-heavy" branches are credited with revenue at these rates applied to the amount by which their demand and time deposits exceed their loans. "Loan-heavy" branches are charged at a rate related to one of these two rates according to their uses.

2. ISLAMIC BANKING

The most remarkable phenomenon in the financial world recently is, perhaps, the advent of Islamic banking. Not only confined to Muslim countries, Islamic banks have expanded to the Far East, Europe and even as far as the Bahamas.

The first Islamic bank was established in Dubai in 1975, and since then the number has been increasing steadily. Currently there are about a hundred and fifty Islamic banks and financial institutions in not less than thirty countries. In Iran, Pakistan and the Sudan, decrees were issued ordering the Islamisation of the whole financial sector. Moreover, many known conventional banks operating in Muslim countries have established divisions, windows or subsidiaries to offer Islamic banking services (City Bank and ABC in Bahrain, Arab Bank in Jordan, Samba and Saudi-Holandi Bank in Saudi Arabia, etc.).

This background leads us to the question: What constitutes an Islamic bank? The safest definition of an Islamic bank is, perhaps, a bank that is strictly observing the laws of Islam, often called Shariah. Shariah affects banking because the payment and receipt of interest are strictly prohibited as they constitute Riba (usury).

It also provides, as an alternative, an amalgam of Islamic mechanisms some of them are commodity-backed sale contracts of exchange, and the others are profit sharing mechanisms. Siddiqi (1981) explains the latter as follows:

Instead of being promised a fixed return in the form of interest, depositors in saving or time deposits will be promised a definite share in the profits accruing on their deposits as the result of their investment by the bank. The entrepreneurs seeking advances from banks will promise the banks a share of the profits accruing to them. Should the enterprise end in a loss, the loss is regarded as an erosion of equity and banks get back what remains.

For the purpose of this paper it is, perhaps, better to look at an Islamic bank in terms of sources and uses of funds and the cost or return associated with its transactions. I use the term resources to mean deposits and/or any other resources that can be invested.

In order to mobilize resources, Islamic banks use the Mudaraba mechanism, which is merely a profit-sharing arrangement. Islamic banks collect time and saving deposits at no promised rate of interest. Instead, they promise a fixed share of profits, if any. In case of a loss it will be borne by deposit holders. Current deposits are mobilized as Wadia or Quard-Hassan, which means that funds are deposited with the bank for the purpose of safe keeping and are accordingly fully guaranteed. A critical question to ask here is: What is the cost of these funds? The answer to this question is very much related to the transfer-pricing problem.

On the assets side, Islamic banks use different financial instruments to manage relationships with customers. The most famous Mudaraba contract is trust funding whereby the whole capital is provided by the bank, profits are shared according to predetermined ratios but losses are borne by the bank. The Musharaka is a joint venture in which both parties contribute capital. Profits are shared according to agreed predetermined percentages whereas losses are shared according to the mix of capital. The rest of the implemented instruments are sale contracts and Ijara arrangements, although each one takes a different form. Murabaha is the sale of goods at cost plus a margin. In the Salam and Istisna sale contracts the bank advances cash as a purchase price of goods to be produced and delivered in the future.

In both cases the price is set and agreed to when the contract is signed. Ijara is an operating lease contract but different, in many respects, to the conventional operating lease. In contrast the Ijara-Wa-Iqtina is an operating lease contract providing for an option of ownership. It is evidently clear that none of these instruments looks like conventional lending where money is advanced at a fixed rate.

From the above review, it is evident that in Islamic banking practice, interest rates do not exist in the mobilization or in the investing of funds. Therefore Islamic banks may not be able to use any of the transfer pricing methods that are based on interest. Hence, the relevant questions to ask are the following: How do Islamic banks price the internal transfer of funds? And what are the implications for performance measurement of responsibility centres and resource allocation?

The rest of this paper is organized as follows. In the following section, I briefly outline research methodology, followed by a description of the results of our empirical work. I then discuss the results in Section 4 and provide some concluding remarks in Section 5.

Transfer pricing in Islamic banking was first reported by Ahmed (1987) in a case study of one of the pioneering Islamic banks in Sudan. This paper builds on Ahmed's propositions, utilizing the potential of the case method which gained much attention and respect in business research.

The researcher studied three Islamic banks in the Middle-East relying mainly on interviews with branch managers and head office senior executives. The cases include one bank in the Sudan, one in Saudi Arabia, and a third in Bahrain. The objective is to examine and describe the organizational structures and processes related to transfer pricing in Islamic banks and, in addition, provide a diagnosis that would lead to conceptualization and generalization (Hagg & Hedlund, 1979).

3. EMPIRICAL EVIDENCE

In this part of the paper, transfer pricing systems in three Islamic banks are described. It has to be noted that the visits to the sample banks and the interviews were conducted during the period 1996 to 1999.

EL-Tadamon Islamic Bank (EIB)

El-Tadamon Islamic Bank (EIB) was established in the Sudan in 1981 as a public shareholding company with an authorized capital of US$ 50 million of which US$ 20 million is paid up. The bank has at the moment a network of 22 branches, its total deposits are equivalent to US$ 100 million and total assets are equivalent to US$ 117 million. The bank operates according to the guidelines of the Sharia, and has a Sharia Supervisory Board.

EIB draws on the basic ideas and purposes of conventional transfer pricing, although the Islamic principles and the regulatory environment (ceiling policy enforced by the central bank) affect its operations very much. The transfer pricing system is based on three factors:

(1) The central bank has enforced a ceiling policy on the utilization of funds whereby half of the funds available stay idle.
(2) The management established a central pool at headquarters and structured it as a center responsible for approving investment ventures that are normally large funding requirements beyond the scope of branch managers.

(3) The Murabaha, being the dominant Islamic instrument in EIB business, has a rate ascertainable in advance.

Based on these factors, the transfer pricing system works as follows: The head office allocates ceilings to all branches from the total ceiling authorized by the central bank. The amount a branch gets is based on its administrative scale, regardless of its volume of deposits. The scaling of branches was assumed to have taken care of their deposit potentials. Normally about 30% of the total ceiling of the bank is not allocated but kept by headquarters pool for two purposes:

(1) To meet the need for funds at headquarters to facilitate top management investment decisions. Headquarters pool is in itself a profit center.
(2) To keep a reserve to allocate to efficient branches when needed. It is impossible to claim back part of the ceiling if it is already allocated to the branches. This allows continuous control of investment funds at head-quarters for efficient use.

To illustrate how the system works, I collected two sets of data from the books of the central pool. Branch (A) approved ceiling of ten million dinars was exhausted during the first eight months of the year. However, the balance of branch deposits to date was thirty million dinars. Head office approved an additional two million dinars, to be funded from the branch own excess deposits retrieved from headquarters. The branch was not charged for this amount because it used its own resources. The additional ceiling would come from the central pool reserve kept back by headquarters. Branch (B) approved ceiling of five million dinars was exhausted during the first nine months of the year. The balance to date of branch deposits was exactly five million dinars.

The branch had no more resources, but many investment opportunities. The branch manager obtained approval to advance a further one million dinars and the funds were drawn from another branch through headquarters. Branch (B) was charged a fee for the use of transferred funds calculated at the minimum required rate on the Murabaha operations which was (2%) per month. The corresponding credits of these charges are normally pooled and allocated later, on a pro-rata basis, to branches with excess deposits. The investment manager, commenting on this transfer pricing system, asserted that:

> The system is needed for management purposes. It permits headquarters to allocate the investment ceiling efficiently and rewards branches whose excess deposits have been used elsewhere.

The reward is mainly in terms of the internal competition between branches for resources. Branches compete over the budget, staff and the investment ceiling as well as seeking the branch promotion to a higher scale and accordingly an increase in the branch-managers' discretion to approve funding facilities

National Commercial Bank (NCB)

National Commercial Bank (NCB) was the first Saudi bank to be established with 100% local capital. It started operations in Mekka (the Muslims' holy city) in mid-forties and gradually expanded into a multi-branch commercial bank. Although it started as a pure conventional bank, NCB management opted for partial Islamization in 1990.

To implement the new strategy, a division for Islamic banking services was established headed by an assistant to the chief executive officer. There are, at the moment, 57 branches in this division, mostly newly established Islamic units. The remaining units are converted into conventional branches. The conventional side of the bank (composed of two hundred branches) is still doing business as usual. The overall deposits of the bank are about fifty billion Saudi Riyals (equivalent to 13.4 billion U.S. dollars).

The flow of funds between the branches in NCB is a daily routine controlled by a computerized accounting system. Each branch has a control account with the head office and it keeps a control account for head office in its general ledger.

All transactions involving the payment or receipt of money between a branch and another and between a branch and head office are recorded in these control accounts. If the balance of a branch account with head office is in credit this means that the branch has excess cash advanced to other branches through head office. A debit balance, of course, means deficiency covered by advances from other branches.

The pricing of the transferred funds is based on the Saudi Inter Bank Overnight Rate (SIBOR), which is, at the moment, 4% per annum. Branches with excess funds, as reflected in the monthly average balance of the control account, are credited at the SIBOR after deducting 7% for the legal reserve. Deficient branches are debited with an amount based on the multiplication of the same rate by the balance of the control account but without accounting for the legal reserve.

The Islamic branches can not use SIBOR or any other rate as Islamic funds do not carry predetermined fixed rates. Although the Islamic branches are still part of the computerized accounting system and maintain control accounts with head office, the excess or deficiency of funds are managed by divisional management and not head office. Total excess funds minus any deficiencies and legal reserve are the funds under divisional management. In fact all of the Islamic branches have had excess funds all through the years, except for one case when a branch recorded a deficiency in August 1996.

Islamic Divisional Management utilizes available net excess resources on behalf of the branches on the basis of the Mudaraba arrangement. The resources are, directly or indirectly, invested following Islamic banking instruments with more emphasis on Murabaha, Musharaka, and Istisna. After deducting direct Mudaraba expenses, Islamic Divisional Management allocates the profits to the branches, on a pro-rata basis, according to individual branch contributions adjusted for legal reserve. It is worth noting that the allocated profits are actually realized, not figures plugged in for control purposes only. Profits allocated to a branch comprise a significant part of its revenues, accordingly, they affect its performance.

Deficient branches in any specific month are charged with a negative figure, accounted for in the branch profit and loss account, to be offset by future profit figures. The calculation of this figure is based on the multiplication of the rate of return of the excess funds, for the same month the branch has a deficiency, by the amount of the deficiency. Divisional management calls this "the opportunity cost."

Faysal Islamic Bank of Bahrain (FIBB)

FIBB is a Bahraini public holding company established in 1982 with authorized capital of two hundred million dollars of which one hundred is fully paid-up. Dar Al-Maal Al-Islami Trust (DMI) holds 53% of FIBB shares leaving the balance to other investors in the region. FIBB holds both an onshore and an offshore banking license issued by Bahrain Monetary Agency.

FIBB follows a unique investment strategy whereby customers' resources are separated from the bank's own resources. Customers' resources are further segregated in separate accounts or funds according to maturity. This strategy is generally known as the "separation of funds method." From the outset customers are required to make a choice of where they would like to have their funds invested. Available types of accounts or funds have different lives ranging from one week to thirty-six months, having ten choices in this range. Each separate account or fund, with a specific maturity, is a separate Mudaraba contract with different profit sharing terms.

A fund or an account is either restricted or unrestricted. In restricted accounts/funds investors put some restrictions on the activities of the bank while investing the funds. Restricted funds are measured in terms of units (unitized).

Unrestricted funds have no such restrictions and are measured in monetary terms (monetized), so they are banking accounts, although they are called funds. Savings mobilized by each fund are separately invested in assets of similar maturity. As funds have different profit sharing terms and asset structures, their rates of return noticeably differ. Rates of return are announced weekly when profits are allocated to investment accounts or units on accrual basis.

Funds are managed at the center by the treasury department, which selects the appropriate earning assets and manages liquidity for each fund. In doing so, liquidity is often transferred from one fund to another, creating a serious internal transfer-pricing problem. A fund that receives liquidity is better off, in terms of return, than another that gives away liquidity. To solve the problem, FIBB established a separate unique fund known as "Treasury Fund." There are no customer accounts in this fund and it is not advertised to the investors. It is merely a management tool to facilitate liquidity management and the internal transfer system. If a fund has excess liquidity, it is sent to this pool. Pooled funds are often invested in highly liquid earning assets that generate modest returns. Then, on the basis of profit-sharing, earnings generated by the "Treasury Fund" are allocated to the participating funds on a pro-rata basis according to the amount of funds transferred.

To transfer liquidity to a deficient fund the Treasury Fund would buy units (for unitized funds) or open an investment account (for monetized funds) in that fund. Therefore, it shares in the realized profits of the deficient fund. The Mudaraba is the Islamic mechanism underlying such profit-sharing arrangements.

4. DISCUSSION

Divisional banking organizations need transfer-pricing systems in order to allocate the shared resource-liquidity economically and efficiently. Margins, objectives, customers and product pricing as well as product policy are all dependent on the set transfer price(s). For the controlled unit, the transfer-pricing system greatly affects performance evaluation, so the choice of an internal pricing mechanism is an important one.

Divisional managers would naturally prefer systems that positively reflect on their financial performance evaluation. However, controllers should be able to ensure that such systems do not allow a division to gain at the expense of another one. The issue of fairness has always been at the heart of the transfer-pricing problem. It is difficult to allocate resources efficiently if the internal pricing mechanism is unfair to some divisions and/or managers.

In the cases I have covered, it has been found that funds and services have been transferred from one branch to another or from one autonomous unit to another. Excess funds of "deposit-heavy" branches and/or highly liquid investment funds are often transferred to deficient units through a central pool. The transferring branches/units pick up the cost of funds whereas the receiving branches/units enjoy the revenue.

The reviewed literature reveals that in conventional banking, interest rates play the major role in pricing the internal transfers. This is so because interest rates can objectively measure the cost and revenue of transferable funds and services. Moreover, interest rates are readily available whether on loans or on deposits.

Views are so much divided on the issue of the cost of funds in Islamic banking. Scholars argue that customers' funds have no cost for Islamic banks because Islamic banks do not promise their customers any returns on their deposits. An example of this view is found in Meeni's (1996) argument that:

> To switch over to Islamic banking, in its true form, it will be necessary that the bankers as well as the investors realize that there is no such thing as the cost of money and that they can not contract for the use of funds at a predetermined cost or rate.

He went on, noting that:

> No one can, however, predict with any certainty if the business will make a loss or a profit, and if the latter, how much. As such, the Sharia considers it unjust that the entrepreneur should bear the entire brunt of the uncertainties by committing to make a fixed return on investors capital. This prohibition strikes at the very root of the cost of money concept. To begin with, all money in a business is invested in the shape of equity. Since it is not known that the business will make a profit or incur a loss, this money may be considered zero cost money.

This view overlooks the fundamental economic principle that finance has a cost. The facts that Mudaraba funds are mobilized on profit sharing basis, and that profits or losses can not be known in advance do not make investment funds zero cost money. Equity finance in conventional markets has similar features as those of the Mudaraba, yet it has a cost. The cost of equity has been defined as the investors' required rate of return. Along the same lines of thinking, but contrary to Meeni's views, Al-Dehani et al. (1999) argued:

> Given that deposit account holders share with shareholders the same portfolio investment risk of the bank, the cost of deposit accounts financing should, ex ante, not be less than the minimum rate of return which shareholders expect to earn from investing their funds in a portfolio of projects of the same degree of risk as those in which the banks funds are invested.

So it is evident that Al-Dehani et al. recognize that deposits in an Islamic bank have a cost, defined as follows:

The minimum rate of return required by Investment account holders given the risk they bear.

In Islamic banking operations, there are no interest-bearing transactions on either side of the balance sheet. The alternative to interest-bearing transactions, for funds mobilization, on the funding side is the Mudaraba, which is a profit-sharing arrangement. On the assets side, there are an amalgam of Islamic instruments including Murabaha, Salam, Istisna and Ijara, which are asset-based sale or leasing contracts. Can any of these instruments serve as an effective mechanism to price the transfer of funds between business units of an Islamic bank?

It is evident that the banks studied for this paper differ in their choice of the instrument to use as a transfer pricing mechanism. El-Tadamon has been using the Murabaha, which is a sale contract with a mark-up, predominantly used to finance corporate and retail customers. Although management is aware that there are no real asset-based sale transactions between the branches of the bank, it uses the Murabaha to price internal transfers. El-Tadamon Islamic bank went for the Murabaha for three reasons: First, because Murabaha, unlike other forms, has readily available mark-up. Second, because Murabaha is the oldest in terms of implementation and the most understood. Third, examining the assets mix of the bank for the year 1998, it can be seen that Murabaha receivables have a noticeable share (21%) in the bank earning assets portfolio. Transfer pricing at El-Tadamon is a one-price Murabaha minimum mark-up system. Branches borrowing from the central pool are charged the minimum Murabaha mark-up of 2% per month on the funds internally received during the period.

The corresponding credit of these charges is allocated pro-rata to the branches transferring the excess funds. Hence the central pool plays a passive role in the system because it is neither a profit center nor a cost center. This factor limits its ability to influence branch behavior because it can neither subsidize nor penalize branches. Given that the maximum Murabaha mark-up on customers, as set by the central bank, is 3% per month, the receiving branches can at maximum generate a net margin of 1% per month on the funds internally received. However, charging customers the maximum Murabaha mark-up puts these branches and the bank as a whole at an extremely disadvantageous competitive position in the market.

Is the Murabaha a suitable and fair mechanism to use for transfer pricing? The answer to this question is not straight-forward. What is peculiar about the Murabaha, vis-à-vis other Islamic instruments, is its readily available mark-up.

But the Murabaha is a mechanism that is only relevant to pricing earning assets and not deposits. In Islamic banking, deposits are raised on the basis of the Mudaraba, which is a profit-sharing arrangement where no definite rates can be offered. Since investors bear the commercial risk of their deposits, the cost to the bank can be estimated as the customers' required rate of return, which in turn can be estimated using historically realized rates of return.

At Al-Tadamon, where Murabaha has been used for pricing the transfer of excess funds, the charge to deficient branches of 2% per month (24% per annum) on the funds received is far more than the average cost of deposits. Realized rates of return on deposits at the bank have never exceeded 12% per annum (8% in 1998).

This makes internally transferred funds far more expensive for deficient branches than customers' deposits. Consequently, if the deficient branches use the Murabaha to invest these funds they will have to charge the maximum mark-up of 3% per month (36% per annum) to generate a gross return of 12% per annum, before allowing for other costs such as bad and doubtful debts.

If they go for other instruments, such as Musharaka or Salam, deficient branches will also have to set prices higher than usual because of the high cost of internal funds. Therefore, because of their higher cost, internally transferred funds can only be used to finance assets with expected high return but also high risk. This may reduce the demand for internal excess funds, and motivate deficient branches to work hard to generate their own deposits.

The reward for the branches transferring their excess funds is a gross return of 2% per month (24% per annum) on the excess funds used by other branches. Since the average cost of deposits has been, at maximum, 12% per annum, then, these branches make a minimum definite net return of 1% per month (12% per annum) shown as internally generated revenue in the branch monthly profit report. As there seems to be no further costs or risks associated with these internal transactions, Murabaha-based internal transfer prices are, perhaps, more favored by the transferring branches than the receiving branches.

Unlike Al-Tadamon, both NCB and FIBB use the Mudaraba to price the internal transfer of funds. It can be seen that NCB Islamic division departed from the transfer pricing system maintained by its conventional mother company (NCB Corporation) because the system was based on SIBOR.

The Islamic division invests net excess funds in the market as Mudarib, i.e. working for a pre-determined percentage share of profits, if any, and the realized return becomes the transfer price. A branch maintaining surplus funds is credited with an amount arrived at by the multiplication of branch excess funds and the realized rate of return generated by the Mudaraba, after adjusting for the required liquidity reserves. A branch maintaining funding deficiency is debited with an amount arrived at by the multiplication of branch deficiency and the same Mudaraba realized rate of return.

To calculate this rate of return, divisional management divides the net income generated by the Mudaraba by net excess funds. The Islamic division central management is the fund manager, whereas the branches maintaining excess funds are the investors. The Islamic division central management plays a passive role. It is neither a profit center nor an investment center.

FIBB uses the Mudaraba to establish a fair transfer price for excess funds. However, the organizational units involved are autonomous funds, not branches. The central pool, called the "treasury fund", receives monthly income from deficient units (monetized or unitized) based on the performance of these units. Deficient monetized units pay the treasury fund income calculated at the average Mudaraba return per monetary unit, whether in dollar, dinar or riyal.

Unitized units pay the difference between cost and net asset value (NAV) multiplied by the number of shares/investment units. In case of surplus liquidity transferred to the "treasury fund", a monetized as well as a unitized unit is credited with an amount calculated by the multiplication of its surplus balance and the Mudaraba rate of return generated by the "treasury fund" in any specific month. The rate of return the "treasury fund" or any other fund generates depends on the maturity and quality of the earning assets of the fund. So rates of return differ from one fund to another and from one period to another.

Is the Mudaraba a suitable mechanism to use for transfer pricing of excess funds? The answer to this question is neither simple nor straightforward because of the complexity of the Mudaraba mechanism itself. Mudaraba is a profit sharing mechanism that has been used both in the assets and funding sides of the balance sheet of an Islamic bank.

On the funding side, depositors place their deposits with the bank in its capacity as Mudarib, i.e. working for a predetermined percentage share of profits, if any. The investors bear the commercial risk of their investments, but not any risks associated with the negligence and/or the misconduct of the Mudarib. Islamic banks, handling investment accounts, have so far differed on two distinct investment strategies; namely, the "pooling of funds strategy" and the "separation of funds strategy" (Karim, 1994).

In the first strategy, resources are pooled in a portfolio of earning assets. The Mudaraba investments pooled with other resources generate an average rate of return, if profits are realized. The Islamic division of NCB, following the pooling strategy, has been distributing profits to its depositors making around 5% average annual rate of return during the period 1994–1999.

In the second strategy, deposits are separated from other resources, and furthermore they are themselves segregated according to maturity, creating a variety of funds, each with its distinct portfolio of earning assets. As profit sharing percentages are also different from one fund to another, different funds generate different rates of return to their investors. Therefore, the separation of funds strategy results in multiple Mudaraba rates of return. FIBB, following the second investment strategy, has been distributing profits on a monthly basis at annual rates of return ranging between 5% and 8% for the different funds. The "treasury fund" has been generating annual rates of return ranging between 5% and 6%.

When Mudaraba is used to establish the transfer price(s) for excess funds, the set price(s) are dependent on the investment strategy of the bank. If the bank adopts the "pooling of funds" strategy, there will be one unique transfer price; the Mudaraba average rate of return for the period.

Our typical case, the NCB Islamic division, applies its unique rate across the borders crediting branches providing liquidity and debiting branches borrowing liquidity. This rate is the same one the division uses to credit Mudaraba investment accounts held by depositors. Since the cost of investment accounts (deposits) is estimated by proxy as the average realized rate of return on the Mudaraba, the transfer price becomes the average cost of funds.

On the face of it that seems fair, but in fact it is not, at least for the branches with surplus funds. Branches maintaining surplus funds receive a credit that may not satisfactorily motivate them, because the credit may just be equal to the cost of their deposits. Thus, the set transfer price may not provide a spread for the branches transferring their surplus funds. For the business units receiving the excess funds the transfer price resembles the cost of deposits.

Accordingly, for these units/branches, externally and internally generated funds seem to have the same average cost. Given the extra efforts and time management exerts on deposit mobilization, internally transferred funds appear to be cheaper and so more appealing. This may discourage unit/branch management from exerting efforts to generate their own customers' deposits; thus, defeating an important organizational goal.

However, if the bank adopts the "separation of funds" strategy, there appears to be multiple transfer prices, because separated funds generate different rates of return. There will be a different transfer price between the "treasury fund" and each of other funds when these funds receive liquidity from the central pool. But, when funds invest their excess liquidity through the central pool there is one transfer price applying across the borders; it is the "treasury fund" realized rate of return. FIBB case, I have at hand, shows that the first group of transfer prices – ranging between 5.5% and 8% – always tends to be larger than the second price – ranging between 5% and 6%.

The reason why the "treasury fund" rate of return is at the lower end is that the " treasury fund" invests considerable amount of its money in highly liquid assets because it is primarily a liquidity management vehicle. Furthermore, it is worth noting that if the separation of funds strategy is adopted, the organizational unit that is emphasized is the fund, which may or may not be a separate legal entity. This analysis leads us to the conclusion that a fund borrowing liquidity from the central pool pays a transfer price that is equal to its average cost of deposits, because this same rate is paid as return to depositors.

So, funds generating higher rates of return pay higher prices than those generating lower rates. This seems fair because, as it is observed at FIBB, the funds generating higher rates of return, and accordingly paying higher prices, have longer maturity.

When funds provide their excess liquidity to the central pool, they all receive the same single price (the treasury fund rate of return) which seems, in most cases, to be less than the fund average cost of deposits.

It seems that this single transfer price policy suffers from two major weaknesses. First, it is inconsistent with the multiple transfer prices controlling the movement of liquidity from the central pool to the funds. Second, a single transfer price is unfair to the funds providing liquidity in larger amounts and/or for longer maturity. A further important implication for the "separation of funds strategy" on transfer pricing is the issue of equity and fairness to investment account holders (depositors).

As each fund is a separate and different contractual relationship, depositors in each fund have to receive their equitable rate of return (including negative returns) as per the signed Mudaraba contract. If liquidity is transferred between different funds, the set transfer price(s) should serve the causes of equity and fairness. It seems that the only way to determine the required equity and to be fair to all parties is to look for market-based transfer price(s).

The view generally taken in transfer pricing is that transfer prices should be based on the outside market rate if the goods or services transferred are of a kind for which an outside market exists (Kaplan & Atkinson, 1990). Is this suitable for a banking organization? One may strongly argue that an outside market exists for the excess funds in banking organizations, yet a bank may not willingly allow its business units to invest surplus funds outside when such funds are needed internally.

There is a dysfunctional effect to such policy as the organization, overall, may be losing money if the deficient units may have good investment opportunities capable of generating returns higher than the market.

This is very likely in conventional banking where surplus funds placed in the market normally produce the money market rates. In contrast, Islamic banks can not place surplus funds in any form except profit sharing investment accounts (based on Mudaraba), which have so far been generating annual rates ranging between 3% and 8%. These rates of return have been in line with the prevailing conventional money market rates for similar maturity, although such accounts, at least theoretically, can also incur losses as per the provisions of the Mudaraba contract.

5. CONCLUSIONS

It is found that EIB has been using the Murabaha to price the transfer of funds between its operating branches, because of the Murabaha readily available mark-up and the noticeable emphasis of the bank on its use to generate earning assets. However, a transfer-pricing system based on Murabaha does not seem to be an efficient one because the Murabaha, being an asset pricing mechanism, may not be applicable for pricing internally transferred deposits.

A transfer price based on Murabaha mark-up may far exceed the average cost of deposits (defined as the realized rates of return on deposits), therefore penalizing the branches transferring excess liquidity.

In sharp contrast to EIB, both the NCB Islamic division and FIBB have been using the Mudaraba to price the internal transfer of funds. However NCB and FIBB differed over their choice of an appropriate investment strategy, to pool or separate resources, which has far reaching implications for transfer pricing systems. NCB has been implementing the "pooling of funds" strategy whereas FIBB has been implementing the "Separation of funds" strategy.

If an Islamic bank adopts the "separation of funds" strategy, the funds become the important control units. For an organization of such units, Mudaraba seems to be the most fair and equitable mechanism to price inter-fund transfer of liquidity. This is because, Mudaraba makes sure that investors in any fund are not offered guaranteed return, therefore preserving a basic Sharia requirement.

Secondly, as internal transfers are carried out at an arm's length, Mudaraba makes sure that a fund and, accordingly its investors, do not profit at the expense of other funds. Thirdly, as the figures indicate, Mudaraba rates of return have been in line with conventional market rates for similar maturity. However, the use of Mudaraba in "a separation of funds" situation results in a differential transfer pricing system. Multiple transfer prices are invoked when the central pool provides deficient funds with liquidity, while a single transfer price is applied when it receives liquidity.

To resolve this inconsistency it seems appropriate if the "treasury fund" segregates incoming liquidity according to maturity, generating different rates of return, and therefore multiple transfer prices.

If the Islamic bank adopts the "pooling of funds" strategy, the Mudaraba is still the most viable mechanism for setting transfer prices. However, because liquidity is pooled regardless of maturity, a single transfer price is worked out and used across the board to charge the branches receiving liquidity from the central pool and to compensate other branches providing their excess liquidity. The worked-out prices may not be fair to the branches transferring liquidity with longer maturity.

REFERENCES

Abdel-Khalik, R., & Lusk, E. J. (1974). Transfer Pricing – A Synthesis. *The Accounting Review,* (January), 8–23.

Ahmed, T. E. (1987). The Impact of Religion on the Management Control Systems of Banks: The Case of Islamization in the Sudan. Unpublished Ph.D. Thesis, University of Bath, U.K.

Al-Dehani, T., Karim, R. A., & Murinde, V. (1999). The capital structure of Islamic Banks under the contractual obligation of profit sharing, *International Journal of Theoretical and Applied Finance,* 2(3), 243–283.

Archer, S. (1991). Management Accounting and Strategic Decisions in the Banking Firm: A Note. Unpublished Paper, University of Wales, Bangor, U.K.

Kaplan, R. S. (1977). Application of quantitative models in managerial accounting: a state of the art survey. In: *Management Accounting – State of the Art.* Robert Beyer Lecture Series, University of Wisconsin Madison.

Kaplan, R. S., & Atkinson, A. A. (1990). *Advanced Management Accounting* (2nd ed.). Englewood Cliffs, USA: Prentice-Hall International incorporated.

Emmanuel, C. (1977). Transfer Pricing: A Diagnosis and possible solutions to dysfunctional decision-making in the divisionalized company. In: J. Sizer (Ed.), *Readings in Management Accounting.* Penguin Modern Management Readings.

Hagg, I., & Hedlund, G. (1979). Case studies in Accounting Research. *Accounting, Organization and Society,* 4(12), 135–143.

Hirshleifer, J. (1956). On the Economics of Transfer Pricing. *Journal of Business,* 29(3), 172–184.

Meenai A. A (1997). Developing New Modes of Investment, *New Horizon* (No. 6), *Journal of the Institute of Islamic Banking and Insurance.* London, U.K.

Karim R. A. (1994). Accounting Aspects of Profit Allocation Methods between Shareholders and Investment Account Holders in Islamic Banks. *Journal of Economics and Administrative Science,* (10), 165–197.

Paik, C. (1963). Use of Reports for Control of Branches: An Analysis of the Determinants of their Effectiveness with Particular Reference to Commercial Banks. Ph.D. Thesis, Harvard Business School.

Siddiqi, M. N. (1981). *Muslims Economic Thinking: A Survey of the Contemporary Literature.* International Center for Research in Islamic Economics. King Abdul Aziz University, Jeddah, Saudi Arabia.

Udoritch, A. L. (1970). *Partnership and Profit in Medieval Islam.* Princeton, NJ: Princeton University Press.

5. ENHANCING COOPERATION BETWEEN THE DEPARTMENT OF ACCOUNTING AT THE UNIVERSITY OF BAHRAIN AND AUDITING FIRMS: AUDITORS' PERCEPTIONS

Hasan Al-Bastaki and Sayel Ramadhan

ABSTRACT

The objective of this study is to examine auditors' perceptions concerning the areas and strategies to enhance cooperation between the Department of Accounting at the University of Bahrain and auditing firms. All auditing firms working in Bahrain (9 in number) were included in the study. A questionnaire was used to collect the data. Of the 91 questionnaires distributed, 63 were returned completed (a response rate of 69.2%). Descriptive statistics were used to analyze the data. The results indicate that the level of cooperation in the area of preparing qualified graduates is moderate, but low in the areas of training, workshops, seminars, consultancy and research. Lack of information about the areas of cooperation is a major obstacle which hinders cooperation. The most important strategies to enhance cooperation are: (1) request professionals in auditing firms to teach and participate in preparing and evaluating the accounting and training programs; (2) exchange visits between the faculty of accounting department and auditing firms; and (3) both the department of accounting and auditing firms should conduct joint research and consultancy services.

Research in Accounting in Emerging Economies, Volume 5, pages 71–94.
© 2003 Published by Elsevier Science Ltd.
ISBN: 0-7623-0901-6

1. INTRODUCTION

Cooperation between accounting educators and accountants in practice has been suggested as an important strategy for enhancing the accounting profession and practices in developing countries. The rapid changes in business environment make it essential for a dynamic partnership to be formed between accounting educators and accountants in practice. Many new accounting issues and problems being faced by developing countries require cooperative research efforts to solve. In addition, the profession must communicate to the academic community, the skills and knowledge necessary for practice and provide feedback on the strengths and weaknesses of accounting graduates. In turn, the academic community will incorporate the feedback received from those in practice, to re-engineer accounting curricula. Also, cooperation in the area of teaching will help by bringing in "real world" problems to classrooms and thus enhance learning and students' judgment and abilities to deal with and solve complex problems. This indicates that accounting educators must be concerned with whether they are educating students to meet the demands of current and future environments.

This study examines auditors' perceptions regarding the areas of cooperation between auditing firms and Departments of Accounting of universities, using the University of Bahrain as an illustration. The strategies for enhancing such cooperation will also be examined. This will strengthen the relationship between them and develop new areas of cooperation. Furthermore, evidence of changes in the practice of auditing would have significant implications regarding the common body of knowledge required for auditing and the future direction of accounting education.

The next section provides information about the current state of accounting education and practice in Bahrain. Section 3 reviews the relevant literature. Section 4 discusses the research method. Section 5 presents the results and their analysis. The last section summarizes the study and provides some recommendations which are likely to enhance the level of cooperation between accounting education and accounting practice.

2. THE CURRENT STATE OF ACCOUNTING EDUCATION AND PRACTICE IN BAHRAIN

Accounting Education

Accounting education in Bahrain is mainly provided by the University of Bahrain and some other specialized training centers such as the Bahrain Institute of Banking and Finance. The University of Bahrain is the only institution that offers a degree in accounting. The Department of Business and Management was established in 1982 within the then newly reconstituted Gulf Polytechnic. The department was given a mandate to update and diversify its curricula to meet the mounting needs of the rapidly expanding business community. The department installed a credit-hour-based program reflecting a one-track two-tier program. Within this program, intended to link student output to actual labor market demand, the department started offering an integrated Associate Diploma – Bachelor of Science track – the twin majors of Business Administration and Accounting. In 1992, a separate accounting department was established. Since then, it has continued to follow the one-track two-tier system at the Associate Accounting Diploma (AAD) and the Bachelor's (B.Sc.) levels.

The undergraduate accounting curriculum includes a number of compulsory and elective courses (66 credit hours in Diploma and 126 credits in B.Sc.). The existence of a clear view of the importance and relevance of curricula to the professional needs is essential.

There is an increasing number of students who choose accounting as their major either when they enter the university or transfer from other departments, within the College of Business Administration, or from outside the college (i.e. other colleges within the university). For example, Table 1 shows the number of students who were admitted to the accounting program since 1994.

The department also grew rapidly to cater for the increase in the number of students admitted each year. In 1992, there were only five faculty members; but in the first semester of the year 1999/2000, the number had gone up to fourteen, with these faculty members holding different academic ranks (four Associate Professors, five Assistant Professors, one Senior Lecturer, three Instructors, and one Teaching Assistant). There is also a plan to hire additional staff from the professorial and other ranks (e.g. a new full professor will join the department in July 2000).

Table 1.   Number of Students Admitted in the Accounting Program.

Year	1st semester	2nd semester	Total
1994/1995	104	28	132
1995/1996	102	16	118
1996/1997	106	20	126
1997/1998	94	46	140
1998/1999	119	35	154
1999/2000	196	22	218

Accounting practice

The Bahraini Commercial Law of 1975 requires that companies prepare a balance sheet and a profit and loss statement. Furthermore, article (184) requires that these statements be audited by independent auditors. Accountants and auditors practicing in Bahrain formed a professional body in 1972 (Bahrain Society of Accountants and Auditors). The Society, however, does not have the power to license accountants or to establish accounting standards. The Ministry of Commerce is responsible for licensing auditors to practice in Bahrain.

There are nine auditing firms in Bahrain. Recently, Price Waterhouse and Coopers merged under a new name PricewaterhouseCoopers (PWC), reducing the number to eight firms. These firms offer many services to their clients such as, audits of financial statements, management advisory service and consultations. Furthermore, Bahraini accountants make up only 15% of all accountants practicing in Bahrain. The Big Five international auditing firms are present in Bahrain with a market share that exceeds 95%.

3. PREVIOUS RESEARCH

Previous research in the areas of cooperation between Departments of Accounting at universities and auditing firms has examined the means of improving the education and training of accountants. It focused on the content levels of accounting courses and the quality of accounting graduates as perceived by the practitioners and the strategies to enhance the accounting profession. For example, Hart (1969) examined the views of practitioners who stated that an accounting curriculum must be under constant review because of the rapid change in the environment. They also referred to the need for future accountants to acquire communication skills which will enable them to function in a changing environment.

Hadley and Balke (1979) concluded that there was an obvious need for practitioners and academics to cooperate with one another with a view to making undergraduate accounting curricula more relevant to "real world" needs. In recent years, there has been a growing demand for significant changes in the design and delivery of accounting education. Professional accountants express dissatisfaction with the state of accounting education (Inman, 1989; Elliott, 1991). Research by accounting academics also found that accounting curricula were not adequately serving the profession's needs (AAA, 1986).

Lyall (1985) surveyed the views of qualified U.K. accountants working in industry and the profession, to rate the level of exposure to accounting topics that they felt was desirable for new recruits in their undergraduate courses. The results showed that accountants in the profession rate auditing and taxation topics more highly than accountants in industry do. This may be true because accountants in the profession give more emphasis to auditing than accountants in industry.

Ramadhan (1992) examined the views of accountants in the profession and industry on the content levels of undergraduate accounting courses. The results indicated that most of the contents of accounting courses are suitable for the needs and requirements of the job. However, there was a narrow gap between the contents of the courses offered by the department of accounting and the professional needs of accountants.

The Accounting Education Change Commission (AECC), as part of its objectives of education for accountants (1990), describes the capabilities specified by the accounting profession that students should develop through the educational process. The desired capabilities are: intellectual, communication, and interpersonal skills, knowledge and professional orientation.

Skills

The cornerstone of professional accounting education is the recognition and development of communication and interpersonal skills. Accounting programs must develop these skills. This will require a change in instructional methods. The traditional format, dominated by lectures and the solving of routine problems, and bounded by what is included in textbooks, must give way to interactive learning. Students must be active participants, not passive receptors of information. They must learn by doing exercises, solving problems, using case studies and simulations. Role-playing and other interactive teaching methods should be made a routine part of accounting education.

Knowledge

A key concept in understanding the nature of universities is that of knowledge strategy. Knowledge strategies underline the basic philosophy of academic disciplines and departments, and each department has to take account not only of the paradigm of its discipline, but also of its knowledge strategy (Brown & Guilding, 1993). Accounting graduates should have a minimum level of knowledge in three areas: general knowledge, organizational and business knowledge, and accounting knowledge. They should also be able to integrate the knowledge in these areas. In addition, they need the ability to increase their level of knowledge when necessary. This requires a basic understanding upon which to build, and an ability to efficiently search for needed information.

General knowledge is necessary to understand the worldwide economic, political, and social forces affecting society and the accounting profession. It allows accounting professionals to interact with diverse groups of people. Business and organizational knowledge allows accountants to understand the internal workings of organizations and how they change. Especially important is the understanding the impact of technology on organizations. Accounting knowledge includes a strong fundamental knowledge of accounting principles and concepts, not a memorization of techniques and professional standards.

Professional Orientation
Accounting students should appreciate their obligations as professionals. They should be dedicated to improving the knowledge, skills and values of members of their profession. They must understand ethics and be able to make value-based judgments. Finally, they should be prepared to address issues with integrity, objectivity, competence and concern for the public interest.

Saudagaran (1996) suggested a new "introduction to accounting course" which will provide students with a broad-based introduction to accounting rather than a narrow bookkeeping perspective offered under the traditional approach. His suggestion attempts to develop judgment, emphasize the need to learn on one's own and address improvement of written and oral communication skills. Tipgos (1987) also proposed a two-tiered accounting education model and called on developing nations to implement it as one of the important strategies for enhancing the accounting profession and practice in developing countries.

Al-Bastaki (1997) examined accounting experts' perceptions on the strategies for enhancing the accounting profession and practices in Bahrain. He found that raising educational requirements for accountants at the entry level to the profession, requiring and providing continuing education for certified accountants, and strengthening the power and responsibilities of the Bahrain Accounting Association, were perceived to be the most effective strategies for enhancing the accounting profession and practices in Bahrain.

Finally, many ways of cooperation between accounting educators and practicing accountants were suggested by researchers addressing the question of enhancing the accounting profession and practices. In this regard, Tipgos (1987) suggested the following specific strategies for cooperation between accounting educators and those in practice.

(1) Establish faculty internship programs.
(2) Have cooperative teaching arrangements between universities and the profession.
(3) Develop plans to encourage coordinated research between accounting faculty and outside parties.

Tipgos argued that adopting these strategies would eventually enhance the accounting profession and practices. Akathaporn et al. (1993) examined the strategies to enhance the accounting education and practice in Thailand. They found that encouraging profession-university cooperation as one of the main strategies.

It can be seen that the literature focuses on three main areas: the content levels of undergraduate accounting courses as perceived by the practitioners, the capabilities specified by the accounting profession that students should develop through the educational process, cooperation between practitioners and academics, and the strategies to enhance the accounting profession.

4. METHOD

Population, Sample and Responses

All auditing firms operating in Bahrain were included in the study (8 firms). The questionnaires were distributed randomly to a sample of 91 auditors. For the purpose of the study, professionals are defined as those who audit clients' accounts. However, auditors in one of the eight firms did not respond. Sixty-three questionnaires were returned; a response rate of 69.23%. Table 2 shows the names of responding firms, the number of questionnaires distributed and received, and the response rate. It is worth pointing out that a large number of responses come from Ernst and Young, KPMG Fakhro, and PricewaterhouseCoopers. The effect of Ernst and Young and KPMG on the results is clear and cannot be ignored (see Table 2). These two firms add up to more than 60% of the total responses. This could have some effect on the results. So, the results should be interpreted in light of this limitation. The reason for this is that these two firms, together with PricewaterhouseCoopers, represent the largest auditing firms in Bahrain. On the other hand, Talal Abu-Ghazala may have no effect on the results because of the very small number of questionnaires completed by them (one questionnaire only).

The Questionnaire

A four-part questionnaire was developed to collect the data needed for the study. Part one covers demographics of respondents. It contains background information about the size of auditing firms as measured by the number of employees, respondents' academic or professional qualifications, years of experience and the services provided by auditing firms to their clients. Part two provides information about the four areas of cooperation examined in the study. Part three

Table 2.   Auditing Firms and Questionnaires Distributed.

Firm	No. of questionnaires distributed	No. of questionnaires returned	Response rate
(1) Arthur Anderson	10	6	60
(2) PricewaterhouseCoopers	16	9	56
(3) Ernst and Young	25	25	100
(4) KPMG Fakhro	20	13	65
(5) Saba	4	4	100
(6) Nabeel Al-Saie	6	5	84
(7) Talal Abu-Ghazala	10	1	10
Totals	91	63	69%

elicits information about the difficulties and obstacles which hinder cooperation between the department of accounting and auditing firms. The last part
collects information about the strategies to enhance cooperation.

Respondents were asked to provide information about the importance of each
criterion on a five-point Likert-type scale ranging from 1 indicating poor, to 5
indicating excellent. The questionnaire was pilot-tested on a small sample of
subjects (four partners in three auditing firms). The results and feedback of the
pilot test were used to refine the questionnaire and a final draft was developed
and distributed to the entire sample.

The Procedure

Access to the firms was obtained through the joint efforts of the researchers
and accounting students. Three students were asked to visit each of the eight
firms and ask the auditors to fill in the questionnaires. The students were paid
for their services because the research was funded by the Deanship of Scientific
Research of the University of Bahrain. Descriptive statistics were used to
analyze and explain the results.

5. RESULTS

Characteristics of Respondents

Size of Auditing Firms
The size of auditing firms as measured by the number of auditors ranged
between 3 and 50. In two of the firms, Ernst and Young and KPMG Fakhro,
the number of auditors is about 50. In PricewaterhouseCoopers, it is about 30.

In the remaining firms, the number is less than 20. However, no inference is drawn from the relationship between size and the strategies to enhance cooperation between auditing firms and accounting departments.

Academic/Professional Qualification of Respondents

Table 3 presents demographic information of the respondents. With regard to the academic qualifications of respondents, the table shows that the majority of the respondents (58.5%) have professional qualifications, mostly CPAs, but some of them have CA or ACCA. Three respondents indicated that they have CIMA in addition to ACCA. Only 24.4% have first degrees.

Years of Experience

Table 3 shows the level of experience of respondents. The majority have experience of more than five years (about 62%). Only 38% of the respondents have less than five years experience. This is an indication of high experience on the part of respondents.

Table 3.   Demographics of Respondents ($N = 63$).

Academic/professional qualification of respondents*	Frequency	Percentage
(a) CPA, CA, ACCA.	48	58.5%
(b) B.Sc.	20	24.4%
(c) Masters	4	4.9%
(d) Ph.D.	3	3.7%
(e) Other qualifications	5	6.1%
Years of experience		
(a) Less than 5 years	24	38.1
(b) 5–10 years	20	31.7
(c) 11–15 years	9	14.3
(d) More than 15 years	10	15.9
Totals	63	100
Services provided to clients*		
(a) Audits of financial statements	61	100
(b) Management advisory services	32	52.5
(c) Tax services	8	13

* Total is more than 63 because multiple responses were allowed.

Services Provided to Clients

Respondents were asked to indicate the services they offer to their clients. Table 3 shows that all respondents (100%) provide the same main service, i.e. audits of financial statements. Next is management advisory service (52.5%). The service least provided to clients is tax services (13%). This is because there is no corporate/personal income tax, and such a low percentage could apply to offshore firms.

Finally, some respondents added services other than those listed in the questionnaire. These are:

		Frequencies
(a)	Special investigations (e.g. acquisition, merger or liquidation, company formation, share registration, fraud investigation)	10
(b)	Legal support	2
(c)	Special reporting and business evaluation	3
(d)	Internal control structure or audit	2
(e)	Recruitment	1
(f)	Setting up accounting systems and procedures	2
(g)	Corporate finance	2

Fields of Cooperation

Preparing Qualified Graduates

Number of Graduates Recruited by Auditing Firms. The total number of students graduating from the Department of Accounting, University of Bahrain who were recruited by auditing firms during the last five-year period (1992–1997) ranged between 5 and 15.

Criteria for Evaluating Graduates

The accounting profession needs a variety of individuals with differing backgrounds and abilities. No one model of accounting education should be put forward as the preferred model (Sundem & Williams, 1992). Nevertheless, there are some basic capabilities that are essential for success in the accounting profession, and they should be included in any accounting education program. According to previous research, these include skills, knowledge, and professional orientation.

Based on this background, the basic capabilities that should be developed in accounting students were included in the questionnaire under these three categories. Respondents were asked to indicate their evaluation of the performance of the graduates of the Department of Accounting, University of Bahrain, who are working in their firms. Survey responses are presented in Table 4. They are reported as a percentage of the total responses on each evaluation criterion.

Table 4. Criteria for Evaluating Accounting Graduates $N = 36*$.

Evaluation criteria	Percentage distribution of responses					Average**	Total
	Poor %	Fair %	Good %	Very good %	Excellent %		(n)
(1) Skills							
(a) Interpersonal skills	0	23.5	58.8	17.7	0	2.94	34
(b) Communication skills	0	40.5	48.7	10.8	0	2.70	37
(c) Time management	2.8	38.9	55.5	2.8	0	2.58	36
(2) Knowledge							
(a) General academic background in accounting	0	19.4	44.4	30.5	2.7	3.17	35
(b) Ability to learn.	0	5.6	52.8	36.0	5.6	3.14	36
(c) Compared with graduates of other universities	2.8	22.2	47.2	22.2	5.6	3.06	36
(d) Competence in the use of Arabic language	0	28.6	42.9	25.7	2.8	3.03	35
(e) Competence in the use of computers	0	16.7	38.9	19.4	0	3.03	36
(f) Creative thinking	0	44.4	38.9	13.9	2.8	2.75	36
(g) Competence in the use of English language	0	22.9	62.9	14.2	0	2.40	35
(3) Professional orientation							
(a) Readiness to cooperate with colleagues	0	5.6	44.4	41.7	8.3	3.53	36
(b) Adaptability to new situations	0	19.4	47.2	30.6	2.8	3.17	36
(c) Initiative and enthusiasm	2.8	28.6	40.0	28.6	0	3.03	34
(d) Dependability and sense of responsibility	2.8	30.5	41.7	22.2	2.8	3.00	35
(e) Knowledge of market conditions	2.8	52.7	41.7	2.8	0	2.44	36
(f) Competence on the job	0	25.0	66.7	8.3	0	2.83	36
(g) Discipline and punctuality	2.7	40.5	43.3	10.8	2.7	2.78	36
(h) Readiness to accept right criticism	0	31.4	60.0	8.6	0	2.77	35
Overall rating						**2.94**	

* It should be pointed out that the total number of respondents is 36 and not 63. The reason is that the other 27 respondents joined their firms recently and they may not be familiar with the work of graduates from the University of Bahrain.

** Average is computed-based on a scale ranging from 1 = poor and 5 = excellent.

The table shows that the graduates achieved just above average scores in some of the criteria – the highest rating being 3.53. None of the criteria received 4 or more rating. Therefore, the overall rating is below the average, i.e. 2.94. This is an indication of relatively average graduates which may reflect negatively on the profession.

The criteria which received the highest ratings are "readiness to cooperate with colleagues", with 3.53, "general academic background in accounting" received a rating of 3.17, "adaptability to new situations" 3.17, "ability to learn" also received just above a rating of 3. This may be because accounting education is remote from business concerns, and is too academic. However, the criterion "compared with graduates from other universities" received just above a rating of 3. This result indicates that respondents perceive University of Bahrain graduates as not different from those of other universities. "Competence in the use of Arabic language" also received an average rating of 3, which indicates that the Arabic language of graduates is poor. This may be because the Arabic courses in the program are not enough (one course only) and all lectures are in English. There is a perceived need for greater emphasis to be attached to the development of creative thinking as well as communication skills. The former requires personal knowledge while the second requires collegial knowledge. It is believed that the development of accounting students' creative thinking and communication skills will be greater if accounting educators exhibit a greater propensity for personal and collegial knowledge strategies.

Some criteria received less than average ratings. Examples of these are: "discipline and punctuality", and "time management". This may be because graduates lack experience in time management. "Competence on the job" received a rating of 2.83, which is below average. This may require a specialized curriculum which develops in students the habits of mind and the skills that will enable them to solve problems when faced with them. "Dependability and sense of responsibility", and "initiative and enthusiasm" both received an average score of 3.00 and 3.03 respectively. This suggests some sort of responsibility on the part of the graduates and willingness to take initiative at work. The criterion "competence in the use of computers" received an average score of 3.03. Graduates are, to a moderate extent, able to use computer applications in their work. The undergraduate accounting program at the University of Bahrain includes three courses in information technology. In addition, instructors ask their students to do some assignments, using computer applications such as EXCEL. This will enhance their personal skills in the use of computers.

The criteria which received the lowest ratings are "knowledge of market conditions" with a score of 2.44, "competence in the use of English language" with a score of 2.4, "communication skills" with a score of 2.7, and "creative thinking" with a score of 2.75. The low score for "knowledge of market conditions" may be due to the fact that the graduates have little experience and are not yet familiar with market conditions. The low scores for "competence in the use of English language" and "communication skills" may be due to some weaknesses in the undergraduate program as it does not include enough English courses which can help students to develop their communication skills. Competence in the use of English language is required because almost all business transactions are carried out in English. It is the dominant language of communication used by Bahraini companies in conducting business. Moreover, if graduates want to obtain professional qualifications in accounting, they need to improve their English language skills. Furthermore, English is the language of instruction for business and accounting courses in the College of Business Administration at the University of Bahrain. All courses and textbooks are in English. Finally, most faculty members graduate from USA or U.K. The existing accounting curriculum includes three English courses at the Diploma level, namely, English for business I and II and Report-writing for business. There are no English courses at the B.Sc. Level. In addition, some graduates may not be competent in the use of English because they were not exposed to enough English courses at school. In such an environment, it is not surprising to find that auditors rank these qualities as the lowest. Massoud et al. (1996) believe that colleges of business and management in the Gulf states must introduce at least a new course in business communication in order to develop the communication skills of their graduates.

Some respondents also emphasized the importance of qualified graduates in order to be prepared to achieve professional qualifications such as CA and CPA. However, some respondents indicated that they are not qualified to comment on the graduates' competence in the use of Arabic language because they themselves cannot speak and write in Arabic (e.g. Indians).

The findings are not surprising, considering the current state of accounting education and practice in Bahrain. Some firms recruit unqualified and incompetent accountants. Some of them, perhaps, do not hold the first university degree (i.e. B.Sc.). Therefore, accounting experts must raise the educational requirements at the entry level to the profession. This is because accounting requires a breadth of capabilities (Arthur Anderson and Co. et al., 1989) and individuals have a variety of learning styles Kolb et al. (1986). The importance of bringing a broad range of knowledge to bear on the education of accounting students would appear to be self-evident. Therefore, it is believed that the accounting curricula at the University of Bahrain may need continuous revision in the light of the practitioners' views. Moreover, the various constituents of accounting education are increasingly demanding that the curriculum emphasizes the analysis, oral and written communication, and inter-personal skills (Williams, 1991).

Participation in Preparing Curriculum. With regard to participation in preparing or modifying the curricula and programs offered by the Department of Accounting, only one firm indicated that they participated in this process. In fact, auditing firms did not participate in the preparation of the curriculum in accounting. In some cases, respondents were asked to indicate whether they believe that they should participate in preparing and modifying the curricula and programs offered by the Department of Accounting. About 66% said yes, the remaining 34% said no. Table 5 shows that all reasons are related to each other. The main reasons why respondents feel it is important for them to partic-ipate in preparing accounting curricula are: "to reduce the gap between theory and practice", "to make curricula closer to the business needs", "to acquaint students with the problems of business world", and "to strengthen cooperation between the university and auditing firms".

Allowing auditors to participate in developing accounting curricula will help academics to incorporate courses required by practitioners in such a way that they will bridge the gap and meet the needs of the profession. In addition, professionals will exchange views and ideas with academics which will reflect positively on accounting programs offered by universities. The reason "to enable auditors to update their background on new developments in accounting" was not considered as important by the majority of respondents. This may be because auditors feel that they are up to date in their field and do not need to participate solely for this reason.

Other reasons added were: "to prepare and equip students to deal with practical and real life business situations" (which is similar to a large extent to reason (c) in Table 5), "to improve their sense of ethics and responsibilities", and "to enable them to sit the exams for professional qualifications". The last reason is related to those mentioned in Table 5 because exchanging views and ideas when preparing accounting curricula will help accounting graduates to sit for the professional accounting examinations.

Teaching Accounting Courses by Respondents. Auditing firms were asked to indicate whether they sent some of their auditors to teach any accounting courses on a part-time basis at the University of Bahrain. Two firms indicated that they did. These firms are: Ernst and Young and Arthur Anderson, who nominated five of their professionals to teach auditing courses during the second semester 1997/98 and the first semester 1998/1999 under the University of Bahrain cooperative teaching scheme (professionals are those who possess professional qualifications in auditing, e.g. CPA, ACCA).

Table 5. Reasons why respondents want to participate ($N = 40^{*,+}$).

		Frequencies	%
(a)	Reduce the gap between theory and practice	31	77.5
(b)	Make curricula closer to the needs of business firms	24	60.0
(c)	Acquaint students with the problems of business firms	21	52.5
(d)	Strengthen cooperation between the University and business firms	21	52.5
(e)	Enable auditors to update their background on new developments in accounting	16	40.0

* Total is more than 100% because multiple responses were allowed.
+ Auditors in one firm did not respond to the question.

Internship for Accounting Students. The accounting curriculum at the University of Bahrain includes two credit hours of internship. These two credits are not included in the cumulative GPA, but a student is required to do some training for eight weeks at one of the local institutions. The Professional Relations Division at the university, together with the college coordinator for training, finds suitable placements for students who register for training, each semester. Normally, training should be taken in the summer semester, because students are not allowed to register for any other course during the training period.

Auditing firms were also asked to indicate if they provide practical training (internship) for the Department of Accounting students. Five firms indicated that they do provide training. Those firms that provide training were asked to indicate whether they provide feedback to the Department of Accounting, about the students who have completed their internship with them. They said that they do. However, some firms added that they provide feedback only during their busy sessions and not in the "quiet" summer months. Others provide feedback on request. Some of them also issue a certificate of internship. However, all firms offering training are now required to fill in a report about the performance of the trainees. Moreover, the trainees themselves are also required to prepare reports about their training.

Training Programs, Workshops and Seminars
Auditing firms were asked to indicate if they participated in any training programs, workshops, or seminars organized by the Department of Accounting of the University of Bahrain during the last five-year period (1992–1997). Only two firms indicated that they participated. Those who participated were asked to specify the number of workshops and seminars which they had participated

in. The two firms indicated that they had participated in one or two workshops and seminars.

Auditing firms that had participated in workshops and seminars were asked to indicate, on a five-point scale, the extent to which they are satisfied with the training programs, workshops and seminars. They all indicated that they were satisfied with the material presented at these workshops.

Consultancy Services

Auditing firms were asked to indicate if they carried out consultancy services for business firms, in collaboration with the Department of Accounting of the University of Bahrain, over the last five years (1992–1997). None of them reported that they had carried out any consultancy services. Therefore, there were no responses regarding the duration, nature of the consultancy services, and the number of consultancy services which they had conducted in collaboration with the Department of Accounting.

Research and Studies

Auditing firms were also asked to indicate if they carried out any market research or field surveys in cooperation with the Department of Accounting of the University of Bahrain over the last five years (1992–1997). Only one firm reported that they did and that they participated in one research project.

Barriers to Cooperation

Respondents were asked about the difficulties and obstacles which are likely to hinder the degree of cooperation between auditing firms and the Department of Accounting of the University of Bahrain. Table 6 shows the results. All the difficulties, except one, received above the rating of 3. "Lack of information about the training programs which the department can conduct" and "lack of information about the availability of a list of professionals' capabilities in the department" received an average rating of 3.8. This indicates that there are no proper communication channels between the academics and the accounting profession regarding workshops. This could be true because normally, workshops and training programs are meant for people working in local firms who need to enhance their skills in specific areas. So, auditing firms would not be contacted. "Lack of information about the availability of a list of professionals' capabilities in the department", "lack of prompt liaison", and "lack of information about the consultancy services offered by the department" received the highest ratings. The last difficulty/obstacle, i.e. "the faculty of the department are busy with teaching and research" is not perceived as an important problem. It received below the average rating of 2.87.

Table 6.   Difficulties hindering the degree of cooperation ($N = 56$).

Difficulty/Obstacle	Not Important 1 %	2 %	Moderate 3 %	4 %	Extremely Important 5 %	Average
(a) Lack of information about the training programs and workshops which the department can conduct	3.6	1.8	33.9	32.1	28.6	3.80
(b) Lack of information about the availability of a list of professional capabilities of the department's faculty members	0	8.2	34.6	28.6	28.6	3.78
(c) Lack of prompt liaison	0	9.4	35.8	30.2	24.6	3.70
(d) Lack of information about the consultancy service offered by the department	5.3	5.3	32.2	30.4	26.8	3.68
(e) Lack of appropriate experience by the faculty in the department	7.4	7.4	42.6	25.9	16.7	3.37
(f) The instructors in the department are very busy with teaching and research	11.5	11.5	59.7	11.5	3.8	2.87

Degree of Importance Placed on Selected Strategies to Enhance Cooperation

Respondents were asked to rank, on a five-point scale (strongly disagree = 1 and strongly agree = 5), the degree of importance that they place on various strategies to enhance cooperation between auditing firms and the Department of Accounting in each of the four areas of cooperation identified in the study (i.e. strategies to improve the quality of accounting graduates, training programs, workshops, seminars, consultancy and research). The results are reported in Table 7.

The table shows that all the strategies, with the exception of "both the department and auditing firms should conduct consultancy services", received above average ratings. This indicates that auditors perceive these strategies important

Table 7. Strategies to Enhance Cooperation (*N* = 60).

Strategy	Percentage distribution of responses					Average
	Not Important 1 %	2 %	Moderate 3 %	4 %	Extremely Important 5 %	
(1) Improving the Quality of Accounting Graduates						
(a) Auditing firms provide internship for the Department of Accounting students	0	3.4	6.9	46.6	43.1	4.29
(b) Exchange visits between the faculty of the department and auditing firms	0	1.7	11.7	55.9	30.7	4.15
(c) Conduct seminars between the faculty of accounting department and auditing firms	0	1.7	19.0	48.3	31.0	4.09
(d) Request professionals in auditing firms to participate in preparing and evaluating the programs offered by the Accounting Department	0	3.3	15.0	53.3	28.4	4.07
(e) Request professionals in auditing firms to teach some accounting courses at both the Diploma and B.Sc levels	0	1.7	23.3	40.0	35.0	4.08
(f) Admit staff from auditing firms as members of the College/Department Council	0	3.4	20.3	49.2	27.1	4.00
(2) Training Programs, Workshops and Seminars						
(a) Request professionals in auditing firms to participate in the training programs, and workshops offered by the department	0	3.4	8.6	67.3	20.7	4.05
(b) Request professionals in auditing firms to participate in preparing and developing training programs	0	8.9	32.1	41.1	17.9	3.96

Table 7. Continued.

Strategy	Percentage distribution of responses					Average
	Not Important 1 %	2 %	Moderate 3 %	4 %	Extremely Important 5 %	
(3) Consultancy Services						
(a) Establish consultancy which include members from both the department and auditing firms	1.8	8.8	31.6	40.3	17.5	3.63
(b) Department should be aware and appreciate the expertise and range of services provided by auditing firms	0	5.5	40.0	41.8	12.7	3.62
(c) Both the department and auditing firms should conduct all consultancy services	5.4	23.2	42.8	23.2	5.4	3.00
(4) Research and Studies						
(a) Conduct applied research in collaboration with auditing firms	0	7.3	32.7	40.0	20.0	3.73
(b) Use the faculty members as advisors during course assignments	1.8	7.3	32.7	43.7	14.5	3.62
(c) Use only students of the department to carry out surveys	3.7	14.8	46.3	22.2	13.0	3.26

for enhancing cooperation between accounting education and accounting practices. The strategy that received the highest rating is "auditing firms should provide practical training to accounting students", with a rating of 4.29. As mentioned earlier, some auditing firms do provide internship in summer to accounting students. Novin and Baker (1990) also reported that providing training to accounting students during their college education and encouraging profession-university cooperation are two important strategies for enhancing the accounting profession and practices.

This is perceived as an important strategy because it gives students a real world experience and reduces the training period required when they graduate and join auditing firms. One respondent indicated that the internship period should be more than eight weeks. "Exchange visits between faculty of accounting departments and auditing firms" received a high rating of 4.15. The strategies "request professionals in auditing firms to participate in preparing and evaluating the accounting programs" and "request professionals in auditing firms to teach some accounting courses at both the Diploma and B.Sc. levels" received high ratings of 4.07 and 4.08 respectively. These high ratings may indicate that what is covered in the classroom should ultimately be determined by practitioners' needs. Flaherty (1979) and Robinson and Barrett (1988) found substantial differences between what practitioners believe should be taught and topical coverage in the curricula. The gap between what accounting educators teach and what accountants do may have increased in the last five years (Szendi & Elmore, 1993). There is a need for significant changes in the accounting curricula in order to adapt to the new business environment. Other strategies such as, "allow professionals from auditing firms to be members of the college council", "conduct seminars between accounting departments and auditing firms", and "exchange visits between faculty and auditing firms" are also important. This indicates that respondents perceive all strategies as important in enhancing cooperation between the department of accounting and auditing firms. Therefore, academics must be concerned whether they are educating students to meet the current and future needs of their environment. A specialized curriculum will develop in students the habit of mind, and the skills that will enable them to solve problems they are faced with. From the scores given to the various strategies, it is evident that respondents do find that exchange visits between faculty of the department of accounting and auditing firms are important in enhancing cooperation between them. Exchange of visits, joint seminars, the participation of professionals in preparing accounting programs and also in teaching some courses, and allowing auditing firms to be represented in the college council will help in improving the quality of accounting programs in such a way that they would meet the needs of the profession.

It can be seen that all the six suggested strategies that could bring about an improvement in the quality of accounting program offered at the University of Bahrain received high ratings.

Respondents were asked to add any other strategies they felt were also important. Other strategies added by respondents are:

(1) Input from firms on the courses and topics being taught, with particular reference to practical issues and problems.

(2) Presentations made by the audit and accounting firms to the students to introduce them to the profession and to the wide range of areas that the students will work in.

(3) Jointly participate in career workshops where the advantages of a career in the profession can be conveyed to interested students.

5. CONCLUSION AND RECOMMENDATIONS

The study provides some guidelines on the areas of cooperation between the Department of Accounting at the University of Bahrain and auditing firms. Based on the results, close cooperation between academics and professionals is important for any reasonable development in the accounting profession (Abdel-Kareem, 1994). In this regard, Bahrain Accounting Association, academic institutions, The Ministry of Trade, and auditing firms should play a major role in enhancing the degree of cooperation between academics and auditing firms.

The results of the study have important implications for international audience (e.g. accounting educators, auditing firms and accounting students). Each of these groups has the common goal of an undergraduate accounting program that adequately prepares accounting majors to enter the profession.

The implications of the results for accounting educators are that they help in understanding the necessary educational requirements for the accountant in practice. This knowledge will enable academics to streamline their educational programs, research, training, seminars, workshops, and consultancies to serve the needs of the profession, both at home and abroad. As a result of such modification, auditing firms employing accounting graduates will benefit in such a way that these accountants will be able to perform their duties effectively.

The findings of the study also have important implications for accounting students in that cooperation in the area of teaching will reduce the problems in the work environment that accounting students face when they enter the profession. Furthermore, they highlight the roles of both academics and auditing firms in preparing qualified accountants. This role should be emphasized in order to enhance accounting education and provide an appropriate academic background for those who choose auditing as their career.

One limitation of the study is that it applies only to Bahrain. Therefore, the findings may not be generalized to other countries in the region (i.e. the Gulf States). For further research, the perceptions of professionals in other GCC countries and the views of the faculty of accounting departments (the academics) in GCC universities regarding the areas of cooperation between departments of accounting and auditing firms could be examined. In addition, the extent to which auditing firms provide financial support and assistance to the Department of Accounting in each of the four areas of cooperation (e.g. providing partial finance for research projects, teaching, new programs, conferences, seminars, training and consultancies) could also be examined. Furthermore, a study focusing on undergraduate course coverage of the innovations and recent developments in accounting may help in determining if universities should develop and incorporate into their curricula, a new and separate course dealing with these new issues.

Finally, fields of cooperation between the Department and governmental units (e.g. Ministry of Finance and Ministry of Trade) which supervise the accounting profession, and other organizations such as Bahrain Accountants Association, which monitor and promote the profession, may also be examined.

Recommendations

In light of the result, the authors recommend the following:

(1) There should be cooperation between auditing firms and the Department of Accounting in order to turn out qualified accounting graduates. In this regard, the selection of appropriate material, having certain lectures delivered by professionals, and encouraging regular visits by auditing firms will lend credibility to the university programs.

(2) There should be continuous updating of accounting courses to reflect changes in the environment and the needs of the profession. The competency levels of curricula contents should be conducted periodically. In addition, both the department and auditing firms should revise the syllabuses to incorporate new developments in accounting and supporting disciplines (e.g. good knowledge of computer applications).

(3) Auditing firms should provide training for accounting students to develop their analytical skills and help them solve practical problems.

(4) Joint research, seminars and workshops should be conducted to enhance accounting awareness among the users of accounting information and to make output from academic research appropriate for practice.

(5) There should be summer employment for members of faculty of accounting departments in the form of fellowships in auditing firms (Wallace, 1998). This will provide professional development opportunities for accounting educators. In other words, it will enable them to understand the problems faced by the profession and enhance and explore new areas of cooperation. In this regard, Abdolmohammadi (1988) suggests that one important way to enhance accounting profession in developing countries is to upgrade and train the accounting faculty in these countries. Similarly, Novin and Baker

(1990) suggest that training accounting professors is an important strategy for enhancing the accounting education and profession in developing countries.

(6) The Department should start preparing for a scientific and professional conference on the accounting profession in Bahrain to discuss its past, present and future prospects, including the problems facing the profession and the strategies to overcome them. Businessmen, practitioners in industry, auditing firms and academics should all be invited to participate in the conference.

REFERENCES

Abdel-kareem, N. (1994). The Accounting Profession in West Bank and Gaza Strip: Reality and Challenges. *The Certified Arab Accountant Magazine* (Arabic), *84*(May–June), 16–20.

Abdolmohammadi, M. J. (1988). A Model for Educational Exchange of Accounting Faculty between the Pacific Basin Countries and Advanced World Institutions. *Proceedings of the Fifth Pan Pacific Conference* (pp. 515–517). Singapore.

Accounting Education Change Commission (1990). Position Statement No. 1. *Objectives of Education for Accountants*, (September).

Akathaporn, P., Novin, A. M., & Abdolmohammadi, M. J. (1993). Accounting Education and Practice in Thailand: Perceived Problems and Effectiveness of Enhancement Strategies. *The International Journal of Accounting*, *28*, 259–272.

Al-Bastaki, H. (1997). Strategies for Enhancing Accounting Profession and Practices in Bahrain: Accounting Expert's Perception. *Research in Accounting in Emerging Economies*, *4*, 165–189.

Alsultan, S. M. (1994). Towards a Framework for Co-ordination and Cooperation between the Accountancy Departments and Accountancy Professional Organizations. *Accountancy Magazine* (Arabic), (1), 5.

American Accounting Association: Committee on the Future Structure, Content, and Scope of Accounting Education (The Bedford Committee) (1986). Future Accounting Education: Preparing for the Expanding Profession. *Issues in Accounting Education*, (Spring), 168–195.

Arthur Andersen & Co., Arthur Young, Coopers & Lybrand, Deloitte Haskins & Sells, Ernst & Whinney, Peat Marwick Main & Co., Price Waterhouse and Touch Ross (1989) *Perspectives on Education: Capabilities for Success in the Accounting Profession*. New York: Authors.

Brown, R., & Guilding, C. (1993). Knowledge and the Academic Accountant: An Empirical Study, *Journal of Accounting Education*, *11*(1), 1–14.

Deakin, E. B., & Summers, E. J. (1975). A Survey of Curriculum Topics Relevant to the Practice of Management Accounting, *The Accounting Review*, *50*, 380–383.

Elliot, R. K. (1991). Accounting Education and Research at the Crossroads. *Issues in Accounting Education*, (Spring), 1–8.

Estes, R. (1978). The Profession's Changing Horizons: A Survey of Practitioners' Views on the Present and Future Importance of Selected Knowledge and Skills. *The International Journal of Accounting*, *14*(2), 47–70.

Flaherty, R. E. (1979). *The Core of the Curriculum for Accounting Majors*. Sarasota, FL: American Accounting Association.

Hadley, G. D., & Balke, T. E. (1979). A Comparison of Academic and Practitioners' Views of Content Levels in Undergraduate Accounting Curriculum. *The Accounting Review*, *54*(2), 383–389.

Hart, D. J. (1969). An Outsider Looks at the Accounting Curriculum. *Journal of Accountancy*, (March), 87–89.

Inman, B. C., Wenzler, A., & Wickert, P. (1989). Square Pegs in Round Holes: Are Accounting Students Well Suited to Today's Accounting Professionals? *Issues in Accounting Education*, (Spring), 29–47.

Kolb, D. A., Rubin, I. M., & McIntyre, J. M. (1986). *Organizational Psychology: An Experimental Approach to Organizational Behavior*. Englewood Cliffs, NJ: Prentice-Hall Inc.

Lyall, D. (1985). Content Level in Undergraduate Accounting Courses: Views from Industry and Profession, *The British Accounting Review*, *17*(Spring), 40–48.

Massoud, M. F., Fahmy, S., & Stevens, W. (1996). Accounting Education: A Blueprint for Change, a Paper Presented at the Gulf Cooperation Council Accounting Department, First International Conference, December 16–18.

Ministry of Finance and National Economy (1991). *30 Years of Economic and Social Development in the State of Bahrain*. Manama, Bahrain.

Novin, A. M., & Baker, J. (1990). Enhancing the Accounting Education and the Accounting Profession in Developing Countries. *Foreign Trade Review*, (Oct.–Dec.), 247–257.

Ramandhan, S. (1992). Practitioners' Views Concerning the Content Levels of Undergraduate Accounting Courses. *Abhath Al-Yarmouk*, *8*(3), 9–25. Jordan.

Robinson, M. A., & Barrett, M. E. (1988). The Content of Managerial Accounting Curricula. *Accounting Educator's Journal*, *1*, 49–60.

Saudgaran, S. M. (1996) The First Course in Accounting: An Innovative Approach. *Issues in Accounting Education*, *11*(1), 83–94.

Shank, J. K., & Govendarajan, V. (1989). *Strategic Cost Analysis: The Evolution from Managerial to Strategic Accounting*. Homewood, IL: Irwin Publishing Co.

Shkri, I. (1993). The Role of Professional Organizations and Accounting Associations in Enhancing Accounting Proficiency. *The Certified Arab Accountant Magazine*, (84)(October), 26–29.

Sundem, G. L., & Williams, D. Z. (1992). Changes in Accounting Education: Preparing for the Twenty-First Century, *Accounting Education*, *1*(1), 55–61.

Tipgos, M. A. (1987). A Comprehensive Model for Improving Accounting Education in Developing Countries. *Advances in International Accounting*, *1*, 383–404.

Wallace, R. S. O. (1998). Coordination and Cooperation between Departments of Accounting and Professional Accounting Firms in GCC Countries. Paper Presented at the Seminar on Coordination and Cooperation between Departments of Accounting and Professional Firms in GCC Countries, November 7, 1998, Manama, Bahrain.

Williams, D. Z. (1991). The Challenge of Change in Accounting Education. *Issues in Accounting Education*, (Spring), 126–133.

6. MANAGEMENT ACCOUNTING PRACTICES IN THE GCC PETROCHEMICAL COMPANIES: AN EXPLORATORY STUDY

Khalid Al-Khater and John Innes

ABSTRACT

This detailed questionnaire survey of 24 companies, combined with eight unstructured interviews, explored the management accounting practices of GCC petrochemical companies in the areas of product costing, pricing, budgetary practices and standard costing. The results show that the most important objective of the product cost systems was to provide relevant information for managerial decision making. However, many respondents accepted that the use of volume-related bases (such as direct labour hours) to allocate overhead costs to products meant that product cost information provided to managers was inaccurate. The most important reasons for allocating overhead costs were for cost control and for external reporting purposes. More than half of the companies had a transfer pricing system and almost all the companies had a comprehensive budgetary system with the most important reason for such a system being to control costs, but only 42% of the companies used flexible budgets. The use of standard costing was widespread for cost control, help in setting budgets and improving performance. Respondents identified overhead costs and

Research in Accounting in Emerging Economies, Volume 5, pages 95–124.
© 2003 Published by Elsevier Science Ltd.
ISBN: 0-7623-0901-6

cost allocation in terms of both product costing and cost management as
major areas of concern.

INTRODUCTION

There is a lack of management accounting research in the Gulf Co-operation
Council Countries (GCC Countries namely Bahrain, Kuwait, Oman, Qatar,
Saudi Arabia, and United Arab Emirates). In contrast, several studies have
examined financial accounting issues such as the standard setting process in
these countries (Al-Basteki, 1995; Needles, 1997; Mirghani, 1998). The absence
of management accounting research in the GCC Countries can be attributed to
three main reasons. Firstly, most companies in the GCC Countries are very
small and often family-owned and some accounting researchers consider that
there is a lack of knowledge about management accounting techniques in these
companies. Secondly, the number of management accounting researchers in
these countries is limited. Thirdly, management accounting and particularly
costing are more sensitive issues in the GCC companies than in the West and
managers often try to avoid discussing such issues with outsiders.

This study attempts to identify the most important issues related to management accounting in the GCC petrochemical companies. This paper is organized
in the following manner: Section 1 discusses the purpose of this research project
and the research methods used. Section 2 presents relevant prior research.
Section 3 describes the current practices of product costing, and pricing
decision practices are discussed in Section 4. Sections 5 and 6 are concerned
with budgetary practices and the current practices of standard costing systems
respectively. Finally, the conclusions are given in Section 7.

1. PURPOSE AND RESEARCH METHODS

This research project is an exploratory study and a first attempt to explore management accounting practices in the petrochemical companies in the GCC
Countries, in particular, product costing and cost management. The petrochemical industry in the GCC Countries was chosen as the industry to be studied
because it has become a very significant sector in the GCC Countries. After the
oil crisis of 1973 and the enormous increases in the price of oil, GCC governments made great efforts to change the structure of their economies because they
wished to diversify their economic resources and expand their export earnings
away from the oil sector. The GCC Countries looked towards the downstream
petrochemicals sector to take maximum advantage of their abundant natural
resources and surplus capital to develop export-oriented hydrocarbon-based

chemical industries. As a result, the petrochemical industry has become an important sector in the development process of the GCC Countries.

Along with the oil sector, the petrochemical sector plays a vital role in these national economies and has become an important export industry. In 1995, about 20% of the total GCC Countries non-oil exports were petrochemical products. This industry is highly capital intensive with only 35 petrochemical companies operating in the GCC Countries. These 35 companies have a total investment of over US$ 19 billion giving an average investment per plant of about US$ 600 million (Al-Sadoun, 1997).

The research methods used were a questionnaire survey and unstructured interviews. A questionnaire survey was used to obtain a general picture of management accounting practices in the GCC Countries and the unstructured interviews provided further detailed information about the current management accounting practices in the petrochemical companies in GCC Countries.

Of the 35 petrochemical companies operating in five of the GCC Countries, 26 were included in this research project based on a random sample of 75% of the population. The questionnaire was pilot tested both in the U.K. and, more importantly, with two financial managers in two petrochemical companies in the Gulf Countries and also with staff members in the Department of Accountancy at the University of Qatar. Feedback on the length of the questionnaire, Likert scale, the sequence of questions, and the language and wording of the questionnaire was obtained during this pilot testing and the questionnaire was amended accordingly.

A personally administered questionnaire was chosen as the research method for this study for two main reasons. First, companies in the Gulf Countries were unlikely to respond to a postal questionnaire and second, there was a risk that a questionnaire received by mail would not be given proper attention. The response rates for mail questionnaires in the GCC countries are generally very low. Also, with 26 petrochemical companies being surveyed in the GCC Countries, it was feasible to use personally administered questionnaires. In addition, this method gave the researchers the opportunity to introduce the research topic and explain the importance of the study to encourage the respondents to complete the questionnaire (Sekaran, 1992, p. 200).

The questionnaire, together with a covering letter from the Qatar government, was personally delivered to a sample of 26 petrochemical companies operating in the GCC Countries. The questionnaires were addressed to the finance manager or other senior executives familiar with these issues in their companies. The total number of questionnaires completed was 24 with two companies deciding not to participate in this survey. The response rate was 92%. The respondents were generally well educated in accounting and had good practical experience with an average 10 years of accounting experience. Most companies were joint ventures with foreign companies and they operated in a highly competitive environment. The researcher conducted unstructured interviews in eight of these 24 companies to obtain further detailed information. Interviews lasted about one hour and involved open-ended discussion on the management accounting techniques used by the respondents' companies.

2. PRIOR RESEARCH (WESTERN LITERATURE)

For the past 20 years, there has been growing interest in the literature (mainly from the United States and the United Kingdom) about management accounting and costing techniques (for example, Otley, 1985; Kaplan & Johnson, 1987; Bromwich & Bhimani, 1989, 1994; Scapens; 1992; Spicer, 1992). During the late 1980s, existing management accounting practices were criticized by academics and practitioners and these criticisms were widely publicized in the professional and academic accounting literature (Drury, 1996).

The gap between academic research and the practice of management accounting has long been recognized by management accounting researchers (Scapens, 1983; Otley, 1985; Mclean, 1988; Edwards & Emmanuel, 1990). Kaplan (1984) argued that many companies still used the same cost accounting and management control systems that were developed decades ago for a very different competitive environment from that of today. Kaplan suggested that the challenges of the competitive environment in the 1980s should encourage companies to re-examine their traditional cost accounting and management accounting systems. Despite changes in the nature of organizations during the past 60 years, there has been little innovation in the design and implementation of cost and management accounting systems. Otley (1985) argued that the recommended management accounting techniques had not been used in practice because they were inappropriate to managers' needs.

A series of articles by Kaplan and Johnson during the 1980s encouraged researchers to study management accounting practices. Scapens (1992) suggested that this gap between theory and practice might attract researchers to explore the nature of management accounting practice. Many academic accounting researchers have become interested in exploring the differences between management accounting in practice and management accounting in theory, for example, Ferreira and Merchant (1992) discussed 82 case studies in management accounting and control which had been published since 1984.

Drury (1992) argued that some writers believed that management accounting was in a critical situation and that changes in practice were required. However, there are differences in opinion on whether significant changes in management accounting are necessary. Innes and Mitchell (1989) studied ten electronics companies in Scotland. They supported the idea that there were changes in management accounting techniques in practice and that academic management accountants should pay attention to such changes.

Coates et al. (1983) studied the management accounting practice in 14 divisionalized companies in the U.S., using a questionnaire survey followed up by interviews. They concluded that there was a substantial gap between theory and practice. For example, these companies used little formal analysis of cost behavior even though some managers considered this to be important. Also, the absorption cost-based system was widely used by most companies and the use of marginal cost analysis was very limited. Finne and Sizer (1983) investigated 22 engineering companies. They found that all the companies used absorption costing systems and that marginal or variable costing systems recommended by management accounting textbooks were not used. Drury et al. (1993) studied the management accounting practices in 303 U.K. manufacturing organizations with a turnover in excess of £10 m. They found that some sophisticated techniques advocated by academics in management accounting such as models for variance investigation, cost behavior analysis, risk analysis and residual income were not widely adopted in practice. On the other hand, they pointed out there was evidence in some areas that practice corresponded with theory, for instance, conventional variance analysis, discounting, the use of demand estimates and participative budgeting.

Clark (1992) examined the cost and management accounting practices and decision-making techniques used in large Irish manufacturing firms. He concluded that there appeared to be a major gap between what was traditionally taught as management accounting topics and what was used in practice. Pierce and O'dea (1998) concluded from a survey of management accountants in Ireland that traditional management accounting techniques continued to dominate management accounting systems. Chenhall and Smith (1998) concluded from a survey of Australia's largest companies that the rates of adoption for traditional management accounting practices were higher than the rates of adoption for recently developed techniques. Also, they found out that the benefits obtained from traditional management accounting practices were higher than those from newer techniques.

Major gaps between theory and practice in some management accounting areas such as allocation of overhead costs and overhead cost management have been mentioned in the literature. Overhead costs have been a major issue for management accounting researchers and practitioners in recent years. Overhead is increasing as a percentage of total product cost while direct labour is decreasing (Johnson & Kaplan, 1987; Innes & Mitchell, 1992). In fact, some companies have placed their direct labour costs into overhead because direct labour represents such a small portion of total manufacturing costs (Cornick et al., 1988). Overhead allocation and control have presented major challenges for cost accountants (Bromwich & Bhimani, 1989).

This paper attempts to explore management accounting practices in an important industry in the GCC Countries. The findings from the interviews are discussed together with the questionnaire results.

3. PRODUCT COSTING

The objective of this section is to obtain a broad picture regarding product costing practices and techniques in the petrochemical companies in the GCC Countries with a particular emphasis on overhead costs and cost allocation.

Current Objectives of Product Cost System

The results of the questionnaire[1] indicated that the most important objective of the current product systems in the companies was to provide relevant information for managerial decision making with a mean of 4.7 on a scale from 1 (not important) to 5 (very important). Most respondents (79%) reported that useful information for managers was a very important objective of the product costing system. Also, the objective of a product costing system of meeting the financial accounting requirements ranked second with a mean of 4.4. Many of these companies responding to the questionnaire (76%) indicated that this objective was very important. However, of all the companies responding, 46% reported that providing a basis for pricing was not an important objective for their product costing system with an overall mean of only 2.7. Table 1 shows how important these three objectives of the product cost system were in these companies.

Table 1. Current objectives of product cost system.

	Finan. accounting requirement		Inf. for managerial decision making		Basis for pricing	
	No.	%	No.	%	No.	%
(1) Not important	2	8	0	0	11	46
(2) Below average importance	0	0	1	4	3	13
(3) Average importance	2	8	1	4	1	4
(4) Above average importance	2	8	3	13	1	4
(5) Very important	18	76	19	79	8	33
Means	4.4		4.7		2.7	

Cost Structure

Although the cost structure varied between companies, direct material costs were the most important element of the total cost. Sixty-five percent of the companies stated that direct raw materials were more than 50% of their total costs. The average product cost percentage for direct raw materials was 55%. This high percentage for direct materials indicated that the companies needed to concentrate on controlling and managing direct raw material costs and the inventory of these materials.

Table 2 shows the relative insignificance of direct labour as an element of the total cost. Eighty-two percent of the companies reported that direct labour was less than 25% of the total cost. The average percentage for direct labour costs was 15% of total costs. Only one respondent indicated that direct labour cost was more than 50% of the total costs. With a questionnaire, it is difficult to know why this particular company had such relatively high direct labour costs.

Overhead costs have become an important element of total costs. Overhead costs are increasing as a percentage of total product costs while direct labour costs are decreasing. For 57% of the petrochemical companies, overhead costs represented over 25% of the total costs. The average percentage for overhead costs was 31%.

During the interviews, a cost accountant mentioned that his company produced ten products. He pointed out that the cost structure clearly varied between these products. For example, in product A, fixed costs represented 62% of operating costs and variable costs represented 38% of operating costs. However, in product F, fixed costs represented 14% of operating costs and variable costs represented 86% of operating costs. Table 3 shows how the cost structure varied between this company's ten products.

Table 2. Proportion of Direct Materials, Direct Labour and Overhead Costs to the Total Cost.

	Direct Materials		Direct Labour		Overhead costs	
	No.	Percent	No.	Percent	No.	Percent
(a) Less than 10%	0	0	11	48	2	9
(b) 11–25%	2	9	8	34	8	34
(c) 26–50%	6	26	3	13	10	44
(d) 51–75%	13	56	1	5	3	13
(e) 76–100%	2	9	0	0	0	0
Total	23	100	23	100	23	100

Table 3.   Cost Structure by Products for One Company.

Costs	Products										
	A	B	C	D	E	F	G	H	I	J	Total
Variable costs	38%	54%	49%	47%	50%	86%	75%	70%	79%	77%	62%
Fixed costs	62%	46%	51%	53%	50%	14%	25%	30%	21%	23%	38%
Production costs	100%	100%	100%	100%	100%	100%	100%	100%	100%	100%	100%

Another interviewee gave an explanation for variations between the different cost elements:

(1) There are three types of petrochemical products: basic, intermediate, and final products. Basic petrochemical products are the initial products of steam feedstock such as Ethylene and Propylene. For example, the company produced Ethylene which was considered as a basic product. This product depended on Ethane as feedstock which was very cheap in the GCC Countries. As a result, variable costs for Ethylene product were less than 40% of production costs and fixed cash costs were more than 30% of production costs. Table 4 shows the elements of production costs for Ethylene as percentages.

This company also produced a Polyethylene product as an intermediate product, with variable costs being more than 50% of production costs and fixed cash costs were less than 30% of production costs.

(2) These plants were highly capital intensive and depreciation related to plants was relatively high and this affected their cost structure.

Cost Classification

The questionnaire indicated that most respondents (88%) used both variable and fixed costs in their cost classification. Product and period cost methods were not widely used in the GCC petrochemical companies and only 21% of the

Table 4.   Elements of production costs for Ethylene.

Costs	Percentages
(1) Variable Cost	38%
(2) Fixed Cash Costs	32%
(3) Plant Depreciation	30%

companies used this method. Some companies used more than one method for cost classification.

Types of Product Cost Systems

In general, a process costing system was the most popular type of product cost system employed by the GCC petrochemical industry with 83% of these companies using a process costing system. Although the job order costing system was not widely used in this industry, 22% of the companies employed this system. In other words, some companies used both systems (process costing and job order costing). During the interviews one finance manager mentioned that his company used a job order costing because some customers sometimes asked about specific job orders. For example, some customers asked for specific raw materials (such as chemicals) to be added to their orders. Costs were therefore collected for such specific orders.

Cost Allocation Methods

Seventeen percent of respondents used a plant wide overhead rate (blanket overhead rate) method to allocate overhead costs to products. These companies used just a single allocation base and this was adequate for their financial accounting requirements such as inventory evaluation. However, in most circumstances it did not provide accurate product costs for managerial decision making. Cost center rates (departmental rates) method was used by 83% of the companies.

Overhead Allocation Basis

Respondents were asked what bases they used to allocate overhead costs from departments or cost centers to products. Many companies (58%) indicated that they used direct labour costs or direct labour hours as a basis for overhead allocation. Also, units produced were widely used (50%) as a basis for cost allocation. However, only two companies used machine hours as a basis for allocating overhead costs to products. When manufacturing processes were labour intensive, direct labour was appropriate as a basis for cost allocation. However, direct labour was a relatively small component of product costs (less than 15% of total costs for most companies). So, it was surprising that companies operating with a high level of automation used a direct labour basis rather than a machine hours basis for allocating overhead costs to products.

During the interviews, a financial controller in one of the companies explained and identified the cost centers and cost allocation bases that his company used

Table 5.   Overhead Cost Allocation Bases for One Company.

Cost centre	Allocation base
1 – Utility variable cost	Actual consumption quantity
2 – Utility fixed cost	Variable for previous period
3 – Maintenance	Direct labour
4 – Warehouse	Capital costs
5 – Delivery	Direct charge to inventory code
6 – Production control	Capital costs
7 – Technical	Direct labour
8 – Housing	Budget salary and wages ratio

to allocate overhead costs. Table 5 shows that this particular company used multiple costs centers with different bases of cost allocation.

Another financial controller mentioned that his company allocated all indirect fixed costs to the products from cost centers (production departments). The basis of allocation of indirect fixed costs was the direct salaries. Table 6 shows the allocation of indirect costs to products based on the direct salaries that had been planned for one year.

He said that all indirect costs were allocated based on these percentages. In general, this company just used a single base to allocate overhead costs and thus, their product cost system was relatively inaccurate. Another financial manager pointed out that he was not satisfied with the present cost allocation methods, because he considered that the company's cost system did not provide relevant information for managerial decision making. He wished to change these methods, but top management did not support his idea.

Two financial managers suggested that the most important improvement in their cost systems would be to their cost allocation methods. Their cost allocation system was mainly based on volume-related allocation bases such as direct labour costs or hours and units produced. They argued that a logical and

Table 6.   Salaries as an Overhead Cost Allocation Basis for One Company.

Plant cost centre	Direct plant salaries cost (000)	Percent
1	4320	31%
2	4728	34%
3	3744	27%
4	1044	8%
Total	13,836	100

causal relationship should exist between overhead costs and the choice of cost allocation bases.

Reasons for Cost Allocations

Although there were objections to cost allocation in the literature (Thomas, 1975), many textbooks argued that cost allocation was necessary for many reasons such as product cost control, production planning, external reporting, and product pricing (Fremgen & Liao, 1980; Ahmed et al., 1991). The questionnaire gave some reasons for overhead allocation and respondents were asked how important these reasons were. The companies allocated overhead costs for many reasons.

The most important reason for cost allocation in these companies was to control costs with a mean of 4.0. Sixty-three percent of these companies stated that cost control was a very important reason for overhead cost allocation. Also, external reporting was considered by respondents to be an important reason for cost allocation with a mean of 3.5. Thirty-eight percent of these companies reported that external reporting was a very important reason for cost allocation. Production planning ranked third in importance, with a mean of 3.3. Only 25% of companies stated that this reason was very important for cost allocation. However, in the petrochemical industry, product pricing was not an important reason for cost allocation because this industry was based on an international market price. Thirty-eight percent of the respondents reported that product pricing was not important for cost allocation. Table 7 summarizes the importance of different reasons for overhead cost allocation such as product cost control, production planning, external reporting, and product pricing.

Table 7. Reasons for Overhead Cost Allocation.

	Cost control		Production planning		External reporting		Product pricing	
	No.	%	No.	%	No.	%	No.	%
(a) Not important	2	8	6	25	5	21	9	37
(b) Below average importance	4	17	0	0	2	8	3	13
(d) Average importance	1	4	5	21	2	8	3	13
(c) Above average importance	2	8	7	29	6	25	3	13
(e) Very important	15	63	6	25	9	38	6	24
Means	4.0		3.3		3.5		2.7	
Standard deviations	1.5		1.6		1.5		1.7	

The Level of Satisfaction With the Current Cost Methods

Respondents were asked about their level of satisfaction with their existing cost methods on a five-point Likert scale, where 1 indicated not satisfied and 5 very satisfied. In general, respondents had above average satisfaction with a mean of 3.9 and a standard deviation of 0.9. Thirty-three percent of the respondents stated that they were very satisfied with the existing cost methods used. One finding was that only one respondent indicated that he was less than satisfied with the existing cost methods.

Familiarity with Activity-Based Costing (ABC)

Respondents were asked to determine their familiarity with ABC. The rating was on a scale from 1 (know nothing) to 5 (very familiar). Fifty-two percent of the respondents were familiar with ABC. Also, 9% of the respondents indicated that they were very familiar. However, 22% of the respondents knew nothing about ABC. Generally speaking, the results indicated that respondents were familiar with ABC.

Although financial managers were familiar with ABC, one of them mentioned during the interviews two reasons for not implementing ABC:

(1) Top managers were very satisfied with the information that the existing cost system provided. Top managers did not wish to change their cost systems and wished to keep these very simple.
(2) ABC was too sophisticated a system and very time consuming.

Investigation of Activity-Based Costing

Respondents were asked if they had any plan to investigate ABC and they had three options (yes, no, and not sure). The survey indicated that 41% of respondents were planning to investigate ABC. However, 36% of the respondents stated that they were not sure about investigating ABC and 23% of the respondents indicated that they did not have any plans to investigate ABC.

4. PRICING DECISIONS

There are two types of pricing decisions: (a) those for sales external to the company; and (b) those related to prices used for internal transfers between sub-units of the same company (transfer pricing).

Pricing Methods

Most companies (87%) pointed out that the price was determined by market forces. Other pricing methods were not widely used by these companies. Cost plus methods were used by 35% of the companies. Seventeen percent of the companies stated that they established prices based on a cost plus (manufacturing costs) method. Also the questionnaire responses indicated that some companies used more than one method for pricing.

Transfer Pricing System

In the questionnaire, the companies were asked if they had a transfer pricing system. More than half of the companies (58%) indicated that they employed a transfer pricing system. Also, the respondents were asked if they had an international transfer pricing system. However, only two companies stated that they had an international transfer pricing system.

Objectives of Transfer Pricing System

The questionnaire provided a list of possible objectives of a transfer pricing system and the respondents were asked the importance of these objectives. Helping top management judge divisional performance was the most important objective of a transfer pricing system with a mean of 4.2. More than half of the companies (58%) reported that this objective was very important. The second important objective of a transfer pricing system was to ensure an efficient allocation of resources among divisions with a mean of 4.1. Half of the companies considered this objective was very important. Encouraging divisional managers to make decisions ranked third in importance with a mean of 3.8. Table 8 summarizes descriptive statistics on the importance of the above objectives for a transfer pricing system.

Transfer Pricing Methods

Most companies (86%) stated that they used the full cost method for setting transfer prices. The market-based method and the variable cost method were not widely used by these companies. The questionnaire responses indicated that only one company used the variable cost method and another company used the market-based method. No company adopted the negotiated transfer price method.

Table 8.   Objectives of Transfer Pricing System.

	NI[1]		BAI		AI		AAI		VI			
	N	%	N	%	N	%	N	%	N	%	M	SD
(a) To encourage divisional managers to make decisions	1	8	0	0	3	25	5	42	3	25	3.8	1.1
(b) To help top management judge divisional performance	0	0	1	8	3	25	1	8	7	58	4.2	1.1
(c) To ensure an efficient allocation of resources	1	8	0	0	2	17	3	25	6	50	4.1	1.2
(d) To provide a high level of divisional autonomy	3	25	2	17	2	17	3	25	2	17	2.9	1.5

[1] NI = Not Important, BAI = Below Average Importance, AI = Average Importance, AAI = Above Average Importance, VI = Very Important, M = mean, SD = Standard Deviation.

5. BUDGETARY PRACTICES

This section covers several areas in the budgeting system including: reasons for producing budgets, budget preparation, budget manual, budget committee, types of budgets, flexible budgets, and sales forecasting techniques.

Budgetary System

The respondents were asked if they used a budgetary system. The use of a budgetary system was widespread with 96% of the companies operating such a system.

Reasons for Producing Budgets

The most important reason for producing budgets in the companies was to control activities and costs with a mean of 4.7, followed by periodic planning (mean of 4.5), managers' motivation (mean of 4.5), co-ordination and communication (mean of 4.4), and performance evaluation (mean of 4.4). Most companies (96%) stated that the reason "to control costs" was either of above average importance or a very important reason for budgeting. Table 9 summarizes descriptive statistics on the importance of the reasons for producing budgets.

Table 9. Reasons for Producing Budgets.

	Control costs		Periodic planning		Managers' motivation		Coordination and communication		Performance evaluation	
	No.	%	No.	%	No.	%	No.	%	No.	%
(a) Not important	0	0	0	0	0	0	0	0	0	0
(b) Below average importance	0	0	0	0	0	0	0	0	1	4
(c) Average importance	1	4	3	13	1	5	2	9	2	9
(d) Above average importance	4	18	5	21	10	43	9	39	7	30
(e) Very important	18	78	15	66	12	52	12	52	13	57
Means	4.7		4.5		4.5		4.4		4.4	
Standard deviations	0.5		0.7		0.6		0.7		0.8	

Approaches to Budget Preparation

Sixty-eight percent of the companies preferred a more realistic approach where information was exchanged between top and lower level managers (negotiated budgets). Also, 63% of the companies stated that they preferred a 'bottom-to-top' approach where budgets are prepared by lower level managers and then co-ordinated and communicated upward (participative budgets). Only 9% of the companies reported that they adopted a 'top-to-bottom' approach where top management decide the budget (imposed budgets). Many companies adopted more than one approach to budget preparation with more than 40% of the companies adopting both participative budgets and negotiated budgets.

Types of Budgets

The respondents were asked about the types of budgets that the companies prepared. Table 10 shows the types of budgets that these companies prepared.

Table 10 indicates that all the companies had a comprehensive budget approach because they prepared many types of budgets. However, only half of all the respondent companies prepared a Research and Development budget. It would require further investigation to determine why the research and development budget was the least prepared item.

Table 10.   Current Types of Budgets.

	Number of companies	Per cent
(a) Sales	22	96
(b) Production	22	96
(c) Material	22	96
(d) Direct labour	22	96
(e) Overhead cost	22	96
(f) Profits and loss statement	22	96
(g) Balance sheet	21	91
(h) Capital expenditure	22	96
(j) Research and development	13	54
(I) Cash	22	96

Sales Forecasting Techniques

The sales budget tended to be the most important step in the annual budget process because sales forecasting was the starting point for budgeting. Table 11 presents different types of sales forecasting techniques that were currently used by the companies. Market research was the technique most frequently used when forecasting sales volume. Seventy-eight percent of all the respondents reported that they often or always applied market research techniques. Also, the opinions of executives and sales persons ranked second with a mean rating of 3.6. Sixty-one percent of the companies often or always used the opinions of executives and sales persons. Although statistical techniques are advocated in the literature, only 43% of the respondents indicated that they often or always used this tool.

Flexible Budgets, Budget Manual and Budget Committee

The respondents were asked if they used flexible budgets. The literature suggests that flexible budgets should be used when comparing actual with budgeted costs. However, only 42% of the companies used flexible budgets.

A budget manual is helpful for preparing the annual budget. It describes in writing the objectives and procedures of the budget program. To help administer the budget system, 92% of the companies had a budget manual.

The objective of the budget committee is to ensure that budgets are realistically established and reasonably co-ordinated. Seventy-eight percent of the companies reported that they had a budget committee. This indicated that many companies had central guidance for the budget preparation.

Table 11.   Sales Forecasting Techniques.

	Statistical techniques		Market research		Opinions of executives and sales persons	
	No.	%	No.	%	No.	%
(a) Never	6	26	3	13	3	13
(b) Rarely	2	9	0	0	2	9
(c) Sometimes	5	22	2	9	4	17
(d) Often	3	13	4	17	6	26
(e) Always	7	30	14	61	8	35
Total	23	100	23	100	23	100
Means	3.1		4.1		3.6	
S.D.	1.6		1.4		1.4	

6. STANDARD COSTING SYSTEMS

This section included objectives of standard costing, achievement of standards, methods of setting raw material standards, and variance analysis.

Objectives of Standard Costing

Standards were established and used for several objectives. The questionnaire provided a list of possible objectives of a standard costing system and the respondents were asked to indicate the importance of these objectives.

The use of standard costing for cost control, help in setting budgets, and improving performance were the most important objectives with a mean rating of 4.3. Sixty-five percent of the companies reported that cost control and help in setting budgets were very important objectives for using standard costing systems and 55% of the companies indicated that improving performance was a very important objective. Also, evaluating inventory and reducing costs were considered by the respondents as important objectives for standard costing with a mean rating of 3.7. Forty-five percent of the companies mentioned that evaluating inventory and reducing costs were very important objectives for a standard cost system. Only 15% of the respondents reported that managers' motivation was a very important objective for a standard costing system. Table 12 shows how important these objectives of standard costing system were in the companies surveyed.

Table 12. Objectives of Standard Costing System.

	Cost control		Help in setting budgets		Evaluate inventory		Managers' motivation		Improve performance		Reduce costs	
	No.	%	No.	%	No.	%	No.	%	No.	%	No.	%
(a) NI[1]	1	5	2	10	4	20	2	10	1	5	4	20
(b) BAI	1	5	0	0	1	5	1	5	0	0	0	0
(c) AI	2	10	1	5	2	10	5	25	2	10	3	15
(d) AAI	3	25	4	20	4	20	9	45	6	30	4	20
(e) VI	13	65	13	65	9	45	3	15	11	55	9	45
Means	4.3		4.3		3.7		3.5		4.3		3.7	
S.D.	1.2		1.3		1.6		1.1		1		1.6	

[1] NI = Not Important, BAI = Below Average Importance, AI = Average Importance, AAI = Above Average Importance, VI = Very Important.

Revising Standards

The companies in the study were asked how often they revised their standards. The most frequent answer to this question was annually, with 50% of the companies indicating this choice. Twenty percent of the companies revised their standards quarterly, 15% monthly and 5% semi-annually.

Achievement of Standards

The questionnaire asked for a description of the current standard cost system. Half of the respondents described their standard cost system as being "achievable with high level of performance". Forty percent of respondents stated that their standards were achievable with average performance and only 10% of the respondents reported that their standards were arbitrary.

Setting Raw Materials Standards

Raw materials were the most important element of total costs in the petrochemical industry. Most companies (79%) used a historical records method to set raw materials quantity standards. 32% of the companies indicated that they used an engineering studies method to set raw materials standards and only one company stated that it used the trial runs method to determine raw material standards.

Variance Analysis

The respondents were asked about the importance of direct materials variances, direct labour variances, and overhead variances in their companies. The most important type of variance was direct materials variances with a mean rating of 4.6. Most companies (85%) stated that direct material variances were very important or of above average importance. Overhead variances ranked second in importance with a mean rating of 4.4. Most respondents (90%) considered overhead costs variances were very important or of above average importance. Also, many of the companies (80%) stated that direct labour variances were very important or of above average importance (see Table 13).

7. CONCLUSIONS

This research project was an exploratory study of the GCC petrochemical companies where there was no publicly available information about the current management accounting techniques used. This exploratory study was a starting point for exploring management accounting practices adopted by the petrochemical companies in the GCC Countries, in the areas of product costing, pricing, budgetary practices and standard costing. The study was based on: (1) a personally administered questionnaire survey of twenty-four companies; and (2) eight unstructured interviews. The major findings are summarized below:

The most important objective of the current product cost system was to provide relevant information for managerial decision making. Direct raw materials represented the most important element of the total costs (54%) followed by overhead costs (31%) and direct labour costs (15%). Perhaps as expected, most companies used a process costing system. Most companies also

Table 13.   Importance of Material, Labour and Overhead Variances.

	Direct material		Direct labour		Overhead	
	No.	%	No.	%	No.	%
(a) Very important	0	0	0	0	0	0
(b) Below average importance	2	10	3	15	2	10
(c) Average importance	1	5	1	5	0	0
(d) Above average importance	1	5	3	15	6	30
(e) Very important	16	80	13	65	12	60
Means	4.6		4.3		4.4	
Standard deviations	0.1		1.1		0.9	

used departmental overhead rates and were allocating overheads to products by applying volume-related allocation bases such as direct labour hours (or costs) and units produced. Most companies stated that cost control was the most important reason for cost allocation, whereas product pricing was not an important reason. Overhead costs and cost allocation were identified as major areas of concern.

The external price was determined by market forces. More than half of the companies had a transfer pricing system. The most important objectives of the transfer pricing system were to help top management judge divisional performance, to encourage managers to make decisions and to ensure an efficient allocation of resources. The full cost method was the most widely used for transfer pricing.

The use of a budgetary system was widespread in the companies. The most important reason for producing budgets was to control costs, but less than half the companies used flexible budgets. All the companies had a comprehensive budget approach, but only half of the companies prepared a research and development budget. Market research was the most frequently used technique for sales forecasting. The use of a standard costing system was widespread to meet the objectives of cost control, help in setting budgets, and improving performance. Half of the companies described their standard cost system as being "achievable with a high level of performance".

In the area of cost allocation and management of overhead costs, there was a noticeable gap between theory and practice. Although the primary reason for cost allocation was cost-control, these companies applied a traditional costing system based on volume-related allocation bases. Despite the fact that they were familiar with the Activity-Based Costing system (ABC) and its benefits, they were satisfied with the existing costing methods, and they will continue to apply such methods. However, overhead costs were a relatively high percentage of total costs and respondents indicated that overhead costs and cost allocation were issues of major concern.

Detailed case studies are needed in order to investigate the issues which have been raised by the questionnaire results and unstructured interviews. These results are a first step in exploring management accounting practices in the GCC petrochemical companies. Specifically, further research is required to investigate and explore overhead costs and cost allocations in terms of both product costing and cost management.

NOTE

1. A copy of the questionnaire is available from the authors.

ACKNOWLEDGMENTS

The authors gratefully acknowledge the helpful comments of Professor David Hatherly from the University of Edinburgh and colleagues from the University of Dundee and the University of Qatar.

REFERENCES

Al-Basteki, H. (1995). The Voluntary Adoption of International Accounting Standards by Bahraini Corporations. *Advances in International Accounting, 8*, 47–64.

Al-Sa'doun, A. (1997). The GCC Petrochemical Industry: On the Road Toward the 21st Century. *Al Ta'awon Al Sina'e, 68*, 3–23.

Bromwich M., & Bhimani, A. (1989). *Management Accounting: Evolution not Revolution*. London: The Chartered Institute of Management Accountants (CIMA).

Bromwich M., & Bhimani, A. (1994). *Management Accounting: Pathways to Progress*. London: The Chartered Institute of Management Accountants (CIMA).

Chenhall, H., & Smith, K. (1998). Adoption and Benefits of Management Accounting Practices: an Australian Study. *Management Accounting Research, 9*, 1–19.

Clarke, P. J. (1992). Management Accounting Practices in Irish Manufacturing Business: A Pilot Study. *Irish Accounting and Finance Association Proceedings*, 17–34.

Coates, J., Smith, J., & Stacey, R. (1983). Results of a preliminary survey into the structure of divisionalised companies, divisionalised performance appraisal and the associated role of management accounting. In: D. Cooper, R. Scapens & J. Arnold (Eds), *Management Accounting Research and Practice*. London: CIMA.

Cornick, M., Cooper, W., & Wilson, S. (1988). How Do Companies Analyse Overhead. *Management Accounting*, (June), 41–43.

Drury, C. (1996). *Management and Cost Accounting*. London: International Thomson Business Press.

Drury C., & Dugdale, D. (1992). Surveys of management accounting practice. In: C. Drury (Ed.), *Management Accounting Handbook*. London: CIMA.

Drury C., Braund, S., Osborne, P., & Tayles, M. (1993). *A Survey of Management Accounting Practices in U.K. Manufacturing Companies*, ACCA research Occasional Papers, Chartered Association of Certified Accountants.

Edwards K. A., & Emmanuel, C. R. (1990). Diverging Views on the Boundaries of Management Accounting. *Managing Accounting Research, 1*, 551–563.

Ferreira, L., & Merchant, K. (1990). Field Research in Management Accounting and Control: A Review and Evaluation. Accounting. *Auditing & Accountability Journal, 5*(4), 3–34.

Finnie, J., & Sizer, J. (1983. The Apparent Value Placed Upon Product Cost Information in a Sample of Engineering Companies. In: D. Cooper, R. Scapens & J. Arnold (Eds), *Management Accounting Research and Practice*. London: CIMA.

Fremgen, J., & Liao, S. (1981). *The Allocation of Corporate Indirect Costs*. New York: National Association of Accountants.

Innes, J., & Mitchell, F. (1992). A Review of Activity-Based Costing Practice. In: C. Drury (Ed.), *Management Accounting Handbook* (pp. 36–63). London: CIMA.

Johnson, H., & Kaplan, R. (1987). *Relevance Lost: the Rise and Fall of Management Accounting*. Boston, Mass.: Harvard Business School Press.

Kammlade, J., Pravesh, M., & Ozan, T. (1989). A Process Approach to Overhead Management. *Journal of Cost Management*, (Fall), 5–10.

Mirghani, M. (1998). The Development of Accounting Standards in Saudi Arabia. *Advances in International Accounting*, (Supplement 1).

Mclean, T. (1988). Management Accounting Education: Is Theory Related to Practice? (Part 1). *Management Accounting*, (June), 44–46.

Mclean, T. (1988). Management Accounting Education: Is Theory Related to Practice? (Part 2). *Management Accounting*, (July/August), 46–48.

Needles, B. (1997). International Accounting Research: An Analysis of Thirty-Two Years From the *International Journal of Accounting. The International Journal of Accounting, 32*, 203–235.

Otley, D. (1985). Developments in Management Accounting Research. *The British Accounting Review, 17*, 3–23.

Pierce, B., & O'dea, T. (1998). Management Accounting Practices in Ireland – The Preparers' Perspective. DCUBS Research Paper Series 34: Dublin City University Business School.

Scapens, R. (1991). *Management Accounting: A Review of Recent Developments*. London: Macmillan.

Scapens, R., & Theobald, M. (1992). *Research Method and Methodology in Finance and Accounting*. London: Academic Press.

Scapens, R. (1983). Closing the Gap Between Theory and Practice. *Management Accounting*, (January), 34–36.

Sekaran, U. (1992). *Research Methods for Business: A Skill Building Approach*. New York: John Wiley & Sons Inc.

Thomas, A. (1975). The FASB and the Allocation Fallacy. *Journal of Accounting*, (November).

APPENDIX

Part one: (Background information)

1) Your current position in the company is:

_____

2) Your highest educational qualification is:

High school	Bachelor	Master	Other*
1	2	3	4
*Others (please specify):			

3) Your field of study is:

Accounting	Other *
1	2
* Other (please specify):	

4) The number of years worked in this company:

Less than 5 years	5-10 years	11- 15 years	More than 15 years
1	2	3	4

5) The total number of employees in your company:

Less than 100	100 - 200	201- 500	501- 1000	More than 1000
1	2	3	4	5

6) The number of products that your company produces:

1-2	3-4	5-6	More than 6
1	2	3	4

7) The type of ownership:

Government 100%	Private 100%	Joint venture	Other*
1	2	3	4
* Other (please specify):			

8) Annual sales revenues of your company:

$500 million	$501 m- $1 billion	$1 b- $ 5 billions	Over $5 billions
1	2	3	4

9) Please indicate the level of automation of production processes in your company:

Not automated		Partly automated		Completely automated
1	2	3	4	5

10) Please indicate the degree of competition that your company faces:

No competition		Moderate competition		High competition
1	2	3	4	5

11) Does your company operate at full capacity?

Never	Rarely	Sometimes	Often	Always
1	2	3	4	5

12) Which of the following items describe the types of advanced manufacturing technologies that are currently implemented in your company?
(Please circle one or more as appropriate)

a) Mainframe computer	1
b) Personal computer	2
c) Local Area Network (LAN)	3
d) Computerized Production Systems	4
e) Computer Aided Manufacturing (CAM)	6
f) Factory Automation (Robotics) ·	7
g) Total quality management (TQM)	8
h) Just in time systems (JIT)	9
i) Other types of advanced technologies (please specify):	

Part two: (product costing)

1-What is the approximate proportion of the following elements to the total costs?

a) Direct material	%
b) Direct labor	%
c) Overhead costs	%

2-Why does your company classify costs and how important is each reason ?
(Please circle one reason or more as appropriate)

Reasons	Yes	No	Not important	Below average importance	Average importance	Above average importance	Very important
a) Periodic profits			1	2	3	4	5
b) Budgetary planning			1	2	3	4	5
c) Cost control			1	2	3	4	5
d) Pricing policy			1	2	3	4	5
e) Other (please specify):							

3-How does your company classify costs?
(Please circle one or more as appropriate)

a) Variable costs and fixed costs	1
b) Direct costs and indirect costs	2
c) Product costs and period costs	3
d) Other (please specify):	

4-What types of costs are used for product costing in your company?
(Please circle one or more as appropriate)

a) Actual costs	1
b) Standard costs	2
c) Other (please specify):	

5-What are your company's objectives for your current product costing system?
(Please circle one or more as appropriate)

Objectives	Yes	No	Not important	Below average importance	average importance	Above average importance	Very important
a) To meet financial accounting requirements.			1	2	3	4	5
b)To provide useful information for managerial decision making			1	2	3	4	5
c) To provide a basis for pricing			1	2	3	4	5
c) Other (please specify):							

6-What is the product cost system currently used in your company?
(Please circle one or more as appropriate)

a) Job order costing	1
b) Process costing	2
c) Batch costing	3
d) Other (please specify):	

7-How important are the following reasons for allocating overhead costs in your company?

Reasons	Not important	Below average importance	Average importance	Above average importance	Very important
a) Product cost control	1	2	3	4	5
b) Production planning	1	2	3	4	5
c) External reporting (inventory)	1	2	3	4	5
d) Product pricing	1	2	3	4	5
e) Other (please specify):					

8-What are the current overhead cost allocation methods that your company uses?

a) Blanket overhead rate (plant-wide overhead rate)	1
b) Cost center rates (departmental rates)	2
c) Other (please specify):	

9-Which of the following bases does your company use to allocate overhead costs to products?

a) Direct labour hours	1
b) Direct labour costs	2
c) Machine hours	3
d) Number of units produced	4
e) Other (please specify):	

10-How does your company accumulate overhead costs for the purpose of product costing?

a) By activities	1
b) By departments	2
c) Other (please specify):	

11-How satisfied are you with current costing methods?

Not satisfied		Satisfied		Very satisfied
1	2	3	4	5

12-How familiar are you with activity-based costing (ABC)?[†]

Know nothing		Familiar		Very familiar
1	2	3	4	5

13- Do you have any plans to investigate activity-based costing?

YES	NO	NOT SURE
1	2	3

Part three: (pricing decisions)

A- Transfer pricing:

1-Does your company have a transfer pricing system?

YES	NO
1	2

If your answer is NO, please go to section B on page 6.

2-Does your company have international transfer pricing?

YES	NO
1	2

3-How important are the following objectives for your company's transfer pricing system?

Objectives	Not important	Below average importance	Average importance	Above average importance	Very important
a) To encourage divisional managers to make decisions which lead to achieving both divisional and organizational goals	1	2	3	4	5
b) To help top management judge divisional performance	1	2	3	4	5
c) To ensure an efficient allocation of resources among divisions	1	2	3	4	5
d) To provide a high level of divisional autonomy in decision making	1	2	3	4	5
e) Other (please specify):					

[†] Activity-based costing means an approach to costing that focuses on activities as the fundamental cost objects. It uses the cost of these activities as a basis for assigning costs of these activities to other cost objects such as products (Horngren et al., 1994).

4-Which transfer pricing methods do your company use?
(Please circle one or more as appropriate)

a) Market pricing method	1
b) Full cost method	2
c) Variable cost method	3
d) Negotiated transfer pricing method	4
e) Other (please specify):	

B- External price:

1-What pricing method does your company use?
(Please circle one or more as appropriate)

a) Cost plus (variable cost)	1
b) Cost plus (total cost)	2
c) Cost plus (manufacturing cost)	3
d) Market based	4
e) Other (please specify):	

2-How important are the following factors in pricing decisions?

Factors	Not important	Below average importance	Average importance	Above average importance	Very important
a) Customers	1	2	3	4	5
b) Competitors	1	2	3	4	5
c) Costs	1	2	3	4	5
d) Other (please specify):					

3-If your company uses a cost plus pricing method, what kind of mark-up does your company use?

a) A flat percentage to costs	1
b) A variable percentage to costs	2
c) Other (please specify):	

4-If your company uses the full cost pricing method, what are the main reasons for
using this method?

Reasons	Not important	Below average importance	Average importance	Above average importance	Very important
a) It is simple and easy to apply	1	2	3	4	5
b) It ensures that total revenues will be in excess of total costs	1	2	3	4	5
c) It may encourage price stability	1	2	3	4	5
d) It may provide a defensible rationale for price increases	1	2	3	4	5
e) Other (please specify):					

5-Does your company estimate the demand for its products before deciding the price?

Never	Rarely	Sometimes	Often	Always
1	2	3	4	5

6- What kinds of methods are used by your company to separate fixed and variable costs?
(Please circle one or more as appropriate)

a) Regression analysis	1
b) Account classification	2
c) Managers' experience	3
d) Other (please specify):	

Part four: (cost management):
A-budgeting:
1-Does your company use a budgeting system?

YES	NO
1	2

If your answer is NO, please go to section B on page 9.

2-Does your company have a budget manual?

YES	NO
1	2

3-What kinds of techniques does your company use to forecast future sales volume?

Techniques	Never	Rarely	Sometimes	Often	Always
a) Statistical techniques	1	2	3	4	5
b) Market research	1	2	3	4	5
c) A judgmental estimate by collecting the opinions of executives and sales persons	1	2	3	4	5
d) Other (please specify):					

4-How important are the following reasons for producing budgets?

Reasons	Not important	Below average importance	Average importance	Above average importance	Very important
a) Periodic planning	1	2	3	4	5
b) Coordination and communication	1	2	3	4	5
c) Control activities and costs	1	2	3	4	5
d) Performance evaluation	1	2	3	4	5
e) Managers' motivation toward company objectives	1	2	3	4	5

5-Does your company use a computer in the budgeting process?

Never	Rarely	Sometimes	Often	Always
1	2	3	4	5

6-What types of budgets does your company prepare?
(Please circle one or more as appropriate)

a) Sales budget	1
b) Production budget	2
c) Material budget	3
d) Direct labour budgets	4
e) Overhead budget	5
f) Profit and loss statement	6
g) Balance sheet	7
h) Capital expenditure	8
i) Research and development	9
j) Cash budget	10

7-Does your company have a flexible budget?[‡]

YES	NO
1	2

8-What approaches to budget preparation does your company adopt ?

a) Imposed budget (top-to-bottom)	1
b) Participative budgets (bottom-to- top)	2
c) Negotiated budgets	3
d) Other (please specify):	

9-Does your company have a budget committee?

YES	NO
1	2

10-What is the normal planning period for which the budget is set?

a) Quarterly	1
b) Six monthly	2
c) Annually	3
d) Longer than one year	4

B- Standard Costing:

1-How important are the following objectives for standard costing in your Company?

Objectives	Not important	Below average importance	Average importance	Above average importance	Very important
a) To control costs	1	2	3	4	5
b) To help in setting budgets	1	2	3	4	5
c) To evaluate inventory	1	2	3	4	5
d) To motivate managers	1	2	3	4	5
e) To improve performance	1	2	3	4	5
f) To reduce costs	1	2	3	4	5
h) Other (please specify):					

[‡] Flexible budget means some costs vary with activity and the costs in the original budget will be adjusted to the actual level of activity (Drury, 1996).

2- Which techniques does your company use to set standard costs for materials?

a) Past historical records	1
b) Engineering studies	2
c) Trial runs	3
d) Other (please specify):	

3- How often does your company revise its standard costs?

a) Monthly	1
b) Quarterly	2
c) Six monthly	3
d) Annually	4
e) Other (please specify):	

4- How would you describe your current standard cost system?
(Please circle one only)

a) Achievable with high level of performance	1
b) Achievable with average performance	2
c) Achievable with below average performance	3
d) Standards are arbitrary	4
e) Other (please specify):	

5-What types of standard cost variance reports does your company prepare and how important are these variances?

Types	Yes	No	Not important	Below average importance	average Importance	Above average importance	Very important
a) Direct materials variances			1	2	3	4	5
b) Direct labor variances			1	2	3	4	5
c) Overhead variances			1	2	3	4	5
e) Other (please specify):							

6- Please add any comments that you think are important regarding product costing, cost management and pricing decisions: .

_____

_____

_____

_____

7- Would you like a copy of the results of this questionnaire?

YES	NO
1	2

Many thanks for your time and assistance in completing this questionnaire.

PART II:
ACCOUNTING AND BANKING
IN AFRICA

7. ECONOMIES OF SUB-SAHARAN AFRICA AND THE HISTORICAL COST ACCOUNTING MODEL: A DEFINITION OF THE PROBLEM

Casimir I. Anyanwu

ABSTRACT

Most developing economies, especially those of Sub-Saharan Africa (SSA), are bedeviled by high inflation rates. Hyperinflation and the use of the Historical Cost Accounting Model (traditional approach) do not fit together. Inflation renders the traditional reporting model ineffectual. Historical cost accounting remains the practice of choice for most advanced economies. It has been modified by various nations as necessary to reflect the realities of the times, and to better measure corporate and national wealth. Fair market values (fmvs) and mixed models have often been advanced as alternative reporting choices.

An appraisal of selected financial reports of some manufacturing and production firms from Sub-Saharan Africa failed to reveal any special accounting treatment that addresses the impact of inflation. To the extent that the nations of the sub region have not proactively handled inflationary distortions, their financial reports will continue to be suspect. Indeed, the integrity and relevance of these reports will be questioned.

Research in Accounting in Emerging Economies, Volume 5, pages 127–143.
© 2003 Published by Elsevier Science Ltd.
ISBN: 0-7623-0901-6

It is argued in this paper that slavish adherence to the financial reporting methods of the West does not reflect a fair view of the operations of companies in Sub-Saharan Africa. This research has highlighted the need for reporting models that are native to the region; techniques that address the peculiar circumstances of the area. For SSA to be in a vantage position to attract badly needed direct foreign investment, it is further argued that the need for more reliable and more useful financial reports for the region has never been more urgent.

BACKGROUND

Advanced economies have employed historical cost accounting as the preferred financial reporting technique. In spite of its obvious baggage, it remains the valuation model of choice (Choi, 1991; Ryan & Tibbits, 1997). Historical cost stipulates that business transactions must be recorded at their original prices, regardless of prevailing current market values. In that context, a capital asset purchased ten years ago will still be carried in the books today at its original cost, the fair market value notwithstanding. In the *Conceptual Framework Underlying Financial Reporting*, the Financial Accounting Standards Board (FASB, 1976) shed some light on the need to adhere to the tenets of historical cost accounting. The driving force behind the traditional approach is tangibility. Is the measurement objective reliable and verifiable? The historical model is obsessed with such concerns. To demonstrate tangibility, the traditional model often loses sight of the essential ingredients of financial reporting; namely – the *relevance* and *usefulness* of such reports. A stable currency is at the core of the historical approach. The assumption is an economic environment unencumbered by inflation (FASB, 1976). The worldwide inflation of the 1970s and 1980s resulting mostly from the Arab oil embargo created serious doubts with respect to the relevance of financial reports prepared under the traditional model.

Literature is replete with debates, which have debunked the use of historical cost in times of runaway inflation. Bertholdt (1984) argued that inflation has demolished the stable monetary unit assumption of the traditional model. Those professionals who belong in this school of thought had suggested the use of inflation adjusted, market driven methods as alternatives to and, indeed, as more appropriate measurement tools to historical costing. To maintain the relevance of financial reports in the hyperinflation years of the 1970s and 1980s, advanced economies such as the United States modified their reporting instruments to address the problem. Among the techniques suggested by accounting rule-making bodies is a dual report format in which an inflation-adjusted report based on fmvs is presented alongside the historical cost model. Many authors have highlighted specific situations employed by firms to accommodate inflation distortions (Baer, 1980; Woodham, 1984; Simonsen, 1986).

The dual presentation or any other high-breed is irrelevant today in advanced economies such as the United States because inflation is very low. A robust economy with little or no inflation is the ideal setting for the application of the historical concept. Unlike other regions of the world, the worldwide economic prosperity of the past few years has had little positive effect on the nations of Sub-Saharan Africa. Other than South Africa, SSA nations are burdened by unprecedented high inflation rates, stunted economic growth, abject poverty and disease. For example in 1965, the average African received an income equal to 14% of the average of his counterpart in the Western industrialized nations. Today, that figure has dropped to 7% (*The New Republic*, May 1998). In fact, inflation rates in some countries of the sub region have exceeded 100% (Table 1). Some Sub-Saharan nations are members of the International Accounting Standards Committee (IASC) which has stated that reports of financial position and operating performance in hyperinflation environments are meaningless unless key items of financial statement information are restated to deal with inflation (International Accounting Standards (IAS) #29, 1989). In spite of triple digit inflation rates, SSA nations such as Nigeria have continued to use the traditional financial reporting model without any visible adjustments (Holt & Hein, 1998).[1]

Important economic developmental issues are riding on the credibility of financial reports from the region. It might sound academic but Sub-Saharan Africa is being canvassed as the next economic battleground following the 'Asian Tigers'.[2] The United States Congress recently passed the *Africa Growth and Opportunity Act, H. R. Bill #1432 (The Sub-Sahara Africa Trade Bill)* which gives enormous advantages to U.S. companies and individuals wishing to do business in the sub-region (Martin, 1998). It is fair to conclude that for countries that suffer the ravages of inflation including SSA nations, the continued use of the traditional model will produce financial statements that are misleading. This is a problem for a region in desperate need of massive direct foreign investment. It will be difficult for Western investors to identify credible local partners with whom to do business. While inflation is not the only variable that distorts the usefulness of SSA financial reports, it is a major factor and a problem that must be addressed as a necessary first step.

SUB-SAHARAN AFRICA AS FORMER EUROPEAN COLONIES

Accounting and financial reporting techniques that are used in Sub-Sharan African nations are those transplanted from their former colonial rulers

(Saudagaran, 2001). Accounting models of advanced European economies are not a perfect fit for the struggling Third World economies of SSA. Put differently, in Sub-Saharan Africa, First World financial reporting techniques are employed to account for Third World economic transactions. This is a mismatch.

All countries of Sub-Saharan Africa were at some point ruled by a European government. From the European perspective, economic activities in the African colonies were geared exclusively for the benefit of the colonial masters. Economic activities were simple, straightforward trading transactions. They gravitated around the movement of raw materials from SSA to Europe, and the importation of needed finished goods from Europe. In that environment, accounting and reporting practices were also simple. Pre-independence African nations adopted the accounting practices of their respective foreign rulers. Monetary units used in Europe were the same as those used in the colonies. Valuations of business transactions were simple not only because transactions were few, but also because inflation was immaterial. In addition, modern accounting measurement problems such as exchange rates and foreign currency transactions and translations did not exist.

With forty years of political independence, the Sub-Saharan economic landscape has changed markedly. Political independence has not translated into economic independence for these nations. In addition, the economies of the region, especially those of Franco-phone nations, are tied to the umbilical cords of their former colonial rulers. Political independence allowed these nations to acquire some inappropriate investments associated with independence such as major public utility corporations and an assortment of high-ticket, indigenous-owned manufacturing and trading firms. Forty years later, these corporations are aging. Most are in need of massive renovations, and some must be replaced outright or scrapped. Pre-independence Africa knew nothing about the so-called International Monetary Fund (IMF) and World Bank *'Conditionalities'*. Today, SSA nations are burdened with the debts of both the London and Paris Clubs.[3] There is not much to show for these high levels of indebtedness. The nations of Sub-Sahara are pleading for debt reduction and forgiveness. These requests might not be granted for there is no proper accounting for the utilization of resources made available in previous years.

When the rest of the world is enjoying an economic boom, the nations of Sub-Sahara are ravaged by inflation and poverty. Their accounting system, of course, did not make any provisions for the replacement of an aging infrastructure. These nations are saddled with 21st century commitments, but they are unaware that the rules have changed. They have stuck to the accounting and reporting systems which they inherited from the colonial governments. They continue to employ the traditional cost accounting model in the midst of hyperinflation. Swieringa might have been speaking to the leaders of the sub-region when he described how flawed the historical cost model could be if utilized in the wrong context. He likened it to the use of a tool developed in the Industrial Age to address the concerns of today's Wall Street (Swieringa, 1997).

Accounting rule-making bodies in post-independence Africa have failed to address the following problems:

(a) That Western Europe and the United States, whose models they adopted, have extremely low inflation rates.
(b) That during the high inflation years of the 1970s and 1980s, European and North American countries countered inflation distortions by requiring a dual reporting format namely: the use of *fair market value* financial statements alongside the historical cost model.
(c) That when Latin American nations such as Brazil, Argentina, Bolivia, and Colombia, etc. suffered hyperinflation, they employed radical valuation methods such as indexation to keep their financial reports relevant and useful.

RELEVANT LITERATURE

Although the relevance of the traditional accounting model has been questioned, it remains the most popular, the most reliable financial reporting model of choice in most industrialized nations of the world (Materniak, 1984; Ravlic, 1999; Saudagaran, 2001). Two major events in the past quarter of a century have necessitated the call for a reappraisal of this model. They are:

(1) The hyperinflation of the 1970s and 1980s, and
(2) The huge financial assets which characterize the current economic climate.

Many professionals are calling for the adoption of market-based valuation practices. The crusade for the use of *fmvs* received much attention during the high inflation years of the 1970s and 1980s resulting from the Arab oil embargo. The most recent calls for the use of current cost accounting models are in reaction to the demands of a global economy that is characterized by high technology and instant availability of information. The accounting profession is concerned about the effect of these developments on large portfolios of financial assets.

Advocates of the use of the *fmv* concept argue that in today's highly fluid economic environment, significant changes often occur in extremely short periods. There is the belief that in times of high inflation, inflated units of measure are added to or compared with stale or static units. The perception that apples are mixed with oranges can be avoided if homogeneous measuring units such as current values are used in financial statement reports. United Kingdom firms were required in the 1970s and the 1980s to publish supplementary financial statements using the current purchasing power parity (Accounting Standards Committee, 1980). Such financial reports, prepared essentially on fmv basis, would accompany annual reports prepared in the traditional fashion. In the United States, FASB issued some industry specific pronouncements to counter inflation. While the Statement of Financial Accounting Standards (SFAS) #82, *Financial Reporting and Changing Prices: Elimination of Certain Disclosures – an amendment of FASB Statement No. 33* (1984) would deal with inflationary trends in the utilities industry, SFAS #115, *Accounting for Certain Investments in Debt and Equity Securities* (FASB, 1993), would address the same issues in the financial services industry. If the headache of the 1970s and 1980s was inflation, more recent debates are concerned with the volatility of corporate equities and how to value the accompanying huge financial assets. There is almost no inflation in the U.S. economy today. With specific reference to SFAS #115, it was considered prudent to devise better ways of measuring financial assets since they now constitute a large component of corporate portfolios. Advocates of fmv-based measures argue that market-based valuations provide more relevant appraisals of equities and the earning power of firms than historical data. Market determined measurement models are better than historical data for measuring credit, investing and financing decisions. Hooper, Milburn and Swieringa (1997), Shim and Larkin, and Yonetani and Katsuo (1998) have all supported the above position.

Accounting distortions that arise from hyperinflation have also been addressed with respect to Third World nations. The 1980s runaway inflation in Latin American countries such as Brazil (annual inflation rate 1000%), Argentina (3000%), and Bolivia (20000%) has been discussed extensively by (Baer, 1980; Simonsen, 1986; Stacey, 1992; Arterian, 1994). Extremely radical means, including indexation, were employed to handle the crisis. Arterian (1994) had observed that the promise by Emerging Markets of huge profits would quickly disappear with serious inflation and the resultant currency devaluation. Most Latin American nations suffered inflation headaches in the 1970s and 1980s and did swallow the bitter pills then followed by necessary adjustments. Most of Latin America is enjoying economic stability today. This cannot be said of the nations of Sub-Saharan Africa.

Whether market-based valuations are adopted or not, most accounting professionals agree that the traditional model has major deficiencies and, therefore, cannot be implemented in its pure form. The major qualities sustaining the traditional model are *objectivity, reliability, and verifiability.* Advocates of the market approach counter by arguing that the above qualities mean nothing if *relevance* and *usefulness* are compromised. In spite of the attraction of market driven valuation techniques, critics charge that they have their own downside too. They argue that fmv measures are subjective, susceptible to volatility of earnings and are expensive to manage. Grey warned in strong terms that the use of fmvs could result in manipulations of figures to suit the whims and caprices of management (Grey, 1998). Even some proponents of the market approach advocate extreme caution in its application (Bryer & Brignall, 1985; Shim et al., 1998). Notwithstanding these observations, advocates of market based valuations insist that their advantages outweigh the disadvantages. In times of inflation and volatility in the financial markets, valuations that are market based are superior for measuring and evaluating the financial condition of firms than the traditional approach.

In practice, financial reports are not prepared in the pure historical or pure market determined valuations. Therefore, the debate about a pure traditional concept and a pure market approach is, for all practical purposes, academic. Most modern financial reports are mixed; some accounts are measured on the historical cost basis while others are weighed using fmvs (Milburn, 1997; Chrisman, 1998; Hague & Willis, 1999). The use of the Lower of Cost or Market (LOCM) concept to value inventory, and the application of FASB #115 to deal with the valuations of financial assets underscore the fact that current financial statements are a mixed breed of historical cost and current market valuations.

METHODOLOGY

Nigeria was selected as a surrogate for other SSA nations. The choice was made based on the huge size of the country's formal and underground economy. South Africa was left out of this study because of the advanced level of its economy. In fact, South Africa's financial reporting standards are comparable to those of Western Europe.

Financial reports of some selected major Nigerian manufacturing and production corporations for 1996, 1997 and 1998 fiscal years were examined in search of necessary trends. Inflation and its accounting treatment were the driving force for the data collection. The focus was on identifying which accounting reporting models were employed by the firms; namely – historical, market-based, mixed or other methods. Is there uniformity of practice across the board? Specifically, how was inflation handled in the annual reports? In addressing the inflation variable, critical examination was made of how some particular account subheads, which impact inflation, were treated by the valuation models. In that respect, what treatment was given to *short-term securities, inventory and fixed assets?* What depreciation methods were utilized to accommodate the inflation factor? Are accelerated depreciation methods employed to check this variable? What are the positions of the rulemaking bodies on inflation, valuations, and financial reporting in general? This was the general thought process of the inquiry.

Because of the paucity of reliable data and the politics of economic data, information from third parties had to be relied upon; namely – the World Bank and the International Monetary Fund – IMF (Table 1). The bulk of Nigeria's GNP comes from oil revenue. In fact, oil generates about 90% of the country's foreign exchange earnings (Moser, 1997). Nigeria's non-oil local productive capacity is very low. The country is heavily involved in foreign currency transactions on both the export as well as the import side. Therefore, the *exchange rate premium* was utilized in this study as a surrogate for *inflation*. Firms examined in the study are all manufacturing and heavy production companies. The Nigerian economy does not have the capability to manufacture any machinery including heavy-duty equipment. Machinery and equipment are the major asset/expenditure heads of all manufacturing firms. Since these assets must be imported and acquired with scarce hard currency, foreign exchange transactions will heavily influence their business. This reality justifies the choice of the foreign exchange premium as a surrogate for inflation.

Comparisons between the official rate of exchange and the parallel rates were made to determine the approximate rates of inflation. Table 1 highlights the trend of inflation and Table 2 contains data from some Nigerian premier corporate annual financial reports regarding accounting practices. Inflation is measured by the difference between the parallel foreign exchange rate and the official exchange rate (premium). This is shown on line 3 of Table 1.[4]

FINDINGS

Inflation rates for the three years under review – 1996, 1997 and 1998 were 386%, 409% and 400% respectively (Table 1). While these rates are not close to the wild inflation rates in Latin America in 1970s and 1980s (over 1000%), any economy whose inflation rate approximates 400% must qualify as one in distress. When these rates are compared to relatively small inflation rates in the West especially the United States for the same period, one begins to appreciate the level of economic crisis in the Sub-Saharan region of Africa.

Examination of Table 2 reveals that all firms used in the study adopt the following accounting practices:

Table 1. Exchange Rate Averages and Exchange Rate Developments.

	1980	1981	1982	1983	1984	1985	1986	1987	1988	1989	1990	1991	1992	1993	1994	1995	1996	1997	1998
1. Average Official Exchange Rate (Naira/U.S. Dollar)	0.55	0.61	0.67	0.72	0.76	0.89	1.13	4.01	4.48	7.33	8.04	9.91	17.3	22	22	22	22	22	22
2. Parallel (Black Market Rate) Naira/U.S. Dollar	0.8	0.93	3	3	3.25	4	4.02	4.73	8.89	10.5	9.6	13.3	21.1	71	71	85	85	90	88
3. Parallel Rates, % of Official Managed Rates	145	152	448	416	427	449	355	118	198	143	119	134	122	323	323	386	386	409	400

Sources: Adapted from: V. Galbis, IMF Working Paper, 1993; * World Bank: Nigeria – Structural Adjustment Program, 1994; Moser: IMF Occasional Paper No. 148, 1997.

Table 2. Accounting Convention.

Company	Fiscal year	Accounting convention	Fixed asset basis	Valuation convention fixed asset	Year of last revaluation	Years since last valuation	Depre- ciation method
1. Unipetrol, Nigeria, PLC	1996	Historical Cost	Cost or Revaluation of Fixed Assets	Revaluation Of Fixed Asset Allowed	1995	1	Straight Line
2. National Oil PLC	1996	"	"	"	1996	1	"
3. Guinness Nigeria PLC	1998	"	"	"	1997	1	"
4. A.G Leventis PLC	1997	"	"	"	1995	2	"
5. UAC PLC	1997	"	"	"	1992, 1994, 1996	2, 2, 2	"
6. Nestle Foods Nigeria PLC	1996	"	"	"	1992	4	"
7. PZ Industries PLC	1998	"	"	"	1994	4	"
8. Nichemtex Industries, PLC	1996	"	"	"	1987	9	"
9. Nigerian Bottling Co., PLC	1997	"	"	"	1988	9	"
10. SCOA, Nigeria PLC	1997	"	"	"	1986	11	"
11. Nigerian Tobacco Co., PLC	1998	"	"	"	1987	11	"
12. Total Nigeria PLC	1997	"	"	"	N/A	N/A	"
13. Cadbury Nigeria PLC	1997	"	"	"	N/A	N/A	"
14. Mobil Oil Nigeria, PLC	1997	"	"	"	N/A	N/A	"

(a) The *Historical Cost* convention.
(b) All companies in the study sample *reappraise* some fixed assets to current market values. There appears to be no standard with respect to the frequency for these valuations. Appraisals range from one year for some firms to eleven years for others.
(c) All companies employ the straight-line depreciation method. Accelerated depreciation methods are not proactively employed in practice. However, provisions are made within the straight-line method to inject some element of acceleration in writing off some light fixed assets such as motor vehicles and furniture and fixtures. Depreciation rates in the range of 15–20% for this group of assets are common. The rate for heavy-duty machinery and equipment is approximately 10%.
(d) The financial reports were silent on a particular phenomenon of the region i.e. certain depreciable assets such as motor vehicles do, indeed, appreciate with time rather than lose value. Yet, the accounting system would amortize the historical cost of such assets through some form of straight-line depreciation method.

Other items from the financial reports reveal that accounts such as *inventory* and *short-term investments are valued at LOCM.*

The Nigerian Accounting Standards Board (NASB) allows for the revaluation of certain key fixed assets such as heavy machinery (Evans, 1985; Nexia International, 1993). Given this position, it is instructive to quote some policy statements regarding revaluations from *Notes* to the annual reports of selected companies:

In its 1997 annual reports, Nigerian Bottling Company PLC made these observations:

> Freehold and leasehold land and buildings of the company and two of its subsidiaries were revalued by professional valuers in 1976 and 1988 on the basis of free market value. The plant and machinery of the company nationwide were revalued professionally at 30th November, 1993 on an open market basis.

For the 1998 annual report, Nigerian Tobacco Company PLC had this in the section dealing with fixed assets:

> The leasehold properties were valued by Messrs Knight, Frank & Rutley (Nigeria) as at 30th September, 1987 on the basis of open market valuation using the investment method.

Nichemtex Industries PLC in its 1996 annual report had the following notes with respect to fixed assets revaluation:

> The company's fixed assets with the exception of motor vehicles and furniture and fittings were revalued on 11 February, 1987 by Messrs Knight, Frank & Rutley (Nigeria), estate surveyors and valuers, on the basis of open market value with subsequent additions at cost.

NEED FOR RESEARCH

As noted earlier, economic pundits believe that Sub-Saharan Africa will be the next economic battleground after the 'Asian Tigers'. First, SSA is extremely rich in natural and mineral resources. Second, these resources remain essentially untapped. Given the potential for wealth creation in this region, it has been suggested that the region will soon become a focal point of tremendous economic activity. The above thinking justifies why financial reports from SSA must reflect credibility, reliability and above all, relevance. Here are some of the reasons why the region must keep reliable books:

(1) The century old financial reporting techniques inherited from colonial governments are stale for measuring the wealth of SSA nations at the dawn of the 21st Century. Measurement models that are native to the region are more appropriate.

(2) To evolve credible economic reporting models suitable for each country within the region will enhance the determination of national wealth as well as guide the governments in public policy formulation. National pride will be enhanced if a nation's financial reporting system can be trusted. This factor will encourage foreign investment.

(3) If Africa is the next economic arena, the region must be ready to take advantage of potential investment opportunities. With a return on investment (ROI) that averages 28% for SSA compared to 8% for the rest of the world, it is logical that the region will attract major non-native investors, Overseas Private Investment Corporation (OPIC, 1998). Foreign investors will search for local companies as joint venture partners. Such foreign investors will assess the economic worth of their potential local partners by reviewing their financial reports. Must potential investors be forced to spend extra funds to assess the worth of their potential local partners? This additional expenditure could discourage good, small and medium size companies from taking the risk.

(4) The African Growth Opportunity Act which was recently approved by the United States government will surely open many developmental windows for the sub-region. President Clinton's high profile visits to African nations in 1998 and 2000 served notice that the United States government is serious, and is ready to do business with Africa. Are the Africans ready?

CONCLUSIONS, RECOMMENDATIONS
AND LIMITATIONS

Annual inflation rates in Nigeria for the years under review averaged 400% (Table 1). Any economy experiencing that level of inflation must be in distress, and cannot operate under usual business conditions. That kind of economic climate will call for adoption of emergency measures as prevailed in the United States and Western Europe during the oil crises of the 1970s and 1980s. An examination of the annual reports does not indicate any realization on the part of the management of these corporations and their auditors about the magnitude of the problem. If they appreciated the degree of the crisis, these annual reports would have reflected aggressive valuation techniques such as fmv accounting, which would highlight these emergencies.

Although they may be faced with serious economic distress, Nigerian companies still prepare their financial reports under normal business conditions. They have employed the traditional historical cost accounting methodology sprinkled with some mixed models. The mixed model comes from the use of the LOCM concept for measuring inventory and short-term securities. The straight-line depreciation method is used where rates of 15–20% of the original cost were applied for light machinery and 10% for the very large machinery and equipment. To continue to depreciate at cost on a straight-line basis, an asset whose replacement cost is more than triple its original cost, is to overlook a fundamental economic fact. If a triple digit annual inflation rate impacts heavy machinery as in the sample, what is the logic in depreciating the asset in the first place? If replacement cost is so high, does the concept of amortizing the asset have any theoretical and practical merit? By applying a 10% annual depreciation rate on the original cost, the useful life of the asset is extended over a ten-year period. Experience has shown that in high inflation periods, most fixed assets appreciate rather than depreciate in value. Depending on the degree of inflation, a case can be made for a radical write-off of the original cost. With special reference to Nigeria where an inflation rate of 400% is common (Table 1), one can defend the practice of expensing fixed assets in the year of acquisition rather than capitalizing them. On the other hand, if revaluation of fixed assets can be normalized across the board in the economy, some form of accelerated depreciation method can be applied on reappraised values. For Nigerian companies to continue the current practice of depreciating fixed assets for 5–10 years of cost merely to fulfill an accounting theory, is to woefully miss the mark.

Since Nigeria is a member of the IASC, which recommends the use of current value accounting in periods of hyperinflation, Nigerian companies are expected to revalue fixed assets to prevailing market prices (IAS #16). In practice, this is not necessarily the case. For example, the three firms – Nigerian Bottling Company PLC, Nigerian Tobacco Company PLC and Nichemtex Industries PLC, whose revaluation policies were quoted in this report, had fixed asset appraisals that ranged from nine to eleven years old. In an environment of runaway inflation, what could be the usefulness of revaluations that are so old? If appraisal must be done, why not perform the exercise every year? Other firms in the sample study such as Unipetrol PLC revalue their fixed assets every year. From Table 2, we observe that valuation practices could be as current as one year and as stale as eleven years. Some companies in the sample are silent on the issue of revaluation of fixed assets. It can be inferred from their silence that those firms do not revalue fixed assets in accordance with the prevailing NASB guidelines. One can also conclude that there is no coherent, properly articulated standard policy guiding the practice of fixed asset revaluation. If a policy does exist, there is no enforcement mechanism.

The rationale for the depreciation of fixed assets by Nigerian companies in an environment of hyperinflation has been questioned. The only argument to justify depreciation and the methods employed in the financial reports must be that NASB has so decreed. It is unsettling that the practices are at variance with prevailing economic realities in Nigeria. Also of concern is the notion that while the NASB recommends the reappraisal of fixed assets, it has not stipulated any uniform guidelines for implementation. In an environment characterized by *laissez faire*, how can the messages contained in corporate annual reports be interpreted? Is it feasible to make meaningful comparisons between the financial reports of one company against those of another?

The above concerns call to question the competence of the regulatory agencies such as the Nigerian Stock Exchange, The Nigerian Securities and Exchange Commission and the NASB. What roles do they play in standards setting to guarantee a sound financial reporting system? Is it not the responsibility of the regulators to guide practitioners by promulgating the rules of engagement? How could independent auditors do a good job if there are no uniform standards to go by? It is concluded that the regulatory agencies have not demonstrated strong leadership both in promulgating and enforcing guidelines. The agencies must be reminded that crisis situations call for extraordinary measures.

In this study, the analysis has been focused on those issues in financial reporting, which heavily impact inflation. The reports in the sample have other major flaws, but those concerns will be addressed in another exercise. However, the mismanagement of the inflation factor overwhelmingly casts serious doubt with respect to the credibility of Nigerian corporate financial reports. These lapses will result in financial reports that do not fairly present the results of operations and the economic condition of firms. These lapses will also lead to poor valuations, huge paper profits, wrong conclusions and wrong decisions.

One is not sure of the proper recipe that will deal with SSA's financial reporting problems. One thing is certain, namely – that the transplanted European techniques currently used in the region are not appropriate. A good starting point is to reappraise the practicality and the usefulness of the models borrowed from the former colonial rulers. SSA economies are different from those of the West, and there must be a difference between the accounting and reporting practices of the developed and the developing economies. In other words, there must be a package of reporting practices, which are not only *native* to Sub-Saharan Africa, but which suit the economic environment of the region. More research must be done to determine the ideal fit. Meanwhile and until an appropriate model evolves, the nations of Sub-Saharan Africa must, at the minimum, begin to proactively address inflation in their financial reporting.

Finally, it must be acknowledged that certain factors might limit the findings, analysis and conclusions drawn from this study. First, to the extent that Nigerian data were used to generalize for all SAA nations, the findings and conclusions might not be as robust. Second, to the extent that the exchange rate premium was used as a surrogate for the real inflation factor, the conclusions could also be limited. However, how else could one deal with the politics and paucity of data collection in the Third World?

NOTES

1. Other countries mentioned along with Nigeria as not proactively accounting for inflation are: Canada, France, Germany, Hong Kong, India, Italy, Japan, Korea, New Zealand, Norway, South Africa, Spain, Sweden and Switzerland. Nigeria is the only Third World nation in this list.

2. *Asian Tigers* is a term used to refer to the economically strong Emerging Markets of South East Asia such as – Hong Kong, Indonesia, S. Korea, Malaysia, Philippines, Singapore, Taiwan, and Thailand. It is being suggested that Africa with its vast natural and mineral resources will soon follow in the footsteps of the emerging Asian nations to economic prosperity.

3. The *London Club* refers to the association of commercial bank creditors, and the *Paris Club* refers to bilateral, government to government loans.

4. Exchange Rate Premium=Difference between the parallel rate of exchange and the official rate. The parallel rate is likened to the black market rate namely – the rate a willing seller and a willing buyer of foreign exchange can do business at an arm's length. For some political/economic reasons, the Central Bank of Nigeria (CBN) could peg the conversion rate of the local currency, Naira (N) at below the prevailing market rate. When this happens, the naira is given an artificial higher value than its true worth in a free market. For example, between 1993 and 1999, the CBN pegged the exchange rate

@ N22 to US$1 when the market was offering between N70–N90 for $1. In other words, a buyer of hard currency was willing to pay as much as N90 for $1 but would prefer to pay CBN's N22. At N22, there were hardly any dollars to buy whereas at N90, there were enough dollars in the market. It is envisaged that by the year 2001, the prevailing exchange rate would be N125 to $1.

REFERENCES

Accounting Standards Committee (1980). *Statement of Standard Accounting Practice No. 16.* London: ASC.
Arterian, S. (1994). Accounting for Hyperinflation. *CFO, 10*(8), 61.
Baer, W., & Beckerman, P. (1980). The Trouble with Index-Linking: Reflections on the Recent Brazilian Experience. *World Development, 8*, 677–703.
Bertholdt, R. H. (1984). Why Business Needs to use Inflation Accounting. *Cashflow, 5*(3), 56.
Bryer, R. A., & Brignall, T. J. (1985). The GAAP in the Inflation Accounting Debate. *Accountancy, 96*(1105), 32.
Chisman, N. (1998). The politics of the true and fair view. *Accountancy, 122*(1261), 73.
Choi, F. D. S. (1991). *Handbook of International Accounting* (pp. 17.5–17.7). New York, NY: John Wiley and Sons, Inc.
Epstein, B. J., & Mira, A. A. (1997). *Wiley IAS 1997. Interpretation and Application of International Accounting Standards.* New York, NY: John Wiley and Sons, Inc.
Evans, T. G., Taylor, M. E., & Holzmann, O. (1985). *International Accounting and Reporting.* New York, NY: Macmillian Publishing Company.
Financial Accounting Standards Board (FASB) (1976). *Conceptual Framework for Financial Accounting and Reporting: Elements of Financial Statements and Their Measurement.* Stamford, CT: FASB.
FASB (1984). *Financial Reporting and Changing Prices: Elimination of Certain Disclosures – an Amendment of* FASB #33. Stamford, CT: FASB.
FASB (1993). *Accounting for Certain Investments in Debt and Equity Securities.* Stamford, CT: FASB.
Grey, S. (1998). A quiet revolution that's about to get bloody. *Accountancy, 121*(1255)(March 6).
Galbis, V. (1993). *IMF Working Papers: Experience with Floating Interbank Exchange Rate Systems in Five Developing Economies.* Washington, D.C.: IMF.
Hague, I. P. N., & Willis, D. W. (1999). Old price or new? *CA Magazine, 132*(1), 47–49.
Holt, P. E., & Hein, C. D. (1998). *International Accounting* (3rd ed.). Houston, TX: Dame Publications.
Hooper, K. (1997). Statement of Financial Position . . . What's in a Name? *Chartered Accountants Journal of New Zealand, 76*(3), 37–40.
International Accounting Standards Committee (IASC) (1989). *International Accounting Standards (IAS) #29: Financial Reporting in Hyperinflationary Economies.* London: IASC.
IASC (1998). IAS #16 (Revised 1998). *Property, Plant and Equipment.* London: IASC.
Martin, W. (1998). Dictated Trade: The Case Against the African Growth & Opportunity Act. *Review of African Political Economy, 25*(77), 531–532.
Materniak, D. R. (1984). Current Value Accounting. *Review of Business, 6*(2), 8.
Milburn, A., & Hague, I. (1997). A Need for Uniformity. *CA Magazine, 130*(3), 45–47.
Monahan, T. F., & Huang, J. C. (1985/1986). Specialized Reporting in an Inflationary Environment. *The Mid-Atlantic Journal of Business, 24*(1), 1.

Moser, G., Rogers, S., & van Til, R. (1997). IMF Occasional Paper No. 148: Nigeria Experience with Structural Adjustment. Washington, D.C.: IMF.

Nexia International (1993). *International Handbook of Financial Reporting*. London: Chapman and Hall.

Overseas Private Investment Corporation (OPIC) (1998). OPIC and Africa: Partners in Growth. *OPIC Highlights*, (June). Washington, D.C.: OPIC.

Ravlic, T. (1999). Japan looks to higher standards. *Australian CPA, 69*(10), 48–49.

Ryan, J., & Tibbits, G. (1997). Counting the cost: HCA and Intangibles. *Australian CPA, 67*(9), 54–55.

Saudagaran, S. M. (2001). *International Accounting: A User's Perspective*. Cincinnati, OH: South-Western College Publishing.

Shim, E., & Larkin, J. M. (1998). Towards Relevancy in Financial Reporting: Mark-to-Market Accounting. *Journal of Applied Business Research, 14*(2), 33–42.

Simonsen, M. (1986). Indexation: Current Theory and the Brazilian Experience in Dornbusch. R. Simonsen & M. Simonsen (Eds). Cambridge, MA: MIT Press.

Stacey, R. (1992). Managing Inflation Brazilian Style. *Management Accounting, 70*(6), 14.

Swieringa, R. J. (1997). Challenges to the current accounting model. *The CPA Journal, 67*(1), 26–32.

The New Republic (1998). Trading Up. *The New Republic, 218*(19), 9–10.

Yonetaui, T., & Katsuo, Y. (1998). Fair value accounting and regulatory capital requirements. *Economic Policy Review-Federal Reserve Bank of New York, 4*(3), 33–43.

Woodham, J. (1984). CCA-A Proposal for Reform. *Accounting and Business Research, 14*(55), 257.

World Bank (1994). *Nigeria –Structural Adjustment Program: Policies, Implementation and Impact*. Washington, D.C.: World Bank.

8. REGULATING BANKS IN COLONIAL NIGERIA: THE ABSENCE OF ACCOUNTS*

Chibuike Ugochukwu Uche

Before the Banking Ordinance of 1952, banking in Nigeria remained largely unregulated.[1] The accounting provisions that existed for the control of banks could be found in the Companies Ordinance (Nigeria) of 1922. The Ordinance, for instance, required each limited banking company to prepare a half yearly statement of its liabilities and assets and a copy of this statement had to be exhibited in a conspicuous place in all the offices of the company.[2] It further provided for the investigation of the affairs of such banks by Inspectors under certain circumstances[3] and the audit of such institutions by persons other than their directors or officers.[4] The regulations described above applied only to companies registered in the Nigerian Colony. Foreign companies operating in the colony were simply required to file yearly, with the Registrar, a statement in the form of a balance sheet in the format similar to that required from companies registered under the 1922 Nigerian Companies Ordinance. The auditing provisions clearly did not apply to such foreign companies. There was thus no provision for checking the authenticity of the figures provided.[5]

In 1952, the first Banking Ordinance was promulgated in Nigeria. This fundamentally altered the playing field for some banks in the British Nigerian Colony especially the indigenous ones. In general, the ordinance required these

* An earlier version of this paper was presented at the 11th Accounting, Business and Financial History Conference (Cardiff, Wales, 15–16 September 1999).
A Bank of England Research Grant helped fund some aspects of this research.

Research in Accounting in Emerging Economies, Volume 5, pages 145–163.
ISBN: 0-7623-0901-6

indigenous banks to: (1) have a nominal share capital of at least £25,000 of which not less than £12,500 should be paid up; (2) be licensed by the Financial Secretary in order to be able to carry on banking business; (3) abstain from granting loans and advances on the security of their own shares and granting unsecured loans and advances in excess of £300 to any one or more of its directors or to a business in which it or any one or more of their directors had any interests; (4) maintain adequate cash reserves; (5) maintain a reserve fund out of net profit of each year of not less than 20% of such profits until the reserve fund equals the share capital; (6) refrain from paying dividend until all their capitalised expenditure not represented by tangible assets had been written off; and (7) make periodic returns to the Financial Secretary.[6] The Ordinance however allowed existing banks three years either to comply with its provisions or discontinue business.[7] Remarkably, this pioneer banking ordinance contained few new provisions for the regulation of banks through accounts. Indeed the promulgators of the Ordinance were more interested in controlling entry, through licensing, rather than in policing the activities of banks. This paper attempts to explain the absence of some significant provisions in the ordinance. The article will also critically examine the authenticity of the various reasons that have been proffered for the near absence of regulation through accounts in this maiden banking ordinance in the Nigerian colony. Emphasis is placed on the underlying processes and forces that influenced the provisions of the legislation. To achieve its aim, the paper is divided into three parts. Part I discusses the banking environment in pre-independence Nigeria which led to the establishment of indigenous banks and subsequently brought to the fore, the need for some form of regulation in the Nigerian banking industry, while Part II examines the intertwining of political, social and economic factors that influenced both the provisions and the absence of accounting provisions in the 1952 banking Ordinance. Part III concludes the paper.

I

Commercial banking in the Nigerian Colony commenced, in 1891, with the advent of the African Banking Corporation. In 1894, the operations of the bank were taken over by the Bank of British West Africa (BBWA).[8] In 1899 a second foreign bank, Bank of Nigeria, was established.[9] This bank was however absorbed by the BBWA in 1912.[10] For the next four years, BBWA had the banking field in Nigeria to itself. All this changed in 1916 with the advent of the Colonial Bank.[11] Barclays Bank entered the Nigerian banking arena, in 1925, through the merger between the Colonial Bank, the Anglo-Egyptian Bank (which it already owned) and the National Bank of South Africa, to create Barclays Bank (Dominion, Colonial and Overseas).

The advent of colonial banking in the Nigerian Colony was initially to provide banking services for the Government and the British Commercial enterprises then in existence.[12] It was therefore not surprising that at the time, these banks were registered in London, head-quartered in London, and controlled from London. These colonial banks thus fell under the regulatory jurisdiction of London and had little need for host territory regulation. The lack of any form of accounting regulation in the colony was therefore to their benefit. There was thus little pressure for change from this group. Perhaps because of the origins of these foreign banks, they did not aim to meet the needs of the indigenous population who they generally perceived as unworthy of credit.[13] It was in these circumstances that indigenous banks sprang up all claiming the economic emancipation of the indigenes as their main objective.

The first indigenous bank in Nigeria commenced operation in 1929 with the acquisition by some African businessmen[14] of the Industrial and Commercial Bank which was originally established as an Overseas bank in London with the aim of carrying out banking business overseas. The original bank, however, did not take off because of the outbreak of World War One.[15] The philosophy which animated the founding of the Industrial and Commercial Bank was summed up by one of its founding members as follows:

it is evident that there is no law to prevent the African from disposing of the efforts of his labour; therefore, provided with an international business link, he can market his own products, exchanging the proceeds there-from for the purchase of foreign merchandise he may require. These are facilities that as a race we cannot expect these corporations organised for the purpose of exploitation to supply; but it is obvious that the opportunity exists for mutual organisation. It is the foundation for that organisation that the Industrial and Commercial Bank Limited with its affiliations have brought . . .[16]

This bank was however short-lived and went into liquidation in 1930. Very little was known of the internal operations of this bank and indeed most early indigenous banks.[17] For instance, though the liquidators established that the paid up share capital was £100,000, the state of the company's record was so chaotic that they could not determine the proportion of the share capital that was paid up.[18] It was further claimed that:

the managing Director of the so called bank was a man with a very shady past. The prospectus originally issued by the "bank" was a highly misleading document. It gave prominence to the names of the company's solicitors, auditors and secretary, who were leading London firms. Those firms had never been informed that their names would appear on the prospectus and when their attention was drawn to it, they ceased to have any dealings with the company . . . . The liquidators found it impossible to produce anything approaching the accurate statement of the position. The liabilities (some of which related to trading operations) were estimated at £25,000. Of book debts estimated at £12,000, only £40 was collected. Included in the book debts were two substantial loans to the managing director and a company under his control – not a penny of which was recovered. It was also disclosed that the company was a share pushing establishment of the most blatant description; the accounts of many illiterate depositors were found to have been debited with monies due on application and allotment of shares in respect of which no formal application could be traced. A petition submitted to H.E the Governor by shareholders and creditors stated that there were 3570 depositors with claims amounting to £13225. None of the depositors received anything.[19]

The second indigenous bank that came into operation – The Nigerian Mercantile Bank – also had a short and chequered life-span. Established in 1931, it had a share capital of £10,000 of "which £909 seems to have been paid up in cash initially." Here again, the main activity of the company appears to have been "share pushing."[20] By 1936, the bank had failed. In 1933, the National Bank became the first successful indigenous bank to be established.[21] In its prospectus, its directors made a nationalistic appeal for patronage by asserting that:

> No people can be respected or regarded as a nation unless it has its own national institutions and the greatest of all national institutions is the financial institution in the form of a bank. This is therefore an appeal to one and all who have the interest of her country at heart and are prepared to work for her progress.[22]

This was followed by the Nigerian Penny Bank which was short-lived.[23] It had an authorized share capital of £5000 of which £287 was paid up in cash. By 1946, the bank had failed. The Official Receiver reported that "neither . . . (the promoter) nor any of his associates had even a rudimentary idea of banking or company practice and the bulk of the so-called assets will prove to be unrealisable".[24] Also, the Director of Audit referred to the "fantastic way in which the affairs of the company were managed."[25]

In 1947, two other banks (African Continental Bank and the Nigerian Farmers and Commercial Bank) were established. Worried by the spate of the establishment of such indigenous banks and not unmindful of past banking failures, the Federal Government, in 1948, appointed Mr. G. D. Paton, an Official of the Bank of England to "enquire generally into the business of banking in Nigeria and make recommendations to the Government on the form and extent of control which should be introduced." Mr Paton submitted his report which was accompanied by a draft Ordinance on the 28th of October 1948. Extensive criticism of the Paton recommendations mainly by the local banks led the government to produce its own report[26] (Barriff Report).[27] This culminated in the 1952 Banking Ordinance.[28]

The 1952 banking regulation was therefore influenced by the advent of poorly capitalized, poorly staffed and in some cases fraud infested indigenous banks into the Nigerian banking arena. Despite the shortcomings of these indigenous banks, such banks had a constituency different from that of the European Banks.[29] As Rowan once noted:

the principal gain from the operation of African banks is the obvious one, namely, that Africans who might otherwise have been unable to obtain bank finance and thus might have been driven out of business or into the hands of money lenders, can obtain the necessary finance at rates that are certainly not unreasonable. In the last analysis, the development of Nigeria must depend upon African enterprise and skill, and both these forces require all the encouragement and assistance they can get.[30]

If the interests of the Africans were paramount and if it was the Government objective to minimize the indigenous banking failures, one would have expected the Government to have invested in regulation, on the lines of detailed banking inspection procedures, and in perhaps manpower development for these indigenous banks.[31] This was however not the case. The recommendation of the 1948 Paton Commission that the Government should assist indigenous banks in the training of staff[32] came to nothing. Even the calls, by Africans, for the establishment of a central bank, one of its main aims being to strengthen the existing African banks, was also opposed by the colonial government which did not consider it important that such a central bank, if established, should concern itself with helping and strengthening the existing African banks.[33] Helping these poorly capitalized and poorly staffed indigenous banks grow was therefore not the objective of the Colonial Government. Given the above, it is therefore not surprising that the Colonial Government, in the main, adopted a regulatory regime that focused on placing barriers to entry and forcing out unsound banks.

Whatever policy the Colonial Government adopted must be judged in the context of the fact that there were no such detailed regulatory provisions in the United Kingdom at the time. Indeed formal legislation regarding the registration, regulation and activities of the banking system in the United Kingdom is a recent phenomenon.[34] Before the 1979 Banking Act in the United Kingdom, there were no specific legal requirements governing the setting up of banks in the United Kingdom. There was also no legal definition of a bank in the United Kingdom. Although the Bank of England Act of 1946 conferred on the Bank of England, the powers to define a 'banker' and authorized the Treasury to issue directions to such parties, no such definition or directions were ever issued. A bank remained legally undefined with no prescribed legal requirement for the setting up of depository institutions.[35] Other legislation of the time however gave some guidance as to which institutions were generally perceived as banks by the authorities. For instance, the Exchange Control Act of 1947 provided a list of authorized banks permitted to deal in foreign exchange. Also, the Companies Act of 1948 authorized the Board of Trade to exempt banking companies from the obligation to publish accounts in full (schedule 8 banks). In other words, they were allowed to maintain secret reserves. The criteria for being a schedule 8 bank were largely subjective. The status was usually offered where the Bank of England believed that the bank in question would be an acceptable member of the recognized banking community.[36] It was therefore only banks in these two categories, sometimes partly overlapping, that the Bank of England maintained regular contact with.[37] Such supervision was based on custom and acceptance rather than legal authority under the Bank of England Act.[38] Depository institutions not recognized under the Exchange Control Act and the 1948 Companies Act (fringe banks), were thus outside the scope of banking regulation.

In most British Colonies, where British laws were almost always transcribed, there was no legal check to the establishment of indigenous banks. Unlike in the United Kingdom, where the Bank of England at least had the choice, if they so wished, to establish contact with the fringe banks, there was no such central bank in place in most of the colonies. The belief, among the Africans, that the colonial banks and indeed the entire colonial structures discriminated against them led to widespread mistrust of colonial initiatives, thus further reducing the chances of success for any informal kind of regulation either from London or from any kind of colonial structure within the colonies.[39] It was therefore difficult for the United Kingdom to transcribe its informal model of regulation to the colonies. Furthermore, the Bank of England apparently transcribed its philosophy of maintaining contact with only 'club members' to the colonies. With most of the indigenous banks too small, in all respects, to achieve 'club membership', the Bank of England did little to encourage informal regulatory contact with such banks.

Because of the relatively late development of formal banking regulation in the United Kingdom, the Colonial Government had no ready 'technology' to transfer in the 1940s, when they considered regulation for the banking system of colonial Nigeria to have become necessary.[40] The Colonial Government therefore had to take a cue from the banking regulation developments at the time in other British Colonies especially, India and Pakistan which had enacted banking laws following their independence.[41]

The next section examines the intertwining of the political, social and economic factors that influenced both the provisions and the absence of accounting provisions in the 1952 banking ordinance.

II

Section 8 of the Paton report recommended the appointment of a Bank Examiner who should be an Officer of the Government. He should have power to call for and examine the books of these banks in addition to the returns the banks will be making to the Financial Secretary, the main purpose being to satisfy himself as to the liquidity of each bank. The report went on to further explain that if the degree of liquidity was found to be insufficient, the Government Officer would advise the bank as to the policy it should adopt with a view to improving its liquidity position. The degree of liquidity which banks should maintain, and which would vary according to the changing financial conditions, local and international, would be a matter for consideration by the advisory committee.[42] A minimum cash ratio was not recommended by the Paton Report on the grounds that a system of supervision primarily designed to ensure the maintenance of an adequate degree of liquidity is the most effective method of reducing the risk of banking failures. In many countries, the report argued, there was already in place, at the time, legislation providing for a minimum cash ratio, but the cash reserve of the bank is no criterion of the general liquidity, particularly in less advanced countries where local liquid assets may not be available and where small banks may be under incompetent management.[43]

The above claim that the cash reserves of a bank is no criterion of its general liquidity at first was taken with some scepticism by officials of the Bank of England. The Bank was of the opinion that although a minimum cash reserve is admittedly no criterion of general liquidity but at least it would prevent the sort of situation disclosed in his report where a bank's only realizable asset included a bicycle and a sewing machine.[44] By 1950, however, the Bank of England had shifted its position in support of the Paton report. It argued that:

> it is questionable whether provisions for minimum cash reserves are desirable in simple legislation or in the conditions of Nigeria where a cash ratio would not necessarily be a guarantee of liquidity. The advances made by a bank operating in the territory might not be so easily callable nor the collateral so readily realizable as in a more advanced country and it might show a perfectly satisfactory cash position according to local law but still be in a poor state of liquidity .... It is a very moot point whether the advantages of fixing minimum cash reserves by law are not outweighed by its disadvantages. The keeping of the right amount of cash against liabilities call for experience and skill and what may be right in one country may be quite inappropriate elsewhere.

It went on to suggest that:

> the danger here is that the inexperienced or bad bank may regard the extremely low percentage in the law as its maximum and may shelter behind the law when it gets into trouble. I would far rather see a section in general terms which required the banks to maintain as proper liquidity and to hold at all times an adequate cash reserves against their obligations.[45]

While the Barriff report implicitly adopted the above view of not fixing the minimum liquidity ratio, it went ahead to expunge the provisions relating to the appointment of a bank examiner and an advisory committee. The Report rather replaced these with an extensive set of provisions which basically transferred the duty of bank inspection to the financial secretary.[46] The Bank of England described this Barriff recommendation as:

> some rather vague provisions for inspection of banks, on application from members or at the discretion of the financial secretary.[47]

The Bank of England report went ahead to state that:

> in view of the fact that no minimum cash ratio is provided in the draft, some continuing control and supervision of banks is, in the circumstances of Nigeria, clearly necessary. This is very necessary from the situation disclosed in the Paton's report, and I think that we should ask Barriff the reasons why a Controller and an advisory committee were repugnant to Nigeria and put it into his mind that if these reasons were not very cogent, it will be as well to reconsider Paton's suggestion which seems not only necessary but also very sensible and flexible.[48]

On the issue of banking inspection, the Bank of England, perhaps because of pressures from British banks then operating in the Nigerian colony, later adjusted its position and backed down from its demand for banking inspection along the lines recommended by Paton. Its main reason for this change of mind was made explicit in a letter to the Colonial Office. Here, it was asserted that:

> over 90% of the banking business is conducted by two powerful British banks who need no control; no system of full audit or inspection could ignore any particular bank and both these banks would therefore rank equally with the weakest. With the present state of political feeling in the colony, it might even be dangerous to place such a measure before the legislative council and so precipitate a demand for complicated banking control which might be objectionable and cause undesirable and unnecessary interference with the two chief banks.[49]

Another reason proffered by the Bank of England was the fact that lack of competent examiners in the Nigerian colony would make nonsense of legislating detailed bank inspection.[50] This however was no more than an afterthought. If assisting the indigenous banks was a government policy objective, lack of competent examiners could in no way be an insurmountable obstacle.

It is therefore clear that the main reason why the Colonial Government failed to legislate for bank inspection in the 1952 ordinance was the fact that any such regulation would have had to be uniformly applied to all banks (indigenous or foreign) irrespective of what their past records had been, lest they are accused of discrimination. The Colonial Government, thus not surprisingly, opted for a regulatory regime that emphasized entry barriers (licensing) which made it difficult for Africans, who usually lacked the necessary capital and expertise, to establish banks. As noted by a Bank of England Official:

The 1952 banking Ordinance is designed to achieve the stability of existing banks and to prevent the growth of 'wild cat' banks.[51]

Such a regulatory regime did not only focus on entry barriers, it was also an effective instrument in ensuring the liquidation of many of these poorly capitalized indigenous banks.

Contrary to the view of the Bank of England, the likely reason for the mass failure of the indigenous banks was the enactment of the 1952 Banking Ordinance.[52] The very fact that banks were given three years to meet with the conditions of the Ordinance or face liquidation may have sent a warning signal to the depositors of these unlicensed banks. This may have subsequently led to a run on these unlicensed indigenous banks. In the case of the Nigerian Farmers and Commercial Bank, for instance, it was noted that:

From the moment the Licence was refused us, it meant we had to close down either immediately or gradually . . . the importance attached to the Banking Licence made customers to doubt the continuity of our Bank. They embarked on withdrawal and withdrawal . . . that no licence was being granted to the [Farmers and Commercial] bank was always being pointed to. Even no time was allowed for fixed deposits to stay for the specified period: yet it was impossible for the bank to recover the money given out as overdrafts immediately . . . . Were it that we had a Banking Licence, nothing could have made the customers withdraw their money in thousands as they did . . .[53]

It is difficult to blame the depositors for their action given the fact that at the time, there was no deposit insurance scheme in place. As has already been mentioned, the Colonial Government did not implement the recommendation of the United Nations, at the time, that such a scheme be established.

Despite this recommendation not to legislate bank inspection, the Bank of England still believed that unsound banking practices could be prevented. Measures such as licensing, minimum capital requirements, reserve provisions and the examination of returns should afford sufficient safeguards and prevent the growth of mushroom banks. If despite these precautions, a close inspection of a bank became necessary, administrative action should then be taken under plenary powers embodied in the Ordinance, rather than through the slow complicated machinery of the courts.[54]

The final draft bill put forward to the legislature did not therefore provide for bank examination. Section 8 of the draft Ordinance however provided for banks to maintain 'adequate' cash reserves as recommended in the Paton report.[55] This was passed by the legislature unamended but not without the protest voice of Anthony Enahoro who wondered whether it was indeed right for the Financial Secretary to have powers to decide whether banks reserves are inadequate or not, even if his opinion conflicted with those of expert bankers.[56]

It was not until 1958 (with the imminence of political independence, subsequent to the African Continental Bank Crisis[57] and concurrent with the establishment of the Central Bank of Nigeria) that formal bank inspection and the appointment of a bank examiner was legislated in the Nigerian colony.[58] The fears of the foreign banks that such bank inspection could constitute unnecessary interference with their activities soon materialized and these banks did not hesitate in showing their irritation. In a letter to the Deputy Governor of the Central Bank of Nigeria, subsequent to the coming into force of the 1958 Act, An executive Director of the Bank of West Africa wrote:

> I would just like to place on record the point recently discussed with you by the General Manager of Barclays Bank and myself in connection with the functions of the Banking Examiner. You will recall that we expressed some concern over the fact that recently the Banking Examiner and/or his Assistant have in our opinion gone outside the orbit of what we would regard as their normal duties, in that they have resorted to the practice of examining customers accounts in some detail. I would hope that recent examinations in this connection may be regarded as exceptional as, in my view, a continuance of this practice, even if in fact this might be covered by existing legislation, would lead to serious loss of confidence in the banks by members of the public.[59]

Another regulatory issue considered by Paton, in his 1948 Report, was the types of accounting returns to be made by banks. Section 10 of the Paton report recommended that banks furnish to the Financial Secretary, a quarterly statement of its assets and liabilities and a half yearly analysis of loans and advances. The report went ahead to suggest that such a statement of assets and liabilities is the basic feature of the system of supervision of banks by a bank examiner. The report concluded that since banking statistics provide essential material for the comprehensive survey of economic conditions of a country, such figures should be published in aggregate form for the information of the public. In reference to the above Paton recommendation, the Bank of England commented that it is a:

> basic requirement of Colonial Banking Legislation as recommended . . . . Provision is made for a statement of assets and liabilities and a breakdown of advances to be submitted quarterly. Paton recommended that the latter be submitted half yearly but if the local administration do not consider quarterly submission unreasonable, so much the better. These provisions apply to all banks indiscriminately.[60]

This provision, that banks submitted returns to the Financial Secretary, was aptly explained by him as necessary in order that:

> he could find out, or probably find out, what they are doing.[61]

While the need for banks to file returns was generally perceived to be desirable by the legislature, the frequency of these returns was perceived by some as undesirable. Dr. Kingsley O. Mbadiwe, while proposing an amendment so that returns can be filed twice yearly argued that:

> the four returns – balance sheet returns – is far too much for this young country, because you are fully aware here that the technical skill here is woefully lacking and once you want a young bank just beginning to submit four returns plus other returns to the Registrar of Companies and other forms to be made, that bank will just spend its time compiling those reports.[62]

He then concluded that:

> reports submitted two times a year are quite adequate, once this country grows and we begin to have more technical skill, there is no reason why that more periodic returns should not be adopted but at this particular period of our development . . . I feel that the Financial Secretary wishes to have the cooperation of the banks and not to put them under great disadvantage and handicap, that a method be devised whereby for the meantime, half yearly returns are submitted.[63]

This proposed amendment was supported by A. Enahoro on the grounds that it will be too much of a financial burden on banks especially those with many branches. He asserted that:

> It has been suggested to me that in some cases it might cost as much as £500 and in other cases it might be £100 or £200. . . . You have to employ a Chartered Accountant and qualified people like that. What would happen in the case of a bank which has say, like the Continental Bank or the Farmers bank, twenty branches, and which has to prepare this return every quarter, if it has to pay £100 or £200 to prepare one for each branch? you find that they have to spend at least £10000 to £50000 every year on these returns. I think that this is certainly discouraging to African Banks.[64]

Chief S. L. Edu also supported the amendment arguing that the quarterly production of reports by banks was bound to be expensive and could lead to either an increase in the percentage of interests or a call on the Government to bear the relevant expenses.[65] Chief M. Aboderin, while supporting the motion, cited section 433 paragraph (1) of the 1948 Companies Act of England.[66] He went on to assert that:

> I am also informed that throughout the civilised world, these returns are submitted twice annually and not quarterly.[67]

The Financial Secretary while stating categorically that the Government would not accept such an amendment, argued that:

> It is on the basis of these returns that the Financial Secretary or any one else will know what action to take when a bank is going wrong . . . the whole object of this ordinance is to try and stop banks going wrong. It is not to find out when it is too late that they have gone wrong because these advances or reserves have got out of line.[68]

On the suggestions that the schedule would impose a heavy cost on the banks, he argued that:

these schedules are what any ordinary bank should fill in every week for its own information. The manager must keep this information up to date to know how to run his bank and
to see that everything is secure.[69]

On the issue of the clause being repressive, the Financial Secretary suggested
that it was not. He then went ahead to assert that:

There are at least two Nigerian Banks who send me the information set out in the first of
these schedules every quarter and they don't have to do it. They do it just because I ask
for it. I think that if they can do it voluntarily, others can do it without repressive measures.[70]

The question that quarterly returns should not be demanded out was then put
to vote and the result was negative. The provisions of this section of the draft
Ordinance[71] was therefore passed by the Legislature without amendment.

Section 11 of the Paton Report recommended the exhibition and publication
of banks balance sheets. According to the report, most banks of standing publish
such reports whether or not they are required by law to do so. The report went
on to justify its recommendation of publishing and exhibiting such reports on
the grounds that:

the man in the street should be given an opportunity of forming his own opinion of the
financial condition of any bank in which he may meditate depositing his money.

The report went on to suggest that:

several private companies are operating as banks. Under the provisions of section 27 (3) of
the Companies Ordinance, a private company is not required to file a copy of its balance
sheet and as far as I have been able to ascertain, the private companies which are carrying
on banking business at present do not publish their balance sheets.[72]

The above views were endorsed by the Barriff draft[73] and then the Bank of
England which described it as 'another basic requirement'.[74]

When the relevant section of the draft Ordinance[75] was tabled at the legislature, Mr. Anthony Enahoro pointed out that this was unnecessary as a related
provision was in existence under existing laws. He suggested that:

under section 108 of the Companies Ordinance, the banks are already obliged to exhibit
throughout the year particulars of their balance sheet as per schedule of the Companies
Ordinance.[76]

He then went on to conclude that the provisions in the Companies Ordinance
was quite adequate and that there was no need to compel the banks to incur
extra expenses by preparing and publishing these balance sheets in Newspapers.
The motion to exclude this section from the banking Ordinance was then put
to vote and defeated. The next section concludes this paper.

III

This paper has attempted an analysis of the underlying processes and forces at work that explains the absence of some accounting and inspection provisions in the 1952 Nigerian Banking Ordinance. Though the need for some form of regulation of the banking industry was conspicuously clear to most of the interested parties, there was still some suspicion especially among Nigerians that such legislation was being used to deter the setting up of local banks and protect the interest of foreign banks. These suspicions were not altogether unfounded. For instance, one of the main reasons given by the Bank of England for not advising on full scale legislation of Banking Inspection was because "it might precipitate a demand for complicated banking control which might be objectionable and cause undesirable and unnecessary interference with the two chief banks." In other words, the absence of any inspection provisions in the 1952 banking ordinance was mainly influenced by the foreign banks which saw such provisions as unnecessary interference with their activities. The political climate in the colony at the time made it difficult for uniform regulation to be applied across banks depending on the risk perception of the individual banks. In other words, no matter how rigorous the internal control mechanism of the foreign banks was perceived to be, it was politically inexpedient not to subject them to the same accounting and regulatory standards applied to the poorly capitalized and poorly staffed indigenous banks. It was thus in the interest of the foreign banks that such banks were not allowed to exist. The Colonial Government therefore adopted a regulatory regime aimed at keeping out poorly staffed and poorly capitalized indigenous banks rather than policing their activities. The indigenous banks however played a part in shaping this regulatory outcome that impeded their existence. Although the indigenous banks may have been better placed to serve the interest of Africans, their actions and practices rarely reflected this. The poor staffing and capitalization of many of these indigenous banks made it difficult for such banks to be engaged in such noble objectives. Fraud was also rampant in some of these indigenous banks. Indeed, some of these banks actually stole from the Africans they were supposed to assist. At least, to this extent, such indigenous banks also influenced the regulation process. The assistance the 1952 banking regulation afforded foreign banks can therefore be viewed as a by-product of indigenous and foreign banks action.

NOTES

1. Uzoaga (1986), Nwankwo (1990) and Teriba (1986).
2. See Section 108.

3. See Section 109.

4. Section 112.

5. The accounts of the Nigerian branches of such foreign registered banks were usually consolidated at the headquarters of such banks. The auditing of such banks therefore fell under the regulatory jurisdiction of the country where such foreign banks were head-quartered.

6. This was the pioneer banking legislation in Nigeria. The Ordinance also applied to foreign banks except for the fact that while the indigenous banks were required to maintain a paid up Capital of £12,500, foreign banks were required to maintain £100,000. Unlike most local banks, foreign banks did not have much difficulty in complying with the provisions of the Ordinance since their headquarters were usually abroad and they had better capital base. For instance, by 1948, the Bank of British West Africa (BBWA) and the Barclays bank had a Paid Up Share Capital of £1,200,000 and £7,121,500 respectively while that of the African Continental Bank was only £5,000 (Paton, 1948, pp. 4–6). The case of some of the indigenous banks that were established between 1948 and 1952 was even more pathetic. For instance, City Bank Limited had a paidup share capital of £105 while that for Onward Limited was £410 (Uche, 1997a, p. 225).

7. See Sections 5 (2) and 6 (2).

8. The name was changed to Bank of West Africa in 1957. For a general review of the circumstances surrounding this take-over, see Fry (1976).

9. Originally the bank was named Anglo-African Bank. This name was however changed in 1905.

10. For a detailed account of the rivalry between these two foreign banks prior to 1912 see (Uche, forthcoming).

11. Before then, the Colonial Bank had a successful operation in the West Indies spanning almost 80 years.

12. Rowan (1952, p. 161).

13. Fry (1976, p. 116).

14. They include W. Tete Ansah (from the then Gold Coast, now Ghana), Candido de Rocha, A. A. Oshodi, P. H. Williams and D. A. Taylor (Nigerians).

15. Ayida (1960, p. 29).

16. Cited in Azikiwe (1956, p. 3).

17. Bank of England Archive File Number (BEAFN) OV68/2, Folio 42, p. 1.

18. Paton (1948, p. 7).

19. Ibid, p. 8. Newlyn and Rowan (1954, p. 97), claimed that at the time of the bank's winding up, in 1930, its deposit liability was estimated at £11,735. This was later raised to £13,000.

20. Paton (1948, p. 8).

21. Lack of support and lack of profit led to a split among the directors of the Mercantile Bank. T.A Doherty, Dr A Maja and H. A. Subair subsequently resigned from Mercantile Bank and founded National Bank (Hopkins, 1966, p. 146).

22. Quoted in Azikiwe (1961, p. 209).

23. The exact year of its establishment is not known.

24. Quoted in Paton (1948, p. 8).

25. Ibid.

26. Financial Secretary's statement in the House of Representatives debate (1952, p. 1111).

27. Named after Mr R. A. Barriff who prepared the report. He was then the Assistant Director (Commerce), Department of Commerce and Industries, Lagos Nigeria.

28. Preceding the enactment of the 1952 law, Africans, fearing the imminent clampdown on the establishment of commercial banks following the setting up of the Paton inquiry, had rushed to establish more banks before the advent of regulation. The result was that by 1952, at least 24 local banks had been established. Most of them failed after the 1952 Ordinance came into force.

29. Scholars are in general agreement that European banks were not very helpful to the natives of the British West African colonies, at least, in terms of providing them with credit facilities. The contentious issue, however, is the question of whether these European banks deliberately discriminated against the African natives or whether the natives were, in most cases, not credit worthy. See Uche (1996) for a review of the debate.

30. Rowan (1951, p. 248).

31. It was of course possible that no amount of regulation and control could have saved some of these indigenous banks. Some of these banks were so poorly capitalised that their long term survival, without explicit Government support was doubtful (BEAFN OV68/4, folio 56c).

32. P.17.

33. Uche (1997a, pp. 225–226).

34. A former Deputy Governor of the Bank of England once asserted that he never remembered hearing the word "supervision" used in the bank before 1974. Quoted in Nwankwo (1990, p. 1).

35. Norton (1991, p. 11).

36. Grady and Weale (1986, p. 36).

37. At the time, the British banking system was dominated by a cartelized oligopoly consisting of the London Clearing Banks and their associates in Scotland and Northern Ireland. Together they held 85% of all commercial banking businesses in sterling – domestic and foreign. The absence of effective supervision over the fringe banks was partly because it was wrongly supposed, in Bank of England circles, at the time that these institutions would be absorbed by the primary banks (BOE, Sept 1983, pp. 363–365).

38. Norton (1991, p. 11).

39. The widespread mistrust of the British colonial system by the Africans was not altogether unfounded. The colonial government sometimes did not implement expert recommendations aimed at helping the Africans. A United Nations report in 1950, for instance, recommended the setting up of deposit insurance schemes in developing countries. Apart from depositors, such a policy, no doubt, would have benefited indigenous banks most. As for the existing foreign banks, the report further recommended that they should be encouraged to reinvest profits which would otherwise go abroad (United Nations, 1950, pp. 2–3).

40. It would be foolish to impose the same system of banking supervision on countries with diverse banking structures. Compare for instance, the U.K. and the USA: the former is a small integrated country with fewer than ten large domestic banks all with large branch networks and a large number of relatively small merchant banks. The USA, on the other hand, has a federal structure and contains 14000 deposit banks all of them confined to particular states or smaller areas (Blunden, 1977, p. 326).

41. The Banking Companies (Control) Act was introduced in Pakistan in 1948 while the Banking Companies Act was introduced in India in 1949.

42. Paton recommended that an advisory committee be set up. Such committee was to advise on all matters affecting banks and banking which may be referred to it by Government or raised by the committee itself. The recommended membership of the committee included: (a) a senior government official with financial experience as chairman; (b) a senior government official with economic qualifications; (c) a representative of Nigerian banks; (d) a representative of the British banks; and (e) the official charged with the duty of supervising the banks under the proposed Paton Ordinance. This recommendation was not adopted by the Government (Paton, 1948, pp. 12–14).

43. Ibid, pp. 14–15.

44. BEAFN OV68/1, p. 189.

45. BEAFN OV68/2, p. 14. The bank in question was the Nigerian Penny Bank which went into liquidation in 1946.

46. See clauses 7 to 14 of the barriff draft Ordinance (BEAFN OV68/1, pp. 179–180).

47. BEAFN OV68/1, p. 189.

48. Ibid.

49. See letter from W. J. Jackson of the Bank of England to W. Hulland of the Colonial office dated 22nd May 1950 (BEAFN OV68/1, p. 193).

50. Ibid.

51. BEAFN (OV68/2, p. 42).

52. According to the Bank of England, most of these bank failures "cannot properly be attributed to the requirements of the banking legislation or to any positive action on the part of the Financial Secretary. Such action as has so far been taken has been limited to the collection and scrutiny of the statutory returns and to the issue of licences to five banks to which no official publicity was given" (Undated Commentary, BEAFN OV68/2, Folio 43E, p. 2).

53. Quoted in Newlyn and Rowan (1954, p. 239). The bank was refused a banking licence because they failed to meet the requirements set out under the 1952 Banking Ordinance.

54. Bank of England internal memo by J. B. Loynes, dated 15th February, 1957 (BEAFN OV68/4, p. 47).

55. Section 8 of the draft ordinance presented to the legislature recommended that: (1) Every banking company shall at all times maintain by way of cash reserves such amounts as is necessary to ensure an adequate degree of liquidity and to provide adequate cash reserves against its commitments, and the Financial Secretary may from time to time require the banking company to furnish to the Financial Secretary a statement in writing setting out the cash reserve and the time and demand liabilities of the banking company at a date specified by him. (2) If it shall appear to the Financial Secretary on the examination of such statements that adequate cash reserves are not being maintained, he shall direct that steps be taken to increase the ratio of the cash reserves to the demand and time liabilities in such manner and within such time as shall be stated in the direction, and if such direction is not fully complied with he may at his discretion cancel any licence granted to the bank under Section 6 of this Ordinance.

56. House Debates (1952, p. 1141).

57. See Uche (1997b) for a detailed analysis of the African Continental Bank crisis and the regulatory issues raised.

58. See Sections 11–14 of the 1958 Banking Ordinance. Other provisions of the 1958 Ordinance include: the submission, to the central bank, of monthly reports detailing the

breakdown of the bank's assets and liabilities; the submission to the central bank of half yearly reports giving a breakdown of the advances and other assets of the bank; the yearly appointment of an approved auditor by banks (Section 15); no one individual to be granted a loan for an amount equivalent to more than 25% of the bank's share capital (Section 7); prohibited the payment of dividend before a bank's capitalised expenditure, not represented by tangible assets, have been written off (Section 6) and; the mandatory transfer to a reserve fund, of 25% of net profit, in each year whenever the reserve fund is less than the paid up capital (Section 5).

59. Letter to the Deputy Governor of the Central Bank of Nigeria dated 4th September 1962 (BEAFN OV68/10, p. 70).

60. BEAFN OV68/2, p. 9.

61. House Debates (1952, p. 1113).

62. Ibid, p. 1114.

63. Ibid.

64. Ibid, pp. 1141–1142.

65. Ibid.

66. This states that: Every company being a limited banking company or an insurance company or a deposit, provident or benefit society shall, before it commences business and also on the first Monday in February and the first Tuesday in August in every year during which it carries on business make a statement in the form set out in the thirteenth schedule to this act or as near thereto as circumstances admit.

67. House Debates (1952, p. 1143). This claim by S. L. Edu was incorrect. At the time, for instance, it was a requirement of the 1949 Banking Companies Act of India that such reports be submitted monthly (Section 27).

68. Ibid, p. 1142.

69. Ibid.

70. Ibid, pp. 1142–1143.

71. Section 11 of the draft Banking Ordinance stated that: (1) Every banking company shall furnish to the Financial Secretary: (a) not later than forty-two days after the last day of each quarter ending on the 31st March, 30th June, 30th September and 31st December, a statement in the form set out in the first schedule of this Ordinance showing the assets and liabilities of the banking company at the close of business on the last day of the quarter; (b) not later than forty-two days after the last day of March, June, September and December a statement in the form set out in the second schedule to this Ordinance, giving an analysis of advances current and bills discounted as at the 31st March, 30th June, 30th September and 31st December, respectively: Provided that in the case of a banking company which is a company incorporated outside Nigeria, the statements to which reference is made in paragraphs (a) and (b) hereof, shall comprise data only with respect to offices and branches of such company which are situated in Nigeria; and such statements shall be submitted to the manager or agent of the principal office in Nigeria: Provided further that the Governor may by regulation from time to time vary the Form of the first and second Schedules, and the dates as at which the information required in the Second Schedule shall be compiled and forwarded to the Financial Secretary. (2) Any banking company failing to comply with the requirements set out in paragraphs (a) or (b) of sub-section (1) hereof shall be liable to a fine not exceeding five pounds for every day during which the default continues. (3) Where a banking company is liable to furnish the returns set out in sub-section (1) of this section, it shall not be liable to comply with section 108 of the Companies Ordinance.

72. Paton (1948, p. 16).
73. BEAFN OV68/1, p. 177.
74. BEAFN OV68/2, p. 9.
75. Section 12 of the draft Ordinance stated that: (1) Every bank shall: (a) exhibit throughout the year in a conspicuous position in every office and branch of the banking company in Nigeria a copy of its last audited balance sheet; (b) on or about the date of the presentation of such balance sheet to the shareholders in general meetings cause a copy thereof to be published in a daily newspaper circulating in Nigeria; (c) forward to the Financial Secretary a copy of its last audited balance sheet within six months after the close of its financial year. (2) Any banking company which fails to comply with any of the requirements of this section shall be liable on conviction to a fine not exceeding one hundred pounds.
76. House Debates (1952, p. 1143).

REFERENCES

Ajibola, W. A. (1986). The Politics of Banking Development. In: O. Oyejide & A. Soyode (Eds), *Commercial Banking in Nigeria*. Ibadan: Unibadan Publishing Consultants.

Ayida, A. (1960). A Critical Analysis of Banking Trends in Nigeria. *Nigerian Institute of Social and Economic Research Conference Proceedings*. Ibadan: Nigerian Institute of Social and Economic Research.

Azikiwe, N. (1956). *Banking Monopoly in Nigeria: Statement made by the Hon. Premier in the Eastern House of Assembly on 8th August, 1956*. Enugu: Government Printer.

Azikiwe, N. (1961). *Zik; A Selection from the Speeches of Nnamdi Azikiwe*. Cambridge: Cambridge University Press.

Bank of England Archives (Various). *Country Files on Nigeria*. London.

Bank of England (1978). Regulation in the City and the Bank of England's Role. *Bank of England Quarterly Bulletin, 18*, 379–389.

Bank of England (1983). Competition, Innovation and Regulation in British Banking. *Bank of England Quarterly Bulletin, 23*, 363–376.

Blunden, G. (1977). International Cooperation in Banking Supervision. *Bank of England Quarterly Bulletin, 17*, 325–329.

Fry, R. (1976). *Bankers in West Africa*. London: Hutchinson.

Government of India (1949). *The Banking Companies Act*. Delhi: Government Press.

Government of Nigeria (1922). *Companies Ordinance*. Lagos: Government Press.

Government of Nigeria (Various). *House of Representatives Debates*. Lagos: Government Press.

Government of Nigeria (1952). *Banking Ordinance*. Lagos: Government Press.

Government of Nigeria (1958). *An Ordinance to Provide for the Regulation and Licensing of the Business of Banking*. Lagos: Government Press.

Government of Pakistan (1948). *The Banking Companies (Control) Act*. Karachi: Government Press.

Grady, J., & Weale, M. (1986). *British Banking, 1960–1985*. London: Macmillan Press Limited.

Hopkins, A. G. (1966). Economic Aspects of Political Movements in Nigeria and in the Gold Coast 1918–1939. *Journal of African History, 7*, 133–152.

Horton, J., & Macve, R. (1996). Accounting for Banks. Paper Presented at the OECD Seminar on Accounting Reform in the Baltic Rim. Oslo, Unpublished.

Newlyn, W. T., & Rowan, D. C. (1954). *Money and Banking in British Colonial Africa*. Oxford: University Press.

Norton, J. J. (1991). The Bank of England's Lament: The Struggle to Maintain the Traditional Supervisory Practices of "Moral Suasion". In: J. J. Norton (Ed.), *Bank Regulation and Supervision in the 1990s*. London: Lloyd's of London Press Ltd.

Nwankwo, G. O. (1990). *Prudential Regulation of Nigerian Banking*. Lagos: University of Lagos Press.

Paton, G. D. (1948b). Report on Banks and Banking in Nigeria. Unpublished Bank of England File Copy (OV68/I, folio 165).

Rowan, D. C. (1951). The Native Banking Boom in Nigeria. *The Banker, 97*, 244–249.

Rowan, D. C. (1952). Banking in Nigeria: a Study in Colonial Financial Evolution. *Banca Nazionale del Lavoro Quarterly Review, 5*, 158–175.

Rowan, D. C. (1953). Central Banking in the Commonwealth. *Banca Nazionale del Lavoro Quarterly Review, 6*, 130–142.

Teriba, O. (1986). Nigeria's Indigenous Banks. In: O. Oyejide & O. Soyode (Eds), *Commercial Banking in Nigeria*. Ibadan: Unibadan Publishing Consultants.

Uche, C. U. (1996). Credit Discrimination Controversy in British West Africa: Evidence from Barclays (DCO). *African Review of Money Finance and Banking*, 87–103.

Uche, C. U. (1997a). Bank of England vs. The IBRD: Did the Nigerian Colony Deserve a Central Bank? *Explorations in Economic History, 34*, 220–241.

Uche, C. U. (1997b). Banking Scandal in a British West African Colony: The Politics of the African Continental Bank Crisis, *Financial History Review, 4*, 51–68.

Uche, C. U., (1999). Foreign Banks, Africans and Credit in Colonial Nigeria, c.1890–1912. *The Economic History Review, 52*, 669–691.

United Nations (1950). *Domestic Financing and Economic Development*. New York: United Nations.

Uzoaga, W. O. (1986). Legislating Bank Capital in Nigeria. In: O. Oyejide & O. Soyode (Eds), *Commercial Banking in Nigeria*. Ibadan: Unibadan Publishing Consultants.

9. AUDIT MARKETS IN EMERGING ECONOMIES: EVIDENCE FROM NIGERIA

Mark H. Taylor and Daniel T. Simon

ABSTRACT

Several studies have examined the market for audit services and the determinants of audit fees in the United States, United Kingdom, and Australia. In recent years, this line of research has been extended to other countries. However, the markets for audit services in many countries, including Nigeria, have not been examined. This paper examines the audit services market in Nigeria, Africa's most populous country. The findings indicate similarities in the market for audit services between Nigeria and many, but not all, of the countries previously studied. The results indicate that the audit fee premium that has been documented in most of the markets previously studied also exists in the market for audit services in Nigeria. That is, the Big 6 (now Big 5) audit firms receive premium fees relative to other audit firms after controlling for other factors affecting audit fees.

INTRODUCTION

This paper extends prior research into the market for audit services by examining the market for audit services in Nigeria, a country not previously studied in audit fee research. Understanding the similarities and differences

Research in Accounting in Emerging Economies, Volume 5, pages 165–175.
Copyright © 2003 by Elsevier Science Ltd.
All rights of reproduction in any form reserved.
ISBN: 0-7623-0901-6

between the market for audit services in Nigeria and other nations should improve our knowledge of the increasingly interdependent world economy as it relates to accounting. It may also increase our knowledge of the economics of auditing. Another reason for studying Nigeria is that little attention has been focused on less-developed countries or on Africa in audit fee research. In addition, Nigeria is an important country meriting study in its own right. Its population is over 100 million, making Nigeria the most populous country on the African continent, with more than 15% of the entire population of Africa. The recent change from military to civilian rule may lead to increased economic development and increased internal and external investment. Hence, additional information on the economic and accounting environment in Nigeria is warranted. The similarity of audit fee determinants between Nigeria and other countries is analyzed and the extent to which the large audit firm fee premium documented for several other countries exists in Nigeria is examined.

The remainder of the paper is organized as follows. In the next section the results of previous research on the market for audit services in other countries is briefly reviewed. This is followed by a discussion of the institutional background of accounting and auditing in Nigeria. The next section describes the data and the empirical tests. Then the empirical results are presented. The results are discussed and summarized in the final section.

PREVIOUS RESEARCH

Beginning with the work of Simunic (1980), many studies have analyzed the market for audit services in several countries.[1] The majority of these studies have focused on a few highly developed countries – the United States, the United Kingdom, and Australia. Only limited attention has been given to the market for audit services in other countries, especially non-highly developed nations (for a recent exception, see the study of the market for audit services in Bangladesh by Karim & Moizer, 1996). The major results of earlier studies have served to establish the responsiveness of audit fees to variables related to auditee size, audit risk, and audit complexity. In general, these papers have found that these variables explain a large proportion of audit fees.

An additional question which has been addressed in many prior studies is whether a subset of auditors receive premium fees due to their "brand name" reputation for providing high quality audits. Usually this line of research has explored whether there is an audit fee premium paid to "Tier I" auditors, with the term Tier I usually defined as consisting of the very largest international accounting firms. Typically this group of firms has been viewed as being composed of the so-called "Big 6" international firms.[2] The importance of finding a large-firm audit fee premium is that it provides evidence of supplier differentiation in the market for audit services.

The concept of supplier differentiation suggests that accounting firms which have invested in what economists refer to as "reputation capital" (e.g. recruitment of highly qualified personnel, employee training programs, firm publications, and advertising) may be able to obtain a return on this investment through higher prices for their services. To date a large audit-fee premium has been documented in the United States (Palmrose, 1986; Francis & Simon, 1987; Simon & Francis, 1988; Turpen, 1990; Balachandran & Simon, 1993), the United Kingdom (Taffler & Ramalinggam, 1982; Chen et al., 1993; Brinn et al., 1994), Australia (Francis, 1984; Francis & Stokes, 1986; Craswell et al., 1995), India (Simon et al., 1986), Hong Kong and Singapore (Simon et al., 1992), Bangaldesh (Karim & Moizer, 1996) Pakistan (Simon & Taylor, 1997), and Japan (Taylor, 1997), and South Korea (Taylor et al., 1999). However, while a majority of studies have found a large-firm audit fee premium, this has not been the case for all countries studied. For example, studies of New Zealand (Firth, 1985) and Malaysia (Simon et al., 1992) did not provide evidence of a general large-firm audit fee premium. Analyses of the Canadian audit services market have been mixed: Anderson and Zéghal (1994) found a large-firm audit fee premium while Chung and Lindsay (1988) did not. Thus, it is possible that the market for audit services may differ significantly across countries, with a general large-firm audit fee premium characterizing only certain countries. That is, the inconclusive results of previous studies suggest that the degree of audit supplier differentiation may vary significantly across countries. This study addresses this question in Nigeria.

INSTITUTIONAL BACKGROUND

The accounting and auditing environment in Nigeria is broadly similar to that in many other countries, especially current and former members of the British Commonwealth. However, compared to many countries, official recognition of the accounting profession is relatively recent. For example, it was not until 1960 that the Association of Accountants in Nigeria was organized under the Nigerian Companies Act (Ogundele, 1969). The Association did not receive statutory recognition until 1965 when the Federal Parliament of Nigeria created the Institute of Chartered Accountants of Nigeria. Moreover, accounting education in Nigeria did not receive the emphasis given to other disciplines at the university level until the University of Nigeria, Nsukka, began offering classes in 1960 (Oseigbu, 1987). Hence, the accounting profession in Nigeria is relatively young. One taxonomy (Mueller, Gernon & Meek, 1997) placed

Nigeria in the "British-American Model" classification, based on accounting measurement and disclosure practices. A classification scheme that hypothesized that the legal system of a country is a good predictor of its accounting orientation (Salter & Doupnik, 1992) categorized Nigeria as part of the "Dutch/British Commonwealth group."

The similarity of the Nigerian accounting environment to other current or former British Commonwealth countries can be seen in the use of the term Chartered Accountants to designate firms conducting audits and in the format of the financial statements; for example, "stocks" and "debtors" are classifications of assets in the balance sheet, as compared to the terms "inventories" and "accounts receivable" which are used in the United States (e.g. Coopers & Lybrand, 1993). A study of financial disclosure regulation (Cooke & Wallace, 1990, p. 96) suggests that Nigeria can be considered as a "regulated" country, an intermediate category between "moderately regulated" and "highly regulated" countries.

A unique feature of the audit environment in Nigeria is the requirement that the annual financial statements include a report by the firm's audit committee. This is unusual. For example, in the United States most publicly-traded firms are required by the stock exchanges on which they are listed to have an audit committee, but inclusion of the audit committee's report with the annual financial statements is rare.[3] In Nigeria, inclusion of a report by the audit committee in the financial statements is the norm rather than the rarity it is in the United States. This report, generally included on the same page as the independent auditor's report, indicates that the audit committee has reviewed the scope and planning of the audit, the audit report, and the ethical and legal appropriateness of their firm's accounting and reporting policies.

In terms of the importance of the largest international accounting firms, Nigeria is somewhat similar to many countries previously studied. All of the Big 6 international firms have a presence in the country. In 1991, each of these firms had at least one office in the country. With the exception of Arthur Andersen, each of the Big 6 had multiple offices. The number of partners in the country ranged from a low of three for Arthur Andersen, to a high of 20 for KPMG Peat Marwick (CIFAR, 1993, Vol. 2, pp. 239–240). The market share of the Big 6 as measured by client size was in excess of 75% of the market for audits of publicly traded clients. Many of the middle fifteen international firms are also present (Okike, 1994).

Although the development of the accounting profession in Nigeria is similar to that of other former British Commonwealth countries, it has changed from its strict emulation of the United Kingdom (Wallace, 1992) and has experienced some unique periods. Most notable was the recent enactment *and* relatively swift repeal of a requirement that a legal practitioner must counter-sign the auditor's report. This requirement was enacted by the Companies and Allied Matters Decree of 1990, which took effect January 2, 1990. Although in large part the Decree was a carbon copy of the United Kingdom's Companies Act of 1985, it contained this unusual provision. Due to the confusion created, the Companies and Allied Matters (Amendment) Decree of 1991 repealed the provision in November of 1991. Hence, the countersignature requirement was effective for only a single year (see Okike, 1994, for an analysis of the reporting outcomes of this requirement).

Aside from a few differences in the recent past, in terms of its general accounting policy orientation and the importance of the largest international firms, Nigeria's accounting institutions and policies are broadly similar to many of the other countries examined in prior studies of the market for audit services. This similarity suggests that many of the determinants of audit fees in Nigeria may be similar to those of countries previously studied.

DATA AND METHODOLOGY

Because audit fees are required disclosure in Nigerian financial reports, as is true for most current or former members of the British Commonwealth, audit fee data were collected directly from annual reports.[4] This eliminates the need to obtain data by questionnaire as has been necessary in studies of several other countries (e.g. the United States). The data set consisted of 157 annual reports by 49 different firms in the period 1990–1996.[5] Because Nigerian data is not included in machine-readable data sources such as Standard and Poor's Global Vantage database, the data used in this study were largely obtained by examining annual reports. Most of these reports were obtained from the companies directly via mailings. Others were obtained from the online data-base LEXUS/NEXUS.[6] The basic research approach is to develop a regression model of audit fees similar to those used in most prior studies of audit fees. Typically, as in this paper, audit fee has been placed as a dependent variable to be explained by various characteristics of the audit engagement. Among the client characteristics found most important in explaining audit fees in previous studies, are size and variables related to the complexity of the audit, such as the number of subsidiary firms and the relative proportion of assets that require more auditor effort to verify (e.g. inventory and receivables). These models have consistently explained a considerable proportion of audit fees in studies of Canada, the United States, the United Kingdom, Australia, New Zealand, Hong Kong, Malaysia, Singapore, Bangladesh, Pakistan, Japan, and India. This basic regression model will therefore serve as a useful benchmark for assessing the similarities and differences in the audit services market in these countries as compared to Nigeria.

As in many prior studies, the basic regression model used to explain audit fees is:

$$AUDITFEE = b_1 + b_2 \, ASSETS + b_3 \, SUBSIDIARIES + b_4 \, INVREC + b_5 \, BIG6$$

with the variables defined as:

AUDITFEE	= audit fee paid to the independent auditor
ASSETS	= total assets of the client
SUBSIDIARIES	= the number of consolidated subsidiaries
INVREC	= the proportion of total assets represented by inventories and receivables
BIG6	= a variable which has a value of one if the company is audited by a Big 6 audit firm

The first explanatory variable (ASSETS) represents the size of the audit client. Auditee size is clearly an important determinant of audit fees since larger clients will require more audit effort.[7] The next two variables (SUBSIDIARIES and INVREC) relate to audit risk and audit complexity. For example, more subsidiaries means that the auditors will have to expend more time and effort. Similarly, a greater proportion of assets which are difficult to audit such as inventory and receivables will require more auditor effort and hence increase fees. Inventories and receivables are both more expensive to audit (e.g. sending confirmations and observing inventory) as well as being more "risky" (e.g. uncollectible receivables and potentially obsolete inventory). Therefore, ASSETS, SUBSIDIARIES, and INVREC should be positively related to audit fees. Prior studies (for a summary, see Simon et al., 1992 or Walker & Johnson, 1996) find that Big 6 auditors receive premium fees in many countries, perhaps due to a perception of higher quality associated with their audits. Therefore, the BIG6 variable is used to control for the effect of audit firm type on audit fees. This variable assesses the extent, if any, of a general large audit firm fee premium as an indication of the degree of supplier differentiation in Nigeria. Based upon research findings for other countries, the BIG6 variable is expected to be positively related to audit fees. This expectation is consistent with previous studies which generally have found evidence of a large audit firm fee premium; no studies have found a fee discount on audits performed by large accounting firms. This regression model will allow assessment of the extent to which the results of previous studies apply to the determination of audit fees in Nigeria.

EMPIRICAL RESULTS

Table 1 presents descriptive statistics for the sample. The considerable variation that exists in the explanatory variables is sufficient to test the effects of these variables on audit fees. Table 2 presents the results of the basic regression equation which is similar to the models used in studies of other countries. The overall results suggest a very good linear fit in which a large proportion of the variation in audit fees is explained. The value of the F-statistic is significant at better than the 0.01 level. The value of adjusted R^2 is 0.72, indicating that the model explains more than two-thirds of the variation in audit fees. This value of the R^2 statistic is similar in magnitude to those found in studies of

Table 1. Descriptive Statistics ($n = 157$).

Variable	Mean (Std. Dev.)
Audit Fee (thousands of Nigerian naira)	606 (798)
Assets (millions of Nigerian naira)	1590 (2537)
Subsidiaries	1.19 (1.91)
Proportion of Assets in Inventory and Receivables	0.49 (0.20)
Percentage of Firms Audited by:	
Arthur Andersen	5.7%
Coopers & Lybrand	5.1%
Deloitte & Touche	11.5%
KPMG	29.9%
Price Waterhouse	8.3%
Other	39.5%

Industry Classification of Sample Firms

Industry	Percentage
Agriculture ($n = 4$)	2.5%
Banking and Finance ($n = 4$)	2.5%
Oil & Gas ($n = 2$)	1.3%
Construction ($n = 14$)	8.9%
Manufacturing ($n = 123$)	78.4%
Retail ($n = 2$)	1.3%
Other ($n = 8$)	5.1%

Table 2.   Regression Results for Basic Model ($n = 157$).

Variable	Coefficient (t-statistic)
INTERCEPT	1.89 (7.11)**
ASSETS	0.49 (14.03)**
INVREC	0.46 (1.80)*
SUBSIDIARIES	0.23 (3.85)**
BIG6	0.52 (4.59)**
Adjusted R^2	0.72
F-Statistic	100.66**

* Significant at the 0.05 level.
** Significant at the 0.01 level.

most other countries. In order to assess possible collinearity problems, Variance Inflation Factors (VIF) were calculated. A VIF in excess of 10 indicates that multicollinearity may be unduly influencing least squares estimates (Neter et al., 1990). None of the VIFs approach this level. Further, none of the VIFs even approach the conservative threshold of 5 suggested by Montgomery and Peck (1982). Thus it does not appear that the results are influenced by multicollinearity among the variables in the sample.[8]

An examination of the t-statistics for the individual explanatory variables suggests considerable similarity between the determinants of audit fees in Nigeria and the countries studied in previous research. The client size variable (ASSETS) is statistically significant at better than the 0.01 level. The audit complexity variables, INVREC and SUBSIDIARIES, have the predicted signs and are significant at conventional levels. Thus, the results for the auditee size and audit complexity variables indicate that there is considerable similarity in the determinants of audit fees in Nigeria and the countries studied in previous research. The auditor-size variable, BIG6, is highly statistically significant (at the 0.01 level) indicating that there is an audit fee premium for Big Six firms in Nigeria, as has been found in a majority of countries previously studied.

CONCLUSIONS

The results demonstrate that the auditee size and audit complexity variables found to be important in studies of other countries are also important in explaining audit fees in Nigeria. Thus, most of the major client-specific factors which determine audit fees in other countries have similar importance in determining audit fees in Nigeria. In particular, there is an audit fee premium accruing to large international accounting firms, suggesting that these firms have successfully differentiated their services. This result is consistent with similar findings for a majority of (but not all) countries previously studied. A possible direction for future research is to investigate the reasons why product differentiation, as measured by audit fee premia, differs across countries.

NOTES

1. A useful review of this research through the mid-1990s is Walker and Johnson (1996).

2. For the time period of the sample (1990–1996), there were six international firms in the market. With the recent merger of Price Waterhouse and Coopers & Lybrand, there are now five. Since there were six during the period under study, we refer to the Big 6, rather than the Big 5 in the paper.

3. The infrequency of public reporting by the audit committee in the United States is indicated by a search of the National Automated Accounting Retrieval Service (NAARS) database for 1985. Less than 1% of over 4,000 annual reports included an audit committee report.

4. An exception to this generalization is Canada where audit fees are not standard disclosures in firm's annual reports.

5. The number of observations for each of the years in the data set is as follows: 1990: 27; 1991: 32; 1992: 21; 1993: 25; 1994: 30; 1995: 14; 1996: 8.

6. The authors are willing to provide the database of observations to other researchers who may wish to extend our analysis.

7. Logarithmic transformations of audit fees and client assets are employed because previous research (e.g. Francis & Simon, 1987) indicates that this specification provides a good linear fit in which the assumptions of ordinary least squares regression are satisfied.

8. Previous research has shown that financial institutions usually are associated with lower audit fees. We incorporated indicator variables for financial institutions as well as industrial firms. Further, as inflation was significant during the time period of the sample, we included indicator variables for each the years in the sample (except the last). Each of those variables was significant and indicated a general rise in prices over the time period. However, the results of the basic regression found in Table 2 remained essentially unchanged.

REFERENCES

Anderson, T., & Zéghal, D. (1994). The pricing of audit services: further evidence from the Canadian market. *Accounting and Business Research*, (Summer), 195–207.

Balachandran, B., & Simon, D. (1993). Audit fees and services of large accounting firms. *The Journal of Economics and Management Strategy*, (Fall), 339–348.

Brinn, T., Peel, M., & Roberts, R. (1994). Audit fee determinants of independent and subsidiary unquoted companies in the U.K. – an exploratory study. *The British Accounting Review*, (26), 101–121.

Center for International Financial Analysis and Research (CIFAR) (1993). *International Accounting and Auditing Trends* (3rd ed.).

Chen, P., Ezzamel, M., & Gwillian, D. (1993). Determinants of audit fees for quoted U.K. companies. *The Journal of Business Finance and Accounting*, (November), 765–786.

Chung, D., & Lindsay, W. (1988). The pricing of audit services: the Canadian perspective. *Contemporary Accounting Research*, (Fall), 19–46.

Cooke, T., & Wallace, R. (1990). Financial disclosure regulation and its environment: A review and further analysis. *The Journal of Accounting and Public Policy*, (Summer), 79–110.

Coopers & Lybrand (1993). *The Accounting Profession in Nigeria*. New York: American Institute of Certified Public Accountants.

Craswell, A., Francis, J., & Taylor, S. (1995). Auditor brand name reputations and industry specializations, *The Journal of Accounting and Economics*, (December), 297–322.

Firth, M. (1985). An analysis of audit fees and their determination in New Zealand. *Auditing: A Journal of Practice and Theory*, (Spring), 23–37.

Francis, J. (1984). The effect of audit firm size on audit prices, *The Journal of Accounting and Economics*, (August), 133–151.

Francis, J., & Simon, D. (1987). A test of audit pricing in the small-client segment of the U.S. audit market. *The Accounting Review*, (January), 145–157.

Francis, J., & Stokes, D. (1986). Audit prices, product differentiation, and scale economies: Further evidence from the Australian market. *The Journal of Accounting Research*, (Autumn), 383–393.

Karim, A. K. M. W., & Moizer, P. (1996). Determinants of Audit Fees in Bangladesh. *The International Journal of Accounting*, *31*(4), 497–509.

Montgomery, D., & Peck, E. (1982). *Introduction to Linear Regression Analysis*. New York: John Wiley & Sons.

Mueller, G., Gernon, H., & Meek, G. (1997). *Accounting: An International Perspective*. Chicago: Irwin.

Neter, J., Wasserman, W., & Kutner, M. H. (1990). *Applied Linear Statistical Models*. Chicago: Irwin.

Ogundele, B. (1969). The Accounting Profession in Nigeria: An International Perspective. *The International Journal of Accounting*, (Fall), 101–106.

Okike, E. N. M. (1994). Curious Auditing Regulations in Nigeria: A Case Study of Cultural/Political Influences on Auditing Practice. *The International Journal of Accounting*, *29*(January), 78–91.

Oseigbu, P. I. (1987). The State of Accounting Education in Nigeria. *The International Journal of Accounting*, (Spring), 57–68.

Palmrose, Z. (1986). Audit fees and auditor size: Further evidence. *The Journal of Accounting Research*, (Spring), 97–110.

Salter, S., & Doupnik, T. (1992). The relationship between legal systems and accounting practices. *Advances in International Accounting, 5,* 3–22.

Simon, D., & Francis, J. (1988). The effects of auditor changes on audit fees: tests of price-cutting and price recovery. *The Accounting Review,* (April), 255–269.

Simon, D., Ramanan, R., & Dugar, A. (1986). The market for audit services in India: An empirical examination. *The International Journal of Accounting Education and Research,* (Spring), 27–35.

Simon, D., & Taylor, M. (1997). The market for audit services in Pakistan, *Advances in International Accounting, 10,* 87–101.

Simon, D., Teo, S., & Trompeter, G. (1992). A comparative study of the market for audit services in Hong Kong, Malaysia and Singapore. *The International Journal of Accounting Education and Research, 27,* 234–240.

Simunic, D. (1980). The pricing of audit services: Theory and evidence. *The Journal of Accounting Research,* (Spring), 161–190.

Taffler, R., & Ramalinggam, K. (1982). The determinants of the audit fee in the U.K.: An exploratory study. Working paper, City University Business School, London.

Taylor, M. (1997). The market for audit services in Japan. *The Pacific Accounting Review,* (December), 59–74.

Taylor, M., Simon, D., & Burton, F. (1999). A Survey of Audit Pricing in South Korea, *Research in Accounting Regulation,* (13), 201–207.

Turpen, R. (1990). Differential pricing on auditors' initial engagements: Further evidence. *Auditing: A Journal of Practice and Theory,* (Spring), 60–76.

Walker, K. B., & Johnson, E. N. (1996). A Review and Synthesis of Research on Supplier Concentration, Quality and Fee Structure in Non-U.S. Markets for Auditor Services. *International Journal of Accounting,* (31), 1–18.

Wallace, R. S. O. (1992). Growing pains of an indigenous accounting profession: the Nigerian experience. *Accounting, Business and Financial History,* (March), 25–53.

10. AN EXAMINATION OF INTERNAL AUDIT IN THE SUDANESE PUBLIC SECTOR

John A. Brierley, Hussein M. El-Nafabi and
David R. Gwilliam

ABSTRACT

*The National Chamber of Accountants' (NCA) Circular of 28 January 1987
required public sector organisations in the Sudan to institute systems of
internal audit. For the purpose of evaluating the nature and performance
of internal auditing in the Sudanese public sector, a questionnaire was
administered to 61 chief internal auditors working in separate public sector
organisations. The results of this questionnaire are reported here and some
suggestions are made for the future development of internal audit in the
Sudanese public sector.*

*The results reveal that, not withstanding the NCA directive, the majority
of public sector organisations in the Sudan still do not have internal
auditing departments. Those that do exist are generally not staffed with
trained personnel. Internal auditors are often engaged in direct financial
control activities rather than audit and they are frequently used as an
available resource at a time of staff shortages in other departments. Cooperation and coordination between internal and external audit is limited.
Where internal audit departments have been established, consideration
should be given to the need to enhance their profile and capability by*

Research in Accounting in Emerging Economies, Volume 5, pages 177–195.
Copyright © 2003 by Elsevier Science Ltd.
All rights of reproduction in any form reserved.
ISBN: 0-7623-0901-6

means of the recruitment of staff with a greater degree of experience and training. In addition, more extensive use should be made of their authority to access all records and personnel in their organisations and to address and question more senior personnel. Finally it is suggested that the internal audit function in central government, regional government and the public enterprises be brought under the administrative control of a single body.

INTRODUCTION

The Sudan is a developing country, which over the last two decades has experienced continual economic problems. Very high levels of inflation (MFEP, 1990; Sudan Information Office, 1997), and a persistent need for internal and external borrowing to finance government expenditure (MFEP, 1990) have evidenced this. Underlying the weakness of the economy has been political instability and a long-standing and damaging civil war (MFEP, 1990). Since 1990 the government has sought to revitalise the economy through a series of National Economic Salvation Programmes (NESPs).

Although these programmes have the declared ambition of increasing private sector activity, the Sudanese economy is still very much dominated by the public sector. In this context, public sector financial management (defined by the Government Accounting Office (GAO, 1979) as budgetary processes, internal controls, accounting systems and audit) is likely to play an important role in facilitating the attainment of the objectives of the various NESPs and in ensuring that the country's limited resources are used appropriately. In addition, it is likely to reduce the incidence of financial fraud (Hillison et al., 1999).

The management of a public sector organisation should introduce and maintain an effective system of internal control to enable it to fulfil its responsibility for the economic, efficient and effective utilisation of limited public resources. A key aspect of internal control is that it enables the public sector organisation to conduct its own internal affairs with an appropriate degree of competence and good management, that in turn lessens the need for external control and monitoring.

Internal audit within public sector organisations is established by the management to examine, evaluate and report on the adequacy of internal control systems (Dowsett & Morris, 1981). This will normally involve both financial audit and performance audit. The financial audit reports on an organisation's financial records and assesses whether they are completely and accurately recorded and prepared in accordance with prescribed accounting standards. Performance audit relates to the economic, efficient and effective use of resources. However, internal audit must not be considered as a substitute for the management of the organisation. Management must assume responsibility for internal control and for the attainment of the overall goals of the organization. However, internal audit can assist in achieving organisational goals and objectives, prevent problems from occurring, and correct any problems that arise. For an internal audit department to carry out its duties effectively, it needs the support of management. This in turn requires that management understands the role of internal audit (CIPFA, 1990).

The objective of this paper is to detail the nature of internal audit in the Sudanese public sector. Internal audit has been required in public sector organisations since 1987, but its success or otherwise in achieving its intended goals has been subject to little, if any, external scrutiny or academic study. This paper uses a questionnaire-based research approach to examine both its operation, and those factors that militate against its making an effective contribution to overall accountability and control. As such it is hoped that the findings of the study will be of significant value to those with responsibility for the development and practice of internal audit.

The paper is organised in the following way. The first section focuses on the objectives and role of internal auditing. The second section discusses the establishment of internal auditing in the Sudanese public sector and a series of exploratory research questions are developed. The third section describes how the questionnaire survey was conducted. The fourth section presents the results of the questionnaire survey. The fifth section offers some concluding remarks and suggestions for changes to internal audit in the Sudanese public sector.

INTERNAL AUDIT

A general framework within which to examine the role and objectives of internal audit in both the private and public sector can be found in the Standards of Professional Practice of Internal Auditing of the Institute of Internal Auditors (IIA). These standards which were first issued in 1978 cover: the independence of internal auditing departments, the professional proficiency of auditors, the scope of internal audit work, the performance of internal audit work and the management of the internal audit department (IIA, 1997).

In order to provide an unbiased and unrestricted opinion, internal auditors must be independent and be able to report on matters as they see them, rather than from the management's perspective (Ridley & D'Silva, 1997; Ridley & Chambers, 1998; Cosserat, 2000). Internal audit is not part of the line management's structure, and accordingly, it should not participate in any function, activity or system that the internal auditor has a responsibility to audit. Independence would normally require there to be an organizational charter setting out the role and scope of internal auditing, its rights of access to individuals, records and assets, and delineating appropriate reporting channels and responsibilities (Ridley & Chambers, 1998; Moeller & Witt, 1999).

Internal auditors should carry out their duties with that measure of professional care and skill which might reasonably be expected of a competent auditor relative to the specific duties undertaken (Buttery & Simpson, 1987).

An internal audit department is normally required to review, appraise and report on the soundness, adequacy and application of internal controls. Also within the scope of an internal audit department's work there is usually a requirement to report on the extent to which the organisation's assets and interests are accounted for and safeguarded from all kinds of losses arising from extravagance, fraud, inefficiency, waste and the unreliability of financial and other data prepared by the organisation (CIPFA, 1979; Flesher, 1996). More recently a much wider role encompassing aspects of operational performance and effectiveness has been identified (Ridley, 1996).

The effectiveness of the internal audit system is substantially a function of the quality, training and experience of its members. To carry out its work effectively and to satisfy the requirements of each internal audit task, an internal audit department should have an appropriate complement of staff with suitable qualifications and experience. For example, in the USA and the U.K., internal auditors are often members of the Institute of Internal Auditors (see Montondou, 1995). In these professional organisations internal auditors would be expected to maintain their professional knowledge through continuing professional education schemes.

In order to perform their duties properly and effectively, internal auditors should seek to build close working relationships and mutual understanding with the organisation's management, external auditors and any review agencies (CIPFA, 1994; Bickerstaff, 1996; Ridley & Chambers, 1998; Moeller & Witt, 1999).

The internal auditor should ensure that findings, conclusions and recommendations arising from each internal audit are communicated promptly to the appropriate level of management. Little (1987) suggests that the objectives of internal audit reporting are to: (1) alert management as soon as possible to matters of significance arising from the audit; (2) persuade management to implement the recommendations for changes leading to improvements in the system and its performance; and (3) provide a formal record of points raised by the audit and, where appropriate, agreements reached with management. It is important that the channels of communication are to a suitable level of management or management committee. It would normally be appropriate for the internal auditor to report directly to the head of the finance function (Ridley & D'Silva, 1997).

INTERNAL AUDITING IN THE SUDANESE PUBLIC SECTOR

The Sudanese public sector consists primarily of central government, regional governments and public enterprises. Central government comprises the central ministries and semi-autonomous national agencies, such as the Courts Administration, Chamber of Taxation and the Attorney General's Chamber. It is responsible for administering and managing all the national service organisations, formulating and implementing national economic plans, projects and schemes and taking charge of national defence and security. Most of these bodies are located in the Sudanese capital, Khartoum. The regional governments include the regional ministries, provinces and related departments and agencies such as local councils. Regional governments exist in each of the 26 states that were established in the Sudan in February 1994. Public enterprises dominate the country's economic infrastructure and play a leading role in the economy. They are found in activities like agriculture, energy, financial institutions, hotels and tourism, transport and communications, and many industrial sectors. They include industries that are owned solely by the government and those that are owned in partnership with the private sector.

The present system of internal audit in the Sudanese public sector was established by *fiat* by the National Chamber of Accountants' (NCA) (part of the Ministry of Finance and Economic Planning (MFEP)) Circular of 28 January 1987 (MFEP, NCA, 1987a). The Circular was addressed to all national ministries, semi-autonomous national agencies and public enterprises with copies sent to the Regional Governors and the Auditor General's Chamber (AGC) (responsible for external audit in the Sudanese public sector). As a result, a separate administration, the Internal Auditing Administration (IAA), was established within the NCA to administer Internal Auditing Departments (IADs) in central government organisations. IADs were initially planned in 40 out of the 92 central government organisations. An agreement was made with the MFEP to recruit 82 personnel of various civil service ranks to work as internal auditors in the selected 40 organisations. However, by October 1995 even this relatively modest target had not been achieved, with IADs being established in only 30 of the 92 central government organisations.

In 1990, the NCA directed Regional Governors to establish IADs in regional government organisations. The establishment of internal auditing in regional government was no more rapid than in central government. Nahr al-Neel State was the first to establish internal auditing (Osman Al-Naheem, 1994), and Kassala State was second. After the Sudan was divided into 26 states in 1994, the 1987 Circular of the NCA was again circulated to the Governors of the newly established states requiring them to establish IADs in their organisations. However, by October 1995 only 15 out of the Sudan's 26 states had established IADs.

Duties and Reporting Responsibilities

In July 1987, the under-secretary of the NCA issued a Circular to public sector organisations specifying the scope and responsibilities of internal auditing (MFEP, NCA, 1987b). As stated in the Circular, internal auditors are normally required to carry out the following duties:

(1) Ensuring the legitimacy of revenues and expenditures, relative to plans and budget targets, and compliance with rules and regulations. Furthermore, internal auditors have the authority to carry out checks of relevant documentation before actual expenditures take place.
(2) Ensuring that the balances of all accounting books in which financial transactions and activities are recorded are equal to those on the monthly accounts and final accounts or any other information extracted from them.
(3) Carrying out both systematic and surprise checks on cash deposits to ensure that all monies received are recorded correctly and kept in the treasury department of the organisation or transferred to the bank without delay. In addition, internal auditors have to ensure that no more than the permitted amount of money is kept in the treasury department.
(4) Verifying and reconciling bank accounts every month.
(5) Reviewing and reporting on the efficient use of the organisation's available resources, and bring to the attention of management any inefficiency or irresponsible use of such public resources.
(6) Carrying out an inspection and assessment of inventories and report upon storage methods and the suitability of stores.
(7) Ensuring that the recommendations and comments of the AGC on the accounts are dealt with promptly.

In addition, IADs are expected to review and report upon the adequacy of: (1) the design and efficiency of the accounting system, financial and administrative documentation, and the internal control systems; and (2) appropriate application of financial rules and regulations to the organisation's activities.

To achieve the various internal auditing objectives the under-secretary of the NCA, in the same July 1987 Circular, directed all the public sector organisations to allow IADs unrestricted access to all files and offices of the organisation, and the authority to address and/or summon for investigation all senior personnel of the organisation.

Personnel and Training

For internal auditing to play its role effectively as an internal managerial control that can evaluate the adequacy and effectiveness of all other control systems within an organisation, an IAD should be appropriately staffed with qualified and well-trained internal auditors. The lack of a prior history for internal audit meant that the supply of such personnel was very limited in the Sudan. To improve the quality of public sector accountants, the MFEP established the Institute of Accounting Studies (IAS) as a training centre. This institute was placed under the administration of the NCA, and lecturers were selected from experienced public sector accountants. Following the establishment of internal auditing in the public sector in 1987, the IAS undertook the responsibility for training internal auditors by offering short courses lasting about three months. The courses offered by the IAS concentrate on accounting and auditing issues in the public sector. These courses were expected to be of greater relevance to public sector internal auditors than to more widely-based postgraduate accounting studies.

Reporting

According to the Council of Ministers' Decree No. 62 dated 23 August 1989, internal auditing reports should be submitted to the minister responsible for the relevant unit. The submitted reports are general, routine or special reports. General reports detail the overall compliance with regulation and evaluate the financial policies and controls in place in the organisation. Routine reports indicate the financial performance of each unit in the organisation, and should be submitted regularly (e.g. monthly or quarterly). Special reports relate to specific activities or an investigation of suspected fraudulent financial operations. They should be submitted to the authority that sanctioned the investigation and/or any other interested party. Subsequently, the NCA issued a directive to all public sector organisations requiring that both general reports and special reports be submitted to the minister responsible for the relevant unit, with copies to be submitted to the NCA and the AGC. The routine reports should be addressed to the general manager within the organisation, with copies to be submitted to the relevant minister, the IAA and the AGC.

Within the context of exploratory research, a series of questions were designed to gain an understanding of public sector internal auditing in the Sudan. These questions are listed below in terms of seven areas that formed the basis for the research questionnaire.

Objectives and Duties

- What are the main objectives of internal audit work?
- What are the main duties of internal auditors?
- Are internal auditors directly involved in the operation of the accounting system upon which they are ultimately required to report?

Financial and Performance Audit

- Are financial and performance audits carried out by the IADs?

Planning and Work Programme Design

- How much planning is undertaken prior to carrying out internal audit work?
- What work is undertaken on internal audit work programmes?

Size of Internal Audit Departments

- What is the size of the IADs?

Qualifications

- What qualifications do internal audit staff hold?
- What are the preferred qualifications for internal audit staff?

Training

- Where are internal auditors trained?
- What is the preferred training establishment?
- Why is the most preferred training establishment preferred to others?

Reporting

- Who receives copies of internal audit reports?
- What types of special reports are prepared?

Achievements and Problems

- What are the main achievements of the IADs?
- What are the main problems facing IADs?

RESEARCH METHODOLOGY

In a developed country, large quantities of questionnaires can be distributed via the postal service and follow-up procedures conducted via the post and telephone. The inadequacy of the Sudanese communications infrastructure means that this approach is not feasible. The need to distribute and administer the questionnaires by hand has implications both in terms of sample size and whether a sample can be random when many hundreds of miles might have to be travelled in order to pursue a potential respondent. One other fact to consider when carrying out the research is that the continuation of the civil war in Southern Sudan and the endemic armed plundering in Western Sudan made travelling and the collection of data in these regions fraught with danger. As a consequence, it was necessary in the research design to strike an appropriate balance between efficiency, feasibility and what might be desirable in methodological terms.

A questionnaire was designed to answer the research questions referred to above. Due to logistical constraints the survey was restricted to three states. Khartoum State (Central Sudan) was included as all central ministries, most semi-autonomous national agencies and most public enterprises are located in this State. The two other states chosen were Nahr al-Neel State (in Northern Sudan) and Kassala State (in Eastern Sudan). Although the states are not necessarily representative of the generality of Sudanese States, they are representative of the relatively more prosperous and organised states. They have a continuous history of administration and government as single entities compared with the majority of the states newly established in 1994. All the regional ministries and other important public sector bodies in Nahr al-Neel and Kassala States are concentrated in their capitals, Addamar City and Kassala City respectively.

The first draft of the questionnaire was prepared in English. However, the final version of the questionnaire was translated to Arabic (the dominant language in the Sudan) to be easily understood and answered by respondents. To ensure that the questionnaire was free from any ambiguities that could lead to inadequate or misleading responses, the questionnaire was administered to five potential respondents for comment. On the basis of their comments and recommendations minor revisions were made to the questionnaire.

All central ministries were chosen for the survey because they consume most of the central government resources. Regional government organisations were selected for the survey according to the following criteria. All of the regional ministries were selected because they are responsible for administering all the regional services such as schools and hospitals and, as a consequence, consume most of the states' government resources. A number of local councils were included because they are responsible for collecting regional taxes, which in some States contributed about 80% of the states' total revenue. Finally, a number of other organisations were chosen from each administrative sector in the State. The majority of public enterprises have their headquarters in Khartoum; as a consequence 65 of the public enterprises sampled were based in Khartoum, together with three from Nahr al-Neel State and two from Kassala State.

Fifteen recent graduates of the Department of Accounting at Omdurman Islamic University were selected as enumerators to assist in the distribution and collection of the questionnaires. The enumerators were briefed by the second author to ensure that the questionnaire was handed to the chief internal auditor of the IAD of the organisation, to maintain a continuous follow-up of the respondents to complete the questionnaire in time, to report immediately any problems regarding the distribution and collection of the questionnaires, to report any enquiries from any respondent regarding specific questions in the questionnaire and to ensure when collecting the completed questionnaires that all questions had been answered.

To facilitate the distribution of the questionnaires and to encourage the respondents to answer all questions, a covering letter, written in Arabic, was attached to each questionnaire and addressed to the chief internal auditor. The letter detailed the importance and purpose of the survey, and assured respondents of the confidentiality of all responses.

A total of 178 questionnaires were distributed to public sector organisations in the Sudan. A total of 124 responses were obtained (response rate 70%), 63 indicated that they did not have an IAD in their organisation. A breakdown of the 61 organisations with an IAD is given in Table 1. This reveals that internal audit is more pervasive in the public enterprises than in central and regional government. The results of the survey are based on the responses of the 61 chief internal auditors who have experience as chief internal auditors ranging from one to eight years in total, with the modal class of 15 auditors having five years experience.

Table 1.   Number of Public Sector Organisations Sampled.

Type of organisation	Population size	Sample size	Responding entities	Entities with IADs	No. of internal auditors employed
Central government	92	68	49	21	128
Regional government:					
In Nahr al-Neel state	36	23	18	4	27
In Kassala state	27	17	13	6	6
Public enterprises	136	70	44	30	121
Total	291	178	124	61	282

RESULTS

Objectives and Duties

The most commonly identified objective of internal auditing in the Sudanese public sector was checking for compliance with agreed financial rules and regulations. The next three most popular objectives were, detecting corruption, embezzlement and fraud, verifying the accuracy of financial and accounting information, and reviewing the systems of internal control.

The chief internal auditors identified similar duties undertaken by their IADs across all areas of the public sector and these can be summarised as: (1) to carry out detailed checks on different expenditures before payment; (2) to ensure the accuracy of accounts and adherence to accepted accounting and financial procedures; (3) to ensure that all the organisation's revenues and expenditures are consistent with the budget, and financial rules and regulations; and (4) to prevent and detect error and fraud.

This does suggest that internal audit practice is not entirely consistent with the objectives as perceived by chief internal auditors. In particular, internal auditors spend considerable time carrying out checks on expenditure for payment thereby fulfilling a routine control function. Furthermore, a total of 22 chief internal auditors (36%) stated that their department undertook additional accounting duties. These additional duties may be summarised as: (1) Assisting in closing final accounts of the organisation and making necessary adjustments. (2) Assisting in preparing monthly accounts to ensure they are not delayed. (3) Participating in the activities of the accounting department for limited periods when there is a particular shortage of accounting staff. (4) Participating in budget preparation. (5) Assisting in carrying out accounting duties in peak periods. These additional accounting duties provide evidence that internal auditors were reporting upon activities in which they have had some participative role. This participation is likely to affect the independence of internal auditors with regard to their impartiality of reporting on activities.

Financial or Performance Audit?

The types of internal work conducted are shown in Table 2. All of the 13 IADs that carried out performance audits also performed efficiency audit, but in only eight of these departments was the chief internal auditor able to confirm that public funds were in fact used efficiently. Only four departments carried out effectiveness audits. For three of these, this consisted of an evaluation of the effectiveness of a task after it had taken place, while the other department stated

Table 2. Type of Internal Audit Work Undertaken.

Type of internal audit work	Number	Percentage
Financial audits	48	79
Financial and performance audits	13	21
Total	61	100

that it reviewed tasks before they had taken place. None of the departments carried out an on-going review of tasks. Finally, nine departments conducted economy audits.

The relevant chief internal auditors were asked to state why their department did not undertake performance audits. Their reasons can be summarised as: (1) the shortage of internal auditors in each department made it difficult to cover financial audit adequately, let alone conduct performance audit; and (2) a lack of knowledge and experience of performance audit resulting from the absence of training programmes.

Planning and Work Programme Design

Table 3 provides information about the level of planning of audit work. Those departments where audit planning did take place were asked to specify the main focus of their audit programmes. Of the 27 respondents who plan audit work, a total of 22 concentrated planning work on all revenues, expenditures and other financial activities, 18 concentrated on problem areas identified in prior audits, 13 on activities not audited recently, five on a percentage of revenues, expenditures and assets, and in two public enterprises the IAD focused on planning work relating to the major risks facing the enterprise. The production of the internal audit work programme was the responsibility of the chief internal auditor in 19 out of these 27 IADs, while in the other eight departments planning was normally delegated to other staff within the department.

Table 3. Internal Audit Planning.

Length of the planning period	Number	Percentage
Short-term (up to one-year)	24	41
Long-term and short-term	3	6
No plans prepared	31	53
Total	58	100

Size of Internal Audit Department

Of the 61 IADs, over two-thirds had no more than three members of staff and a little over one-third had just one member of staff. Only 10% of the respondents were heads of an IAD consisting of more than eight internal auditors. The break-down of the total number of internal auditors in these 61 organisations is shown in Table 1. This shows that there are 128 internal auditors in the 21 central government organisations. This includes a total of 58 in one organisation, the Ministry of Defence. Thus, in the remaining 20 organisations there is an average of 3.5 internal auditors. This is slightly less than the average of four found in public enterprises. Given that central government organisations are typically larger than public enterprises this result may be indicative of the rather greater relative importance that is attached to internal auditing in public enterprises. As a consequence of the relatively small size of the IADs, it is not surprising perhaps that 53 out of the 61 IADs surveyed felt that they had insufficient internal audit staff and were therefore constrained in carrying out internal audit duties properly.

Qualifications

Table 4 shows that the 282 internal audit staff in the departments surveyed possess a variety of qualifications with 49% possessing a high secondary school: accounting studies qualification. The qualifications seen by the chief internal auditors as the most desirable for internal audit staff were the BSc. in Accounting (preferred by 79% of the 61 chief internal auditors), followed by the high secondary school: commercial studies qualification (18%) and the Postgraduate Diploma in Accounting (3%). Thus, almost half of the internal audit staff working in the departments surveyed do not possess any of these preferred accounting/commercial-based qualifications and this may call into question the overall quality of the internal audit staff. The reality is that persons with accounting/commercial qualifications have a wide variety of work opportunities in the private sector and Gulf countries where salaries are much

Table 4. Qualifications of the Internal Audit Staff.

Type of Qualification	Number	Percentage
High secondary school: Academic studies	138	49
B.Sc. in accounting	87	31
High secondary school: Commercial studies	45	16
Post-graduate diploma in accounting	11	4
M.Sc. or Ph.D. in accounting	1	0
Total	282	100

higher. It is currently not feasible to seek to staff IADs solely with staff with accounting qualifications.

Training

The survey results revealed that internal audit staff had received very little formal training. Only 51 out of the 282 internal auditors in the 61 public sector organisations had attended public sector accounting training courses at the IAS. Fourteen other internal auditors had received training through post-graduate studies in accounting.

In fact for the majority of Chief Internal Auditors (51%) the preferred training place was the training institute of the AGC, while 28% preferred the Sudanese universities and only 21% preferred the IAS. This result is surprising because the IAS was established by the MFEP to train public sector accountants and internal auditors. Chief internal auditors offered a number of reasons for choosing the AGC. The main ones are: first, the AGC's staff have long experience in auditing the accounts of public sector organisations. Second, the AGC is noted for its high quality training, and those trained by them are more able to find lucrative jobs in the private sector and the Gulf countries. Third, their courses are designed specifically to teach public sector auditing techniques, whereas the courses offered by the IAS are for both public sector accountants and internal auditors.

Reporting

Table 5 indicates that there was considerable diversity in the manner in which departments submitted their routine reports. The great majority of IADs in the Sudan follow similar procedures in submitting routine reports to the general

Table 5.   The Methods Used to Submit Routine Reports.

Submission method	Number	Percentage
To the general managers of their organisation	26	43
To the general managers of their organisation with a copy to the IAA at the NCA and the AGC	17	28
To the general manager of their organisation with a copy to the IAA at the NCA	9	15
To the general manager of their organisation with a copy to the respective ministers	5	8
To the chief financial officer of their organisation	4	6
Total	61	100

manager of their organisation, as required by NCA directives. However, there are significant differences with regard to the authorities to which they submit copies of their reports. None of the respondents submitted their reports as required by the NCA to the combination of general manager, appropriate minister, IAA and AGC. Furthermore, the submission of reports to a chief financial officer could be a cause of friction between accounting departments and IADs.

Although routine reports are expected to be submitted every quarter, only one-third of respondents stated that this was actually the case, while the remaining respondents indicated that there were no defined time limits for submitting reports. Two types of special reports were identified by respondents. The first type referred to by 57 respondents, was submitted when the falsification of records, fraud or corruption was discovered. The second special report, referred to by 27 respondents, was submitted when internal auditing recommendations had been ignored such as those relating to minor mistakes or irregularities which had not seriously affected the overall performance of an organisation.

Achievements and Problems

Fifty of the chief internal auditors assessed the main achievements of their IADs. Eighty percent of them identified as a main achievement ensuring the observance of financial rules and regulations and the prevention of errors and fraud. Fifty-four percent referred to keeping management fully informed of what was happening in the organisation through the provision of valuable information on the activities of various departments. Thirty-four percent of the chief internal auditors identified a main achievement as being able to carry out an annual audit of the most important areas of the organisation. Finally, 24% noted the regular evaluation and reporting upon the effectiveness of internal control systems and making recommendations for improvements.

Only 14% identified gaining the confidence of the AGC (the provider of external auditing services) as an achievement. In these cases the external auditors were able to place increased reliance on the work of the internal auditors. However, the fact that such a low proportion of respondents singled this out as an achievement suggests that for the majority of organisations there is little if any collaboration between internal and external audit. Of course the weakness of external audit in the Sudanese public sector is likely to be a factor in reducing the perceived importance of co-operation between internal and external audit.

Worryingly, seven of the respondents were unable to identify a single major achievement of their departments. This was because of the marginalisation of the internal auditor's role in terms of the work they were permitted to carry out and the lack of consideration given to their reports.

The two major problems identified by chief internal auditors in their IADs were low salary levels (identified by 93% of them), which may have contributed to the next major problem of staff shortages (identified by 87%). Another four major problems were identified as, other persons misunderstanding the role of internal audit (80%), lack of staff training (79%), absence of statutes governing and regulating internal auditing work (66%) and the lack of an appropriate infrastructure (61%).

The majority of internal auditors identified the main achievement of their department as ensuring the observance of financial rules and regulations and the prevention of errors and fraud. However, given the limitations and problems in the practice of internal audit identified above, the extent to which these perceived achievements were genuine ones may be open to question. It is likely that there is need for further resolution of these difficulties if internal audit in the Sudanese public sector is to achieve its objectives.

CONCLUSION

Although when a formal requirement for internal audit was introduced in 1987 it was envisaged that internal audit would play a significant role in Sudanese public sector financial management, the reality has been that the development of the internal audit function has been patchy and slow. Most public sector organisations in the Sudan still do not have IADs. The IADs that do exist are generally not staffed with trained personnel. Internal auditors are often engaged in direct financial control activities rather than audit and they are frequently used as an available resource at a time of staff shortages in other departments.

The development of public sector internal auditing in the Sudan is rooted in financial and compliance audit concerned with the examination of financial transactions, accounts and reports, including an evaluation of compliance with applicable rules and regulations. The audit scope has not been expanded to include measurements of economy, efficiency and effectiveness of public expenditures and there is no current intention to develop in this direction. As such public sector internal audit in the Sudan is not progressing in line with models in more developed countries. The evidence presented above suggests that internal audit has been failing to achieve even its more limited objectives in terms of compliance and regularity audit. There is no doubt that it is the combination of a lack of economic and political stability, racial and religious differences, relative poverty, internal migration and civil war which underlie and define the nature of audit and accountability in the Sudan. In many senses conventional 'Western' notions of audit and accountability do not transfer well into a society where impropriety and fraud is endogenous and institutionalized at all levels of society – indeed for many sectors of society it is a necessity to maintain a basic standard of living (Khalid, 1990) – and where a combination of an extended family system and a culture of powerful male leadership (Sandbrook, 1985; Woodward, 1990) inhibit systems of control and accountability. Furthermore, what may be construed as a half-hearted attempt to establish a system of internal audit in the Sudanese public sector was probably doomed to failure because it was established by the NCA. This may have influenced the policy within internal audit departments to concentrate on accounting rather than audit tasks.

In the short-term, a variety of changes may be made to the structure of internal audit through the imposition of internal audit standards based on those issued by the IIA. At the university level there is scope both for increasing and updating the extent of curriculum content within accounting degrees devoted to public sector accounting and auditing. At present the training institute of the AGC is seen as a leader in its field in the Sudan and efforts should be directed toward maintaining and improving its existing reputation. Further seminars, workshops and conferences on internal audit techniques, procedures and standards could usefully augment current training programmes. There is a particular need for the AGC to seek to work with international donor organisations, such as the IIA, to give its auditors the opportunity to benefit from training programmes sponsored by them.

These changes could lead to the development of a minimum set of qualifications for internal auditors such as studying public sector internal auditing under the organisation of the AGC and the need to attend CPE courses. Having said this, any improvement in training is unlikely to have the desired effect when the pay of accountants and auditors in the public sector is significantly lower than in the private sector (Gujarathi & Dean, 1993), this is a problem, however, throughout the developing world not only in the Sudan (Gujarathi & Dean, 1993).

The 1987 Circular called for internal audit to be established within central and regional government organisations and public enterprises. Many such organisations do not have a functioning IAD and this situation should be reviewed with some urgency. There is a need to establish internal audit functions in accordance with the requirements of the Circular. Where IADs have been established, consideration should be given to strengthening them through the recruitment of qualified, trained and experienced staff; through granting internal auditors unrestricted access to all records, offices and personnel of the organisation, and the authority to address and/or summon for investigation high-ranking personnel of the organisation.

For the system of internal audit to be effective in the long-term there needs to be a fundamental, paradigmatic shift in the ethos of and the attitude towards accountability in the Sudan. How and when such a change will come about is an open question and clearly the economic and environmental circumstances are such that it is not going to happen overnight. However, we would argue that there is scope for a gradualist approach to reform and improvement via changes in terms of administrative structure, a review of the aims, and objectives and processes of internal audit in the Sudanese public sector and a greater focus on the training and development of internal auditors. In particular, it would facilitate the development of internal audit in the Sudanese public sector if responsibility for the internal audit function was transferred from the NCA and a separate chamber established within the MFEP. Bringing together responsibility for the internal audit function in central government, regional government and public enterprises under the administrative control of a single body, would allow a comprehensive review of the extent to which internal audit has been established in the Sudanese public sector and to which it is effective in carrying out its stated objectives. Such a review would consider whether the role of internal audit most suited to the needs of the Sudanese public sector was that of an adjunct to the internal accounting and control system, or whether the focus should be on fraud detection and investigation (see Hillison et al., 1999) or on wider issues of performance and management audit. A separation of authority for internal audit and the clear designation of the aims and objectives of internal audit would enhance internal auditor independence and perhaps allow for improvements in processes and working methods away from an approach based on extensive examination of documents, transactions, accounts and vouchers toward one based more upon sampling, identification of control weaknesses and systems review.

The use of questionnaire-based research has inherent limitations both in terms of the extent and representativeness of the coverage and also in the interpretation of the questionnaire responses. As noted above, ethnographic and other considerations prevented the selection of a fully representative sample of public sector organizations. Rather the sample was biased toward organizations which, because of their geographic location and relative stability and prosperity, were expected to be in the forefront of internal audit practice in the Sudan. Again the method of direct distribution used, in part because of the unreliability of internal communications in the Sudan, militated against the size of sample used in questionnaire studies in more developed countries.

REFERENCES

Bickerstaff, M. (1996). It takes two to tango. *Internal Auditing*, (March), 10–11.
Buttery, R., & Simpson, R. (1987). *Internal Audit in the Public Sector*. Cambridge: Woodhead Faulkner.
Chartered Institute of Public Finance and Accountancy (CIPFA) (1979). *Internal Audit Practice in the Public Sector*. London: CIPFA.

Chartered Institute of Public Finance and Accountancy (CIPFA) (1990). *The Client's View of Internal Audit*. London: CIPFA.

Chartered Institute of Public Finance and Accountancy (CIPFA) (1994). *BS5750 and the Internal Audit*. London: CIPFA.

Cosserat, G. W. (2000). *Modern Internal Auditing*. Wiley.

Dowsett, P., & Morris, T. (1981). Implementing CIPFA's Internal Audit Statements. *Public Finance and Accountancy*, (December), 25.

Flesher, D. L. (1996). *Internal Auditing Standards and Practice*. Altamonte Spring, FL: Institute of Internal Auditors.

Government Accounting Office (GAO) (1979). *Training and Related Effects Needed to Improve Financial Management in the Third World*. Washington, D.C.: Government Printing Office.

Gujarathi, M. R., & Dean, P. (1993). Problems of recruiting and retaining qualified government accountants and auditors in developing countries. *Research in Third World Accounting*, 2, 187–200.

Hillison, W., Pacini, C., & Sinason, D. (1999). The internal auditor as fraud-buster. *Managerial Auditing Journal*, *14*, 351–362.

Institute of Internal Auditors (IIA) (1997). *Standards for the Professional Practice of Internal Auditing*. Altamonte Spring, FL: Institute of Internal Auditors.

Khalid, M. (1990). *The Government They Deserve: the Role of the Elite in Sudan's Political Evolution*. Kegan Paul International.

Little, G. (1987). The Hows and Whys of Auditing Reporting. *Public Finance and Accountancy*, (20 March), 7.

Ministry of Finance and Economic Planning (MFEP) and National Chamber of Accounts (NCA) (1987a). *Circular No, 123*, 28 January. Khartoum: MFEP.

Ministry of Finance and Economic Planning (MFEP) and National Chamber of Accounts (NCA) (1987b). *Circular No, 127*, 13 July. Khartoum: MFEP.

Ministry of Finance and Economic Planning (MFEP) (1990). *Economic Review 1989/1990*. Khartoum: MFEP.

Moeller, R., & Witt, H. (1999). *Brink's Modern Internal Auditing*. Wiley.

Montondou, L. (1995). Accountability in municipalities: The use of internal auditors and audit committees. *American Review of Public Administration*, (25), 59–69.

Osman Al-Naheem (1994). Internal Auditing in Nahr al-Neel State. Paper presented at the conference of accountants of Nahr al-Neel state, Atbara, April.

Ridley, J. (1996). One, two and many, *Internal Auditing*, (January), 9.

Ridley, J., & Chambers, A. (1998). *Leading Edge Internal Auditing*. Prentice Hall.

Ridley, J., & D'Silva, K. (1997). A question of values. *Internal Auditing*, (June), 16–19.

Sandbrook, R. (with Barker, J.) (1985). The Politics of Africa's Economic Stagnation. Cambridge University Press.

Sudan Information Office (1997). *Sudan News: A Weekly Information Bulletin*, (4 October), 3.

Woodward, P. (1990). *Sudan, 1898–1989 The Unstable State*. Lynne Rienner.

11. AN EMPIRICAL INVESTIGATION OF THE DEVELOPMENT OF ACCOUNTING EDUCATION AND PRACTICE IN LIBYA, AND OF STRATEGIES FOR ENHANCING ACCOUNTING EDUCATION AND ACCOUNTING PRACTICE IN LIBYA

Mustafa Bakar Mahmud and Alex Russell

ABSTRACT

This paper contributes to the burgeoning literature on the development of accounting education and accounting practice in developing countries. It analyzes the responses of 131 Libyan accounting academics and professionals to a questionnaire designed to elicit views on: (a) the major problems obstructing accounting education and practice in Libya; and (b) the usefulness of certain strategies for enhancing accounting education and accounting practice in developing countries. The analysis shows that: (a) in the opinion of key personnel in Libya, accounting education and practice in Libya is impaired by a series of professional accounting factors

Research in Accounting in Emerging Economies, Volume 5, pages 197–236.
ISBN: 0-7623-0901-6

and educational factors; and (b) there is a need for Libya to reassess its plans for enhancing accounting education and accounting practice if its aims and objectives for these areas are to be achieved. The findings are consistent with those in the international accounting literature.

1. INTRODUCTION

This paper replicates and extends previously published research by empirically investigating the factors which have influenced the development of accounting education and practice in Libya. Further, it investigates how successfully Libya has employed various "strategies" for enhancing accounting education and accounting practice. The use of the word "strategies" needs qualification since it implies that there exists a conscious long-term planning process which may, or may not, be present in Libya. The terminology is taken from the work of Novin and Baker, 1990 and Akathaporn et al., 1993. It enhances the existing research literature on accounting in developing countries in two important ways. First, it extends the research findings of Akathaporn et al. (see Akathaporn et al., 1993) into similar issues in Thailand by deploying their research instruments to the uniquely interesting developing State of Libya. Second, the statistical analysis used in the current paper is more sophisticated than that used in the Thailand study and therefore should be of interest to researchers in this field.

The primary research instrument used was a questionnaire issued to 131 'key personnel' in Libya on the basis that these respondents were likely to be the best source of relevant perceptions on the issues being investigated. Thus the data for Libya are new and they emerge from an analysis of the questionnaire issued to accounting academics, oil sector accountants, State accountants and licensed public sector accountants in Libya. However, the Libyan study is not a straight replication of the Thailand study. For example, Akathaporn et al. asked open-ended questions to help identify the main factors obstructing the development of accounting education and practice in Thailand and ten factors were identified. For reasons explained later, the current authors did not merely ask open-ended questions but, instead, sought respondents' opinions on their strength of agreement or disagreement regarding the application of the ten factors to Libya. This approach led to a much richer set of responses being available for statistical analysis. Questions were included in the questionnaire which related to the strategies thought likely to have had an impact on the development of Libya's accounting education and accounting practice. These strategies were identified from the literature and from discussions with leading academics in Libya. As mentioned above, to some extent the research under-taken replicates the work of Akathaporn et al., 1993, but in the context of a radically different developing country to that of the prior study. One tentative conclusion which can be drawn from the paper is that even an extreme example of emerging nations, such as Libya, seems likely to employ similar strategies to other developing countries to assist with the development of their accounting education and accounting practice. Unfortunately, the ideographic emphasis of the case study imposes limitations which, at the outset, impede any defensible claim to extend the findings from the particular country of study to a wider class of developing country. But the study does add incremental information which should enrich the literature. The remaining part of this section outlines the content of the paper.

Section 2 outlines essential background information on Libya and gives brief details of its educational and professional establishments. Section 3 describes the rationale for undertaking the research. It also indicates previous relevant work in the literature. Section 4 outlines the research methodology deployed. In particular it explains the statistical techniques used to analyze the data. Section 5 presents the results of the analysis of the responses to the question-naires against the backdrop of the environmental/cultural factors affecting Libya. Section 6 presents the summary and conclusion. Section 7 states the limitations of the study. Section 8 suggests some future research avenues. These are followed by details of the references quoted in the paper.

2. BACKGROUND INFORMATION

Libya is a developing country that gained its independence in 1951. Its history has been characterized by a long-period of colonization. For a period of about 3,000 years prior to 1951, Libya was subjected to wave after wave of foreign military invasions and colonization (Mcguire, 1964; Nyrop, 1973; Fisher, 1985). In the aftermath of its independence, Libya's national economy was plagued with severe underdevelopment (Farley, 1971). Further, all socio and economic indicators demonstrated that it was one of the poorest countries in the world (Lindberg, 1952). For five decades prior to 1960, the economy was "deficient" to an extraordinary extent. There were deficits in the budgets of the State, the balances of trade and the balance of payments, and all State projects were operating in deficit (Higgins & Jacqres, 1967 and Higgins, 1968).

Since 1961, when Libyan crude oil was first exported in commercial quantities, annual crude oil revenues, gross domestic product (GDP), and per capita income have increased at an exceptional rate. Further, the surplus in the balance of payments increased each year, making it the most important source of capital formation. The Libyan economy is dominated by the petroleum sector, which accounts for approximately one-third of GDP and almost all of its foreign trade and foreign exchange earnings (Technical Planning Authority, June 1971, Table 1; Central Bank of Libya, 1972, p. 53; 1973, p. 196; 1986, p. 86; and 1991, p. 23; Arab Monetary Fund, 1984, p. 137; 1990, p. 131; and 1993, p. 131). In addition, most of the State's revenues, national economic development budgets and most of the gains registered in the non-oil sectors of the Libyan economy can be traced directly or indirectly to the stimulus provided by crude oil revenues (Elrifadi, 1976).

In 1969, following the September Revolution, the Libyan economy witnessed significant fundamental changes. The State has controlled at least 51% of the petroleum sector, instead of the 100% foreign ownership prior to the Revolution. The whole Libyan economy has been centrally planned since the late 1970s up to 1991 and the State has controlled both the production and service sectors. However, in 1992, to enhance economic development and fight corruption, this policy was reversed through a privatization process (African Development Bank, 1995, p. 113). The continuous annual increase in the State's oil revenues was accompanied by ambitious public sector and economic development investment programmes.[1] Indeed, the average annual investment expenditures increased from $126 million in the 1960s, to $3 billion in the 1970s and over $6 billion in the 1980s. Due to the decline in the international crude oil prices, annual development programmes were dropped to about $2 billion during 1990–1993 (African Development Bank, 1995, p.108). At the 1984 census, Libya had a population of 3,637,488 (Libyan Secretariat of Planning and Economics, 1984, p. 75). The 1995 population was 5,407,000 (Libyan Secretariat of Economics and Planning, 1995, p. 3), giving the country an overall population density of about three persons per square kilometre (about eight per square mile). Thus, the population had grown by 48.6% over a ten-year period which gives added piquancy to the need to review the state of Libya's accountancy education and practice since a healthy accountancy framework may enhance the prospects of Libya achieving its economic objectives for its growing population.

2.1 Accounting Education

From 1957–1976 the accounting education system in Libya was British orientated in all its elements (curriculum, textbooks and faculty members), whereas from 1977 to date, it has been American orientated. The first accounting programme in Libya was introduced at the Libyan University (currently Garyounis University). Its College of Economics and Commerce was established in 1957 and comprises departments teaching accounting, business administration, economics, statistics and political science. The most influential factors impacting upon accounting education in Libya are: (a) the structures and the content of the accounting courses of the College of Economics and Commerce; and (b) the education and background of its accounting academics which are mainly American or British oriented (Bait-El-Mall et al., 1973; Kilani, 1988).

2.2 Accounting Profession

Since the early 1950s, the development of the Libyan accounting profession has been significantly influenced by several factors. These include the inputs from graduands of the Libyan accounting education system, the teaching of accounting academics, the preferences of international companies, the expertise of international accounting firms and to some extent the rapid changes in the Libyan social, economic, political and legal environment. Western influences have caused the Libyan accounting profession to follow the same path as its counterparts in the U.K. and the U.S. (Kilani, 1988. p. 217). Furthermore, applied accounting principles and auditing standards in Libya follow those of the U.K. and the U.S. (Bait-El-Mall et al., 1973, p. 92).

Accounting firms were mostly British or American during the 1950s and the 1960s. By 1970, the majority of the accounting firms became Libyan (El-Sherif, 1978, p. 110). Accounting firms were licensed during the sixties and early seventies by the Libyan Ministry of Treasury. Practising members were required to have a university degree in Commerce and two years of post-qualifying practical accounting experience. As a result of repeated recommendations from the Auditor General, Law No. 116 of 1973 was enacted (Libyan State, 1974) to organize the Libyan accounting profession and establish the Libyan Accountants and Auditors Association (LAAA). Prior to 1973, the Income Tax Law and the Commercial Code were the only legal pronouncements which required financial statements to be certified by an independent auditor. The LAAA member should be Libyan, have a university degree in accounting and possess five years of post-qualifying practical experience in an accounting firm.

According to the provisions of the Law No. 116 of 1973, the LAAA is responsible mainly for registering (licensing) public accountants, maintaining a register of public accountants, raising the standards of its members profession-ally, academically, culturally and socially, suggesting a code of ethics, ensuring adherence to the suggested ethical codes of conduct; conducting disciplinary actions in respect of erring members, holding conferences, seminars and carrying out educational and training programmes for its members (Libyan State, 1974, Articles 3 and 49).

Although the LAAA was formed more than two decades ago, it has done nothing to build any theoretical base for accounting to be a profession in Libya and has not established a code of ethics for its members to abide by. This suggests that the LAAA has failed to regulate itself and to recognize its obligation towards the public interest. Furthermore, it has not achieved its objectives of: (a) furthering activities such as research, conferences, seminars, continuing education and training programmes; and (b) promoting accounting publications to improve the status of the profession and accordingly of its members. All these factors suggest that the status of the Libyan accounting profession is very weak.

Libyan accountants have no defined or formal code of ethics, accounting principles, auditing standards or procedures. There are no uniform audit report requirements and no professional examination requirements. They base their practices mainly on their accounting education (Kilani, 1988, p. 243).

The definition and the objectives of the accounting profession in Libya are the same as those in the U.K. and the U.S. (Kilani, 1988, p. 255). However, the environmental factors of Libya are significantly different from those of the U.K. or the U.S. Currently, the accounting profession in Libya confines itself to external financial reporting and external auditing (Bait-El-Mall et al., 1973; El-Sherif, 1978; Kilani, 1988).

The above discussion shows the deep-seated influence of Western accounting (mainly the U.K. and the U.S.) that dominated accounting education and accounting practice in Libya.

3. THE RATIONALE FOR THIS STUDY

Economic development in a developing country like Libya is based on a successful and monitored planning process (Belkaoui, 1994). A well-established planning process is mainly dependent upon the availability of timely and reliable micro and macro information for measuring, allocating, utilizing and controlling economic activities and economic resources. Further, the absence of such information makes the achievement of successful economic development in a developing country like Libya difficult, if not impossible (Novin & Baker, 1990). Accounting plays a vital role in the provision of such information (Samuels, 1990). Consequently, the efficacy of accounting education and practice in Libya could have a significant influence on the promotion of its economic development (Enthoven, 1973, 1977, 1981a, b, 1983; Perera, 1989; Wallace, 1993). Furthermore, accountability for economic activities through the preparation of relevant accounting reports will give reassurance to both the Libyan State and to foreign investors in the Libyan oil sector.

In the light of the above discussion, it seems reasonable to believe accounting education and practice in Libya have the potential to affect Libya's economic development. Thus, identification and resolution of accounting educational and practice problems may prove useful for Libyan economic development and it may increase Libyan awareness of the strengths and weaknesses of its accounting systems.

Several researchers (e.g. Bait-El-Mall et al., 1973; El-Sherief, 1978; Kilani, 1988) have provided information on the status of the accounting system in Libya. However, the focus of these researchers was generally on the description of the accounting system in Libya, and not the problems it faced or the strategies available to resolve these problems. The main objective of this paper is to present empirical evidence relating to:

- factors obstructing the development of accounting education and accounting practice in Libya;
- the effectiveness of Libya in using various strategies to enhance accounting education and accounting practice in Libya; and
- the provision of relevant accounting curriculum to Libya.

4. THE RESEARCH METHOD

The basic research tool deployed to compile the necessary data for this study was a questionnaire distributed to "key personnel" in Libya. This questionnaire was constructed in the light of the questionnaire used by Novin and Baker in their developing country study and by Akathaporn et al. in their Thai study (see Novin & Baker, 1990; Akathaporn et al., 1993). The questionnaires were personally delivered and collected by one of the researchers. Both English and Arabic languages were used in the survey questionnaire, which was pilot tested twice. In the first pre-test of the questionnaire, the complete questionnaires were delivered to some staff members and postgraduate students in the Department of Accountancy and Business Finance in the University of Dundee to get their views and comments on the questionnaire. Furthermore, the Arabic versions were distributed to those postgraduate colleagues whose native language was Arabic. Many useful and insightful comments were received with regard to the English-Arabic translation. Accordingly, both the English and the Arabic versions of the questionnaire were revised, and modified versions were produced in Dundee.

The second phase of the pilot-work was conducted in Libya. The English and the Arabic versions of the questionnaire (which resulted in phase one of the pilot-work) were personally delivered to fourteen staff members in the accountancy departments in Garyounis University and El-Fateh University. Following the receipt of the responses and comments from participants in the second phase of the pilot-study, the researchers dealt with constructive critical comments and recommendations. Consequently, the Arabic and the English versions of the questionnaire were revised for the second time in Libya and the final versions were constructed. The final Arabic copies of the questionnaire were distributed in the final survey.

The study sought opinions from "key personnel" judged to be most likely to express informed opinions on the addressed issues. The "key personnel" referred to were "accounting academics" (AA); "oil sector accountants" (OSA); "state accountants" (SA); and "licensed public accountants" (LPA). This choice of category of respondents has been used in several survey studies relating to different aspects of accounting in similar developing countries (see, for example, Al-Mousawi, 1986; Wallace, 1988; Al-Amari, 1989; Novin & Baker, 1990; Shashaah, 1991; Akathaporn et al., 1993).

A simple random (probability) sample was employed in this study to select subjects from the groups of accounting academics, State accountants, accountants working in the oil up-stream activities, and licensed public accountants. In this method of sampling, each person in the population has an equal probability of being selected for the sample, and the selection of any one person has no effect on the selection of others. Additionally, under a simple random sample, in selecting such elements to be included in the sample, non-replacement sampling is used in order to avoid the possibility that a participant element could be chosen more than once. This is called sampling without replacement. The rationale behind using this technique is that it: (a) offers the most generalizability or the most representative sample; and (b) has the minimum bias and enables estimates of sampling errors to be made (Bailey, 1978, p. 76; Sekaran, 1992, p. 230).

The population frames of different categories of potential respondents, with the exception of accountants working in the oil sector, were developed by the researchers from available listings in Libya. Population frames were used to draw the samples for different categories. Such a direct recording approach has the advantages of: (a) being as up-to-date as possible; and (b) being a complete list with no biases, individuals or groups omitted.

Summaries of sample size selection for different categories of potential participants.

Table 1.   Summary of the Sample Size for Different Groups.

No.	Groups	PF	Sample %	Sample Size	%
1	Accounting Academics	57	100%	57	13
2	State Accountants	386	48%	186	41
3	Oil Sector Accountants	492	25%	123	27
4	Licensed Public Accountants	105	80%	84	19
Total		1040	43%	450	100

Notes: No. = Number; and PF = Population Frame.

Table 2.   Summary of Usable Response Rates for Different Groups of
Respondents.

Explanations	AA	SA	OSA	LPA	Total	%
Delivered Questionnaires	57	186	123	84	450	100
Collected Questionnaires	40	56	41	37	174	38.6
Excluded Questionnaires	2	14	21	6	43	9.6
Usable Questionnaires	38	42	20	31	131	29.1
Usable Response Rates (%)	66.7%	22.6%	16.2%	36.9%	29.1%	

Notes: AA = Accounting Academics; SA = State Accountants; OSA = Oil Sector Accountants; and
LPA = Licensed Public Accountants.

A detailed summary of and response rates for different groups of respondents shows that both the Libyan state accountants and the oil and gas accountants appeared more reluctant to reply to the Libyan questionnaire.

However, an overall response rate of 29.9% for the study appears not untypical of response rates on questionnaire-based research. For example, it has been reported that typical response rates for postal questionnaires may vary between 10 and 50% (Weisbery & Bowen, 1977). Also, Oppenheim reported that response rates could be less than 40% (Oppenheim, 1992) and the influential study by Lee and Tweedie in 1977 had a response rate of only 15.7% (Lee & Tweedie, 1977). If the oil and gas accountants were excluded from the database then the response rate becomes a relatively high 49%. It could be argued that since the Libyan oil and gas industry is a highly politically sensitive industry, the poor response rate from this sector was not unexceptional. It would also perhaps have been unwise, for political reasons, to question non-respondents regarding the issue. Thus, the possibility of non-respondent bias is a potential limitation of the study. The researchers do not view this limitation as being a serious weakness since they obtained a relatively high response rate from respondents when the oil and gas sector accountants are excluded.

Table 3 indicates that approximately 40% of respondents held bachelor's degrees, 30% held master's degrees, 25% held doctorate degrees and 5% held professional qualifications and other degrees in accountancy. It also shows that more than 50% of respondents received their degrees either from the U.K. or the U.S. Furthermore, the findings indicate that most of the participants have substantial experience in their present occupation with 84% of respondents being employed for five or more years.

Table 3. Background Information on Respondents.

Occupation	No.	Experience in Present Occupation			Latest Educational Qualification				The Latest Place of Education				
		<5 Years	5–10 Years	>10 Years	Bachelor's Degree*	Master's Degree*	Ph.D.*	Other	Libya	U.K.	USA	Other	PQs
AA	38	9	16	13		12	25	1	3	8	21	6	2
%	100%	23.7%	42.1%	34.2%		31.6%	65.8%	2.6%	7.9%	21%	55.3%	15.8%	5.3%
OSA	20	3	5	12	12	6	2		8	4	5	3	2
%	100%	15%	25%	60%	60%	30%	10%		40%	20%	25%	15%	10%
SA	42	4	13	25	24	12	2	4	24	3	14	1	0
%	100%	9.5%	31%	59.5%	57.1%	28.6%	4.8%	9.5%	57.1%	7.1%	33.4%	2.4%	0
LPA	31		8	23	16	9	4	2	13	5	10	3	18
%	100%		25.8%	74.2%	51.6%	29%	12.9%	6.5%	42%	16.1%	32.3%	9.6%	58%
Total	131	16	42	73	52	39	33	7	48	20	50	13	22
%	100%	12%	32%	56%	40%	30%	25%	5%	37%	15%	38%	10%	17%

Notes: * = or its equivalent; AA = Accounting Academics; OSA = Accountants Working in the Oil and Gas Producing Companies; SA = State Accountants; LPA = Licensed Public Accountants; and PQ = Professional Qualifications.

4.1 The Statistical Techniques Used to Analyse the Data

The researchers sought the assistance of a statistical expert for guidance in the use of the statistical techniques to be utilized in analyzing the data. Tests for the normality of the data were carried out to ensure the appropriateness of applying the selected statistical tests. The tests were performed by using the software of the statistical package for social science (SPSS) to produce visual normal probability plots. The results showed either normal or de-trended normal probability plots for all cases. Consequently, it was deemed suitable to use analysis of variance (ANOVA) procedures. Thus, one way ANOVA was carried out to make inferences about the means of the answers of different groups at a 5% confidence level. Furthermore, The Kruskal-Wallis (KW) test was also performed to test the significance of the difference of the means for the four groups. The KW test does not require the assumption of normality that is required by the ANOVA test. Multiple comparison tests (Scheffe's method) with significance at the 5% confidence level were used to detect significant differences among means.

5. THE RESULTS OF THE ANALYSIS

5.1 Factors Obstructing Accounting Development

The purpose of this section is to report respondents' perceptions on 10 problems (factors) viewed to be primary obstructions to accounting development in Libya. These factors are well established in the extant research literature (see, for example, Akathaporn et al., 1993). All the addressed issues were listed in a random order in the original questionnaire. However, for ease of interpretation, the data presented in the subsequent tables are organized in descending overall mean rankings. Consequently, the numbering of the addressed factors in the original questionnaire is different from that in the analysis tables. This policy is applied throughout the rest of this paper. The results of the analysis and the discussions are outlined in the subsequent sections.

5.1.1 Descriptive Statistics

Descriptive tables demonstrate how different groups and aggregate respondents answered Section two of the questionnaire. Tables 4 and 5 present the response frequencies and percentages for the four groups and all respondents. In these tables, the bold figures show the highest response frequencies and percentages for each factor by individual groups and aggregate respondents. They indicate that:

- the highest aggregate response frequencies and percentages for all listed factors, except for factors 9 and 10, were either "agree" or "strongly agree" and that the factors have obstructed the development of accounting education and practice in Libya;
- the top aggregate response frequencies and percentages for factors 9 "low status of accounting profession" (PF) and 10 "lack of sufficient qualified instructors" (EF) were neutral;
- a high percentage of aggregate respondents either agree or strongly agree with the first eight factors. This percentage ranged from 70.5% for Factor 1 "lack of active professional accounting societies" (PF) to 45.0% for Factor 8 "social and cultural influence" (OF); and
- a low percentage of aggregate respondents either strongly disagree or disagree with factors 9 and 10. This percentage ranged from 40.3% corresponding to Factor 10 to 39.5% corresponding to Factor 9.

The rankings of the four respondent groups are given for each main category followed by the overall mean rank. The higher the mean is above 3, the higher the perceived obstruction of the factor to the development of accounting practice in Libya. On the other hand, the lower the mean is below 3, the lower the perceived obstruction of the factor to the development of accounting in Libya. Table 6 presents the results.

The overall results indicate that "professional factors" with an overall mean ranking of 3.54 were perceived to be the most obstructing factors to the development of accounting practice in Libya. Next were the "educational factors" (overall mean rank = 3.41). The "other factors" (overall mean score = 3.36) were classified by aggregate respondents to be the lowest obstructing factors.

Table 7 shows the overall mean of responses and standard deviations for each of the "professional"; "educational"; and "other" factors. All the factors in the list, excluding factors 9 and 10, were assigned overall mean rankings of over 3. In fact, the highest overall mean rank was 3.84 corresponding to "lack of active professional accounting societies" (PF). However, with the exception of factors 9 and 10, the lowest overall mean rank was 3.26 for "social and cultural influences" (OF). Factors 9 and 10 were assigned overall mean scores of 2.87 and 2.84 respectively.

In summary, the aggregate response frequencies, percentages and mean scores suggest that:

- a majority of aggregate respondents agree that the listed "professional", "educational", and "other" factors, excluding factors 9 and 10, have obstructed the development of accounting practice in Libya; and

Table 4. The Response Frequencies of Factors Obstructing the Development of Accounting Education and Practice in Libya.

F No.	Accounting Academics					Oil Sector Accountants					State Accountants					Licensed Public Accountants					Total				
	SDA	DA	N	A	SA	SDA	DA	N	A	SA	SDA	DA	N	A	SA	SDA	DA	N	A	SA	SDA	DA	N	A	SA
1	0	1	1	**20**	15	0	0	4	**8**	7	4	6	10	**13**	9	1	5	6	**10**	9	5	12	21	**51**	40
2	0	0	0	14	**23**	2	5	**6**	**6**	0	3	5	4	**19**	11	3	4	**8**	**8**	**8**	8	14	18	**47**	42
3	0	2	4	14	**17**	4	**5**	0	**5**	**5**	2	5	8	13	**14**	3	5	8	**9**	6	9	17	20	41	**42**
4	0	1	5	14	**17**	0	5	0	**9**	5	3	6	**17**	10	6	2	5	5	**12**	7	5	17	27	**45**	35
5	1	0	3	**20**	13	0	3	2	**12**	2	2	7	9	**14**	10	3	7	7	**8**	6	6	17	21	**54**	31
6	2	1	5	**17**	12	1	2	5	**9**	2	3	9	8	**15**	7	3	6	5	**10**	7	9	18	23	**51**	28
7	0	2	1	**19**	15	0	5	**6**	**6**	0	**15**	5	9	13	2	1	5	10	**11**	4	4	27	26	**49**	21
8	3	8	**13**	**13**	0	1	**9**	2	3	4	2	5	7	**15**	13	2	6	**13**	7	3	8	28	35	**38**	20
9	7	10	**18**	2	0	1	6	**9**	3	0	7	10	3	**14**	8	1	**9**	**9**	**9**	3	16	35	**39**	28	11
10	4	11	**16**	5	1	3	7	**8**	1	0	3	**14**	11	10	4	3	7	7	**9**	5	13	39	**42**	25	10

Notes: Bold figures denote the highest percent of response for each question by the four groups and their aggregate percentage responses; F No. = Factor Number; SDA = Strongly Disagree; DA = Disagree; N = Neutral; A = Agree; and SA = Strongly Agree; PF = Professional Factors; and ED = Educational Factors; and OF = Other Factors.

Number	Factors	Number	Factors
1	Lack of active professional accounting societies (PF)	6	Low status of present accounting publications (PF)
2	Inadequate public understanding of the role of accounting (PF)	7	Low level of State support (OF)
3	Lack of relevant and effective accounting curricula (EF)	8	Social and cultural influence (OF)
4	Lack of and/or outdated accounting textbooks in Arabic language (EF)	9	Low status of accounting profession (PF)
5	Low status of professional ethics (PF)	10	Lack of sufficient qualified instructors (EF)

Table 5. The Response Percentages of Factors Obstructing the Development of Accounting Education and Practice in Libya.

F No.	Accounting Academics					Oil Sector Accountants					State Accountants					Licensed Public Accountants					Total				
	SDA %	DA %	N %	A %	SA %	SDA %	DA %	N %	A %	SA %	SDA %	DA %	N %	A %	SA %	SDA %	DA %	N %	A %	SA %	SDA %	DA %	N %	A %	SA %
1	0	2.7	2.7	**54.1**	40.5	0	0	21.1	**42.2**	36.8	9.5	14.3	23.8	**31.0**	21.4	3.2	16.1	19.4	**32.3**	29.0	3.9	9.3	16.3	**39.5**	31.0
2	0	0	0	37.8	**62.2**	10.5	26.3	**31.6**	31.6	0	7.1	11.9	9.5	**45.2**	26.2	9.7	12.9	**25.8**	25.8	25.8	6.2	10.9	14.0	**36.4**	32.6
3	0	5.4	10.8	37.8	**45.9**	21.1	**26.3**	0	26.3	26.3	4.8	11.9	19.0	31.0	**33.3**	4.7	16.1	25.8	**29.0**	19.4	7.0	13.2	15.5	31.8	**32.6**
4	0	2.7	13.5	37.8	**45.9**	0	26.3	0	**47.4**	26.3	7.1	14.3	**40.5**	23.8	14.3	6.5	16.1	16.1	**38.7**	22.6	3.9	13.2	20.9	**34.9**	27.1
5	2.7	0	8.1	**54.1**	35.1	0	15.8	10.5	**63.2**	10.5	4.8	16.4	21.4	**33.3**	23.8	9.7	22.6	22.6	**25.8**	19.4	4.7	13.2	16.3	**41.9**	24.0
6	2.4	2.7	13.5	**45.9**	32.4	5.3	10.5	26.3	**47.4**	10.5	7.1	21.4	19.0	**35.7**	16.7	9.7	19.4	16.1	**32.3**	22.6	7.0	14.0	17.8	**39.5**	21.7
7	0	5.4	2.7	**51.4**	40.5	0	29.4	**35.3**	35.3	0	7.1	**35.7**	21.4	31.0	4.8	3.2	16.1	32.3	**35.5**	12.9	3.1	21.3	20.5	**38.6**	16.5
8	8.1	21.6	**35.1**	35.1	0	5.3	**47.4**	10.5	15.8	21.1	4.8	11.9	16.7	**35.7**	31.0	6.5	19.4	**41.9**	22.6	9.7	6.2	21.7	27.1	**29.5**	15.5
9	18.9	27.0	**48.6**	5.4	0	5.3	31.6	**47.4**	15.8	0	16.7	23.8	7.1	**33.3**	19.0	3.2	**29.0**	29.0	29.0	9.7	12.4	27.1	**30.2**	21.7	8.5
10	10.8	29.7	**43.2**	13.5	2.7	15.8	36.8	**42.1**	5.3	0	7.1	33.3	26.2	23.8	9.5	9.7	22.6	22.6	**29.0**	16.1	10.1	30.2	**32.6**	19.4	7.8

Notes: Bold figures denote the highest percent of response for each question by the four groups and their aggregate percentage responses; F No. = Factor Number; SDA = Strongly Disagree; DA = Disagree; N = Neutral; A = Agree; and SA = Strongly Agree; PF = Professional Factors; and ED = Educational Factors; OF = Other Factors.

Number	Factors	Number	Factors
1	Lack of active professional accounting societies (PF)	6	Low status of present accounting publications (PF)
2	Inadequate public understanding of the role of accounting (PF)	7	Low level of State support (OF)
3	Lack of relevant and effective accounting curricula (EF)	8	Social and cultural influence (OF)
4	Lack of and/or outdated accounting textbooks in Arabic language (EF)	9	Low status of accounting profession (PF)
5	Low status of professional ethics (PF)	10	Lack of sufficient qualified instructors (EF)

Table 6. Main Categories Obstructing the Development of Accounting Education and Practice in Libya.

Main Categories	Mean of Responses					Standard Deviations					Test of Significance One-Way ANOVA		Significant Relations Among Means Multiple Range Tests: Scheffe Method With Significance Level at 5%
	AA	OSA	SA	LPA	Total	AA	OSA	SA	LPA	Total	P Value	KW P Value	
1. Professional Factors	3.90	3.38	3.43	3.37	3.54	0.37	0.33	0.35	0.49	0.45	0.0000*	0.0000*	AA > LPA; AA > OSA; and AA > SA
2. Educational Factors	3.73	3.07	3.32	3.35	3.41	0.49	0.76	0.53	0.76	0.65	0.0013*	0.0017*	AA > OSA; and AA > SA
3. Other Factors	3.62	3.06	3.33	3.24	3.36	0.64	0.77	0.75	0.72	0.73	0.0351*	0.0283*	No two groups are significantly different

Notes: * = Significance at 5% Level; and > = statistically significantly different at the 5% level; AA = Accounting Academics; OSA = Oil Sector Accountants; SA = State Accountants; LPA = Licensed Public Accountants; and KW = Kruskal-Wallis.

Table 7. Factors Obstructing the Development of Accounting Education and Practice in Libya.

Main Categories	Mean of Responses					Standard Deviations					Test of Significance One-Way ANOVA P Value / KW P Value		Significant Relations Among Means Multiple Range Tests: Scheffe Method With Significance Level at 5%
	AA	OSA	SA	LPA	Total	AA	OSA	SA	LPA	Total	P Value	P Value	
1. Lack of active professional accounting societies (PF)	4.32	4.16	3.40	3.68	3.84	0.67	0.76	1.25	1.17	1.09	0.0006*	0.0028*	AA > SA
2. Inadequate public understanding of the role of accounting (PF)	4.62	2.84	3.71	3.45	3.78	0.49	1.01	1.20	1.29	1.19	0.0000*	0.0000*	AA > OSA; AA > LPA; AA > SA; and SA > OSA
3. Lack of relevant and effective accounting curricula (EF)	4.24	3.11	3.76	3.32	3.70	0.86	1.59	1.19	1.25	1.25	0.0020*	0.0062*	AA > OSA; AA > LPA
4. Lack of and/or outdated accounting textbooks in Arabic language (EF)	4.27	3.74	3.24	3.55	3.68	0.80	1.15	1.10	1.21	1.12	0.0004*	0.0004*	AA > SA;
5. Low status of professional ethics (PF)	4.19	3.68	3.55	3.23	3.67	0.81	0.89	1.17	1.28	1.12	0.0032*	0.0051*	AA > LPA
6. Low status of present accounting publications (PF)	3.97	3.47	3.33	3.39	3.55	1.04	1.02	1.20	1.31	1.18	0.0750	0.0602	No two groups are significantly different
7. Low level of State support (OF)	4.27	3.06	2.90	3.39	3.44	0.77	0.83	1.08	1.02	1.10	0.0000*	0.0000*	AA > SA; AA > OSA; AA > LPA

Table 7. Continued.

8. Social and cultural influence (OF)	2.97	3.00	3.76	3.10	3.26	0.96	1.33	1.16	1.04	1.15	0.0065*	0.0056*	SA > AA
9. Low status of accounting profession (PF)	2.41	2.74	3.14	3.13	2.87	0.86	0.81	1.42	1.06	1.15	0.0148*	0.0251*	SA > AA
10. Lack of sufficient qualified instructors (EF)	2.68	2.37	2.95	3.19	2.84	0.94	0.83	1.13	1.25	1.09	0.0428*	0.0671	No two groups are significantly different

Notes: * = Significance at 5% Level; and > = statistically significantly different at the 5% level; and PF = Professional Factor; ED = Educational Factor; OF = Other Factor; AA = Accounting Academics; OSA = Oil Sector Accountants; SA = State Accountants; LPA = Licensed Public Accountants; KW = Kruskal-Wallis.

• a majority of aggregate respondents disagree that factors 9 and 10 have obstructed the development of accounting practice in Libya.

Question three in section three of the questionnaire was followed by five open-ended questions to allow respondents to identify any other unlisted obstructing factors. However, it is not necessary to give an inter-group analysis of the responses of the four respondent groups because the frequencies of responses for identified factors were relatively small. The analysis in this section therefore is restricted to presenting information on frequently mentioned factors that respondents believe are obstructing the development of accounting education and practice in Libya.

Some respondents indicated that political positions and industry attract relatively big numbers of accounting academics. This is due to the disparity in salaries (and other advantages) between the universities and other places of employment. Further, they identified the lack of full-time accounting academics as another area of great concern to Libya. The lack of qualified academics may be related to two main factors: (1) high student/faculty ratios in the accounting departments; and (2) high obligations of the faculty members outside the university. In 1978 the student/faculty ratio (the ratio) in the accounting department (Garyounis University) was 50:1 (Dau, 1981, p. 273). By 1992, the ratio was increased approximately to 80:1 or even more. The low rates of pay received by academics give little incentive to lecturers to teach full-time. Most Libyan accounting academics supplement their income by consulting or by having their own practices as authorized public accountants. Academics who have heavy obligations outside the teaching area have very little time to devote to advising students, undertaking research, revising curriculum, and attending professional meetings, seminars, and continuing education workshops.

According to the respondents, the content of present university accounting programs falls short of Libyan needs and emphasizes the theoretical frameworks at the expense of practical aspects of accounting. Other obstructing problems identified by some respondents were the poor quality of university students, inadequate library resources and facilities and the low use of computers in accounting curricula. Some participants indicated that management of publicly owned firms and owners of small-sized family-owned enterprises: (a) have a poor knowledge of the role and benefits of accounting; (b) consider accounting necessary only for keeping records of different accounts and for tax purposes; and (c) do not consider accounting information to be useful for decision-making processes. The main reason for low usage of accounting information for decision making may be related to the lack of relevance of present accounting standards, accounting education and accounting practice to

Libyan needs. Arguably more attention should be given to domestic users' needs and their sophistication level when accounting standards and accounting systems are developed. Some respondents indicated that violation of accounting and auditing standards does not carry a heavy financial and custodial penalty in the same way that breaking the tax law does. Furthermore, some participants stated that the LAAA had not played any significant role in developing accounting education and accounting practice in Libya because it: (1) operates with a part-time staff; (2) lacks strong and effective leadership; (3) suffers from the influence of small groups of people on its activities; and (4) lacks support and co-operation from business, academics and state. In addition, some respondents indicated that the main obstructing factor to accounting practice in Libya is the unethical behavior of many accountants and auditors, mainly the LAAA influential groups, who may on occasions utilize accounting and auditing standards for self-benefit.

5.1.2 Inferential Statistics

One-way ANOVA and KW tests of significance, and multiple range tests (Scheffe method) were performed to identify and allocate significant differences between group means at the five% level. The final three columns in Tables 6 and 7 present the results. The results presented in Table 6 show that:

- a majority among each of the four groups and aggregate respondents agree with the listed categories;
- for each of the "professional"; "educational"; and "other" categories, both one-way ANOVA and KW tests of significance identified statistically significant differences between group mean responses at the 5% level;
- for each of the "professional" and "educational" categories, multiple range tests reported significant relations among group means. However, for "other" factors multiple range test showed that no two groups are significantly different at the 5% level;
- for the "professional" factors the mean response of the AA group is significantly different from the mean responses of the LPA, the OSA, and the SA groups. In addition, the mean of responses of the AA group is higher than the mean of responses of the other three groups;
- for the "educational" factors the mean score of the AA group is significantly different from the mean scores of the OSA and the SA groups. Furthermore, the mean scores of the OSA and the SA groups are lower than the mean score of the AA group.

Significant test results for individual factors are presented in Table 7. For all the factors listed, both tests, excluding factors 6 and 10, indicated statistically significant differences between group means at the 5% level. With respect to Factor 10, the one-way ANOVA test showed that there was a statistically significant difference between groups at the 5% level, whereas KW test did not. The results of multiple range tests (Scheffe method) support the KW test results by showing that no two groups are statistically significantly different at the 5% level. Multiple range tests (Scheffe method) were performed to identify significant relations among group means. The results are presented in the final column in Table 7. These results are summarized in Table 9. Tables 7 and 9 show that:

- the mean of responses of the AA group are significantly greater than the mean of responses of the OSA group for Factors 2, 3 and 7; the SA group for Factors 1, 2, 4 and 7; and the LPA group for Factors 2, 3, 5 and 7. For all these cases, the mean of responses of the AA group are greater than the mean of responses of the OSA, SA and LPA groups;
- the mean rankings of the SA group are significantly greater than the mean rankings of the AA group for Factors 8 and 9; and the OSA group for Factor 2. Furthermore, the mean rankings of the SA group are higher than the mean rankings of the AA group (for Factors 8 and 9) and the OSA group (for Factor 2).

Tables 8 and 9 show that for two of the main categories and for eight individual factors, 19 statistically significant differences were observed between group means at the 5% level. In all these statistically significant differences, the mean rankings of the AA group (84% or 16 cases) and the SA group (16% or 3 cases) were higher than the mean rankings of the other groups. These results indicate that most of the strongest opinions regarding all the addressed issues were expressed by the AA group. This is not surprising since the

Table 8. Summary of Statistically Significant Differences Between Groups for Main Categories (Table 6) at 5% Level.

Group	AA	OSA	SA	LPA	Total*
AA		1 and 2	1 and 2	1	5
OSA					
SA					
LPA				·	
Aggregate number of statistically significant differences identified between the group response means at the 5% level.					5

Notes: AA = Accounting Academics; OSA = Oil Sector Accountants; SA = State Accountants; LPA = Licensed Public Accountants and * = Number of statistically significant differences identified between the group and other groups at the 5% level.

Table 9. Summary of Statistically Significant Differences Between Groups for Main Factors (Table 7) at 5% Level.

Group	AA	OSA	SA	LPA	Total*
AA		2, 3 and 7	1, 2, 4 and 7	2, 3, 5 and 7	11
OSA					
SA	8 and 9	2			3
LPA					
Aggregate number of statistically significant differences identified between the group response means at the 5% level.					14

Notes: AA = Accounting Academics; OSA = Oil Sector Accountants; SA = State Accountants; LPA = Licensed Public Accountants and * = Number of statistically significant differences identified between the group and other groups at the 5% level.

addressed matters, as mentioned in the preceding sections, are issues dealing with the accounting profession and with accounting education. The AA group is arguably the most qualified group for dealing with such matters.

5.2 Strategies to Enhance Accounting Education and Practice in Libya

Respondents were asked to indicate to what extent they agreed or disagreed that each of 21 stated strategies are effectively being utilized in enhancing accounting education and practice in Libya. Descriptive and inferential statistics were used to analyze the data. The findings of the analysis of the responses are presented in the following sections.

5.2.1 Descriptive Statistics

The group and the aggregate mean rankings were calculated and listed for each main category (Table 12) and for each strategy (Table 13) followed by the overall mean rank. The categories and the strategies in all the tables were arranged in descending order according to the overall mean rankings. Thus, categories and strategies were listed from "most effectively utilized" to "least effectively utilized" rankings. Tables 10 and 11 present the response frequencies and percentages for each strategy for the four groups and aggregate respondents. The bold figures presented in these tables highlight the highest response frequencies and percentages for each strategy by the four groups and aggregate respondents. The highest aggregate response frequencies and percentages were either: (a) agree (strategies 3, 6 and 9); (b) neutral (strategies number 2, 4, 5, 7 and 8); or disagree (all the other strategies). Furthermore, based on Table 11 it can be concluded that:

Table 10. The Response Frequencies of Strategies to Enhance Accounting Education and Practice in Libya.

St No.	Accounting Academics					Oil Sector Accountants					State Accountants					Licensed Public Accountant					Total				
	SDA	DA	N	A	SA	SDA	DA	N	A	SA	SDA	DA	N	A	SA	SDA	DA	N	A	SA	SDA	DA	N	A	SA
1	1	10	2	10	14	0	2	5	7	5	7	28	5	0	0	0	0	6	15	9	8	40	18	32	28
2	7	15	7	3	5	0	2	6	9	2	0	5	15	13	7	2	8	13	6	1	9	30	41	31	15
3	9	14	8	5	1	0	0	6	10	3	3	7	7	16	7	3	7	9	7	4	15	28	30	38	15
4	7	8	12	8	2	2	4	3	5	5	1	12	11	14	2	2	7	11	8	2	12	31	37	35	11
5	10	12	6	5	4	0	1	6	8	4	3	8	13	12	4	3	9	11	4	3	16	30	36	29	15
6	10	6	12	5	4	0	3	3	11	2	8	11	7	9	5	3	9	6	7	5	21	29	28	32	16
7	7	14	5	4	7	0	2	8	6	3	13	4	9	8	6	3	7	10	7	3	23	27	32	25	19
8	10	6	11	8	2	3	5	7	3	1	2	11	15	9	3	2	8	14	4	2	17	30	47	24	8
9	12	7	6	9	3	2	7	2	4	4	2	9	13	9	1	3	7	7	10	3	25	30	28	32	11
10	6	19	8	3	1	7	7	2	2	1	3	12	7	12	6	3	6	12	8	1	19	44	29	25	9
11	9	10	7	7	4	3	10	4	2	0	8	16	8	6	2	7	9	7	4	3	27	45	26	19	9
12	10	15	5	3	4	6	4	6	2	0	7	18	7	5	3	4	8	7	6	1	27	45	26	16	8
13	8	13	9	5	0	2	6	5	4	1	18	7	10	5	0	6	9	7	4	4	34	35	31	19	7
14	8	14	12	3	2	0	8	7	4	0	12	16	6	6	0	5	13	5	6	1	25	51	30	19	1
15	10	16	6	3	1	0	7	9	3	0	11	19	2	1	7	9	9	8	3	1	30	51	25	10	10
16	8	15	9	4	3	7	8	4	2	0	12	15	5	8	0	5	9	11	3	2	32	47	27	17	3
17	6	13	8	7	3	2	13	4	2	0	13	22	4	1	0	5	13	9	2	3	26	61	23	10	6
18	15	10	4	5	3	6	6	3	3	0	15	20	0	3	2	7	10	4	8	1	43	46	11	19	7
19	11	14	5	5	2	6	9	3	0	1	7	21	3	7	2	8	19	3	0	0	32	63	14	12	5
20	12	9	6	7	3	4	10	2	1	2	12	19	6	3	0	9	14	7	0	0	37	52	21	11	5
21	10	12	8	4	3	5	8	3	3	0	13	24	3	0	0	9	16	5	0	0	37	60	19	7	3

Table 10. Continued.

Notes: Bold figures denote the highest response for each question by the four groups and their aggregate responses; St No. = Strategy Number; SDA = Strongly Disagree; DA = Disagree; N = Neutral; A = Agree; SA = Strongly Agree; N = Number; PS = Professional Strategies; ED = Educational Strategies.

N	Strategies	N	Strategies	N	Strategies
1	Limiting public accounting to certified accountants (PS)	8	Encouraging participation of accountants in societal activities (PS)	15	Encouraging profession-university cooperation (ES)
2	Training and upgrading domestic accounting professors (ES)	9	Setting professional ethics (PS)	16	Providing practical training for accounting students during their college education (ES)
3	Using computers for processing accounting data (PS)	10	Encouraging accounting students' association activities (ES)	17	Requiring and providing continuing education for accountants after graduation from college (PS)
4	Establishing professional accounting organizations (PS)	11	Educating decision makers on how to use accounting information for making economic decisions (ES)	18	Educating State officials about the role and benefits of accounting for economic development (ES)
5	Determining number of accountants needed by country (PS)	12	Determining information needs of users of accounting reports (PS)	19	Having professional accounting examinations and certifications (PS)
6	Developing accounting textbooks in domestic language (ES)	13	Educating businessmen about the role and benefits of accounting (ES)	20	Setting auditing standards (PS)
7	Raising educational requirements for accounting (ES)	14	Writing accounting standards into law (PS)	21	Setting accounting standards (PS)

Table 11. The Response Percentages of Strategies to Enhance Accounting Education and Practice in Libya.

St. No.	Accounting Academics					Oil Sector Accountants					State Accountants					Licensed Public Accountants					Total				
	SDA %	DA %	N %	A %	SA %	SDA %	DA %	N %	A %	SA %	SDA %	DA %	N %	A %	SA %	SDA %	DA %	N %	A %	SA %	SDA %	DA %	N %	A %	SA %
1	2.7	27.0	5.4	27.0	37.8	0	10.5	26.3	36.8	26.3	17.5	70.0	12.5	0	0	0	0	20.0	50.0	30.0	6.3	31.7	14.3	25.4	22.2
2	18.9	40.5	18.9	8.1	13.5	0	10.5	31.6	47.4	10.5	0	12.5	37.5	32.5	17.5	6.7	26.7	43.3	20.0	3.3	7.1	23.8	32.5	24.6	11.9
3	24.3	37.8	21.6	13.5	2.7	0	0	31.6	52.6	15.8	7.5	17.5	27.5	40.0	7.5	10.0	23.3	30.0	23.3	13.3	11.9	22.2	23.8	30.2	11.9
4	18.9	21.6	32.4	21.6	5.4	10.5	21.1	15.8	26.3	26.3	2.5	30.0	27.5	35.0	5.0	6.7	23.3	36.7	26.7	6.7	9.5	24.6	29.4	27.8	8.7
5	27.0	32.4	16.2	13.5	10.8	0	5.3	31.6	42.1	21.1	7.5	20.0	32.5	30.0	10.0	10.0	30.0	36.7	13.3	10.0	12.7	23.8	28.6	23.0	11.9
6	27.0	16.2	32.4	13.5	10.8	0	15.8	15.8	57.9	10.5	20.0	27.5	17.5	22.5	12.5	10.0	30.0	20.0	23.3	16.7	16.7	23.0	22.2	25.4	12.7
7	18.9	37.8	13.5	18.9	10.8	0	10.5	42.1	31.6	15.8	32.5	10.0	22.5	20.0	15.0	6.7	26.7	33.3	23.3	10.0	18.3	21.4	25.4	19.8	15.1
8	27.0	16.2	16.2	21.6	18.9	15.8	26.3	36.8	15.8	5.3	5.0	27.5	37.5	22.5	7.5	10.0	26.7	46.7	13.3	3.3	13.5	23.8	22.2	25.4	6.3
9	32.4	18.9	29.7	13.5	5.4	10.5	36.8	10.5	21.1	21.1	20.0	22.5	22.5	22.5	12.5	10.0	26.7	23.3	33.3	6.7	19.8	23.8	22.2	19.0	6.3
10	16.2	51.4	21.6	8.1	2.7	36.8	36.8	10.5	10.5	5.3	7.5	30.0	17.5	30.0	15.0	10.0	20.0	40.0	26.7	3.3	15.1	34.9	23.0	19.8	7.1
11	24.3	27.0	18.9	18.9	10.8	15.8	52.6	21.1	10.5	0	20.0	40.0	20.0	15.0	5.0	23.3	30.0	23.3	13.3	10.0	21.4	35.7	20.6	15.1	7.1
12	27.0	40.5	13.5	8.1	10.8	33.3	22.2	33.3	11.1	0	17.5	45.0	17.5	12.5	7.5	13.3	26.7	36.7	20.0	3.3	21.6	36.0	23.2	12.8	6.4
13	21.6	35.1	24.3	13.5	5.4	10.5	31.6	26.3	26.3	5.3	45.0	17.5	25.0	12.5	0	20.0	30.0	23.3	13.3	13.3	27.0	27.8	24.6	15.1	5.6
14	21.6	37.8	32.4	8.1	0	0	42.1	36.8	21.1	0	30.0	40.0	15.0	15.0	0	16.7	43.3	16.7	20.0	3.3	19.8	40.5	23.8	15.1	0.8
15	27.0	43.2	16.2	8.1	5.4	0	36.8	47.4	15.8	0	27.5	47.5	5.0	2.5	17.5	30.0	30.0	26.7	10.0	3.3	32.8	40.5	19.8	7.9	7.9
16	21.6	40.5	24.3	10.9	5.4	36.8	42.1	10.5	10.5	0	30.0	30.0	20.0	20.0	0	16.7	30.0	36.7	10.0	6.7	25.4	37.3	21.4	13.5	2.4
17	16.2	35.1	21.6	18.9	2.7	10.5	68.4	21.1	0	0	32.5	37.5	10.0	2.5	17.5	16.7	43.3	23.3	6.7	10.0	20.6	48.4	18.3	7.9	4.8
18	40.5	40.5	10.8	18.9	8.1	31.6	31.6	15.8	15.8	5.3	37.5	55.0	0	7.5	0	23.3	33.3	13.3	26.7	3.3	34.1	36.5	8.7	15.1	5.6
19	29.7	37.8	13.5	13.5	8.1	31.6	47.4	15.8	5.3	0	17.5	50.0	7.5	17.5	5.0	26.7	63.3	10.0	0	0	25.4	50.0	11.1	9.5	4.0
20	32.4	24.3	16.2	18.9	8.1	21.1	52.6	10.5	5.3	10.5	30.0	47.5	15.0	7.5	0	30.0	46.7	23.3	0	0	29.4	41.3	16.7	8.7	4.0
21	27.0	32.4	21.6	10.8	8.1	26.3	42.1	15.8	15.8	0	32.5	60.0	7.5	0	0	30.0	53.3	16.7	0	0	29.4	47.6	15.1	5.6	2.4

Table 11. Continued.

Notes: Bold figures denote the highest response for each question by the four groups and their aggregate responses; St No. = Strategy Number; SDA = Strongly Disagree; DA = Disagree; N = Neutral; A = Agree; SA = Strongly Agree; N = Number; PS = Professional Strategies; ED = Educational Strategies.

N	Strategies	N	Strategies	N	Strategies
1	Limiting public accounting to certified accountants (PS)	8	Encouraging participation of accountants in societal activities (PS)	15	Encouraging profession-university cooperation (ES)
2	Training and upgrading domestic accounting professors (ES)	9	Setting professional ethics (PS)	16	Providing practical training for accounting students during their college education (ES)
3	Using computers for processing accounting data (PS)	10	Encouraging accounting students' association activities (ES)	17	Requiring and providing continuing education for accountants after graduation from college (PS)
4	Establishing professional accounting organizations (PS)	11	Educating decision makers on how to use accounting information for making economic decisions (ES)	18	Educating State officials about the role and benefits of accounting for economic development (ES)
5	Determining number of accountants needed by country (PS)	12	Determining information needs of users of accounting reports (PS)	19	Having professional accounting examinations and certifications (PS)
6	Developing accounting textbooks in domestic language (ES)	13	Educating businessmen about the role and benefits of accounting (ES)	20	Setting auditing standards (PS)
7	Raising educational requirements for accounting (ES)	14	Writing accounting standards into law (PS)	21	Setting accounting standards (PS)

- a low majority of aggregate respondents either agree or strongly agree that strategies numbered 1, 2, 3 and 4 are effectively being utilized to enhance accounting education and practice in Libya. This majority ranged from 32.1% corresponding to strategy 3 "using computers for processing accounting data" (PS) to 47.6% for strategy 1 "limiting public accounting to certified accountants" (PS); and
- a large percentage of aggregate respondents either strongly disagree or disagree with the remaining strategies. The percentage ranged from 36.5% corresponding to strategy 5 "determining number of accountants needed by country" (PS) to 77% for strategy 21 "setting accounting standards" (PS).

Group and overall mean scores are given for each category (Table 12) and for each strategy (Table 13). These should be interpreted by reference to the observation that the higher the mean score is above 3, the higher the perceived effectiveness of Libya in using the listed category or strategy. In contrast, the lower the mean score is below 3, the lower the perceived effectiveness of Libya in using the listed category or strategy. In fact, "related professional strategies" and "related educational strategies" were assigned overall mean scores of 2.62 and 2.61 respectively. The overall mean results show that Libya is not perceived as being effective in utilizing "related professional strategies" and "related educational strategies" for the development of accounting education and practice.

Table 13 presents the mean of responses for each group for each strategy followed by the overall mean of responses. From Table 13 it can be seen that:

- the first four strategies were assigned overall mean rankings mostly slightly over 3.0. These rankings ranged from 3.25 for strategy 1 "limiting public accounting to certified accountants" (PS) to 3.02 for strategy 4 "establishing professional accounting organizations" (PS);
- the remaining strategies were assigned overall mean rankings of less than 3.0. The highest ranking for the remaining strategies was 2.98 corresponding to strategy 5 "determining number of accountants needed by country" (PS). However, the lowest mean rank was 2.04 for strategy 21 "setting accounting standards";
- four of the top five strategies were from "related professional strategies". These were "limiting public accounting to certified accountants"; "using computers for processing accounting data"; "establishing professional accounting organizations"; and "determining number of accountants needed by country" (overall mean = 2.98). However, "training and upgrading domestic accounting professors" (overall mean = 3.1) was the only education strategy included within the top five strategies;

Table 12. Effectiveness Of Libya In Utilising Various Categories To Enhance Accounting Practice (Section Three Of The Questionnaire).

Main Categories	Mean of Responses					Standard Deviations					Test of Significance One-Way ANOVA		Significant Relations Among Means Multiple Range Tests: Scheffe Test With Significant Level at 5%
	AA	OSA	SA	LPA	Total	AA	OSA	SA	LPA	Total	P Value	KW P Value	
1. Related Professional Strategies:	2.57	2.87	2.49	2.7	2.62	0.39	033	0.25	0.21	0.32	0.0001*	0.0003*	OSA > SA; OSA > AA; and LPA > SA
2. Related Education Strategies:	2.46	2.78	2.58	2.73	2.61	0.45	0.27	0.31	0.34	0.37	0.0035*	0.0017*	OSA > AA; and LPA > AA

Notes: * = Significance at 5% Level; and > = statistically significantly different at the 5% level; AA = Accounting Academics; OSA = Oil Sector Accountants; SA = State Accountants; LPA = Licensed Public Accountants; KW = Kruskal Wallis.

Table 13. Effectiveness Of Libya In Utilising Various Strategies To Enhance Accounting Practice (Section Three Of The Questionnaire).

Strategies	Mean of Responses					Standard Deviations					Test of Significance One-Way ANOVA P Value	KW P Value	Significant Relations Among Means Multiple Range Tests: Scheffe Test With Significant Level at 5%
	AA	OSA	SA	LPA	Total	AA	OSA	SA	LPA	Total			
1. Limiting public accounting to certified accountants (PS)	3.70	3.79	1.95	4.10	3.25	1.31	0.98	0.55	0.71	1.29	0.0000*	0.0000*	LPA > SA; OSA > SA; and AA > SA
2. Training and upgrading domestic accounting professors (ES)	2.57	3.58	3.55	2.87	3.10	1.28	0.84	0.93	0.94	1.12	0.0001*	0.0001*	OSA > AA;; and SA > AA
3. Using computers for processing accounting data (PS)	2.32	3.84	3.42	3.07	3.08	1.08	0.69	1.20	1.20	1.22	0.0000*	0.0004*	OSA > AA; and SA > AA
4. Establishing professional accounting organizations (PS)	2.73	3.37	3.10	3.03	3.02	1.17	1.38	0.98	1.03	1.12	0.2133	0.2665	No two groups are significantly different
5. Determining number of accountants needed by country (PS)	2.49	3.79	3.15	2.83	2.98	1.33	0.85	1.10	1.12	1.21	0.0008*	0.0008*	OSA > AA; and OSA > LPA
6. Developing accounting textbooks in domestic language (ES)	2.65	3.63	2.8	3.07	2.94	1.32	0.90	1.34	1.28	1.29	0.0423*	0.0384*	No two groups are significantly different
7. Raising educational requirements for accounting (ES)	2.73	3.53	2.75	3.00	2.92	1.41	0.90	1.48	1.14	1.32	0.1370	0.1134	No two groups are significantly different
8. Encouraging participation of accountants in societal activities (PS)	2.62	2.68	3.00	2.87	2.81	1.26	1.11	1.01	0.97	1.09	0.4552	0.5518	No two groups are significantly different
9. Setting professional ethics (PS)	2.57	3.05	2.65	3.10	2.79	1.39	1.39	1.12	1.18	1.27	0.2379	0.2542	No two groups are significantly different
10. Encouraging accounting students' association activities (ES)	2.30	2.11	3.15	2.93	2.69	0.94	1.20	1.23	1.01	1.16	0.0006*	0.0007*	SA > OSA; SA > AA
11. Educating decision makers on how to use accounting information for making economic decisions (ES)	2.65	2.26	2.45	2.57	2.51	1.34	.87	1.13	1.28	1.19	0.6906	0.8292	No two groups are significantly different

Table 13. Continued.

12. Determining information needs of users of accounting reports (PS)	2.35	2.22	2.48	2.73	2.46	1.27	1.06	1.15	1.05	1.15	0.4308	0.2791	No two groups are significantly different
13. Educating businessmen about the role and benefits of accounting (PS)	2.46	2.84	2.05	2.70	2.44	1.14	1.12	1.11	1.32	1.20	0.0480*	0.0538	No two groups are significantly different
14. Writing accounting standards into law (PS)	2.27	2.79	2.15	2.50	2.37	0.90	0.79	1.03	1.11	0.99	0.0990	0.0832	No two groups are significantly different
15. Encouraging profession-university cooperation (ES)	2.22	2.79	2.35	2.27	2.36	1.11	0.71	1.39	1.11	1.16	0.3431	0.0743	No two groups are significantly different
16. Providing practical training for accounting students during their college education (ES)	2.32	1.95	2.22	2.60	2.3	1.03	0.97	1.10	1.10	1.07	0.1993	0.1738	No two groups are significantly different
17. Requiring and providing continuing education for accountants after graduation from college (PS)	2.68	2.11	1.82	2.50	2.28	1.20	0.57	0.71	1.17	1.03	0.0013*	0.0037*	AA > SA; and LPA > SA
18. Educating State officials about the role and benefits of accounting for economic development (ES)	2.22	2.32	1.93	2.53	2.21	1.34	1.25	1.07	1.22	1.22	0.2219	0.2054	No two groups are significantly different
19. Having professional accounting examinations and certifications (PS)	2.27	2.00	2.40	1.83	2.17	1.19	1.00	1.13	0.59	1.04	0.1135	0.2467	No two groups are significantly different
20. Setting auditing standards (PS)	2.46	2.32	2.00	1.93	2.17	1.35	1.20	0.88	0.74	1.07	0.1366	0.4677	No two groups are significantly different
21. Setting accounting standards (PS)	2.41	2.21	1.75	1.87	2.04	1.24	1.03	0.59	0.68	0.94	0.0102*	0.0814	AA > SA

Notes: * = Significance at 5% Level; and > = statistically significantly different at the 5% level; PS = Professional Strategies; ES = Educational Strategies; AA = Accounting Academics; OSA = Oil Sector Accountants; SA = State Accountants; LPA = Licensed Public Accountants; KW = Kruskal Wallis.

- excluding strategies 1, 2, and 3, the highest mean rank for professional strategies was 2.98 for "determining number of accountants needed by country", while the lowest mean rank was 2.04 for "setting accounting standards";
- excluding strategy number 2 (overall mean = 3.1), the highest mean rank for educational strategies was 2.94, corresponding to "developing accounting textbooks in domestic language", whereas the lowest overall mean rank was 2.21, corresponding to "educating state officials about the role and benefits of accounting for economic development"; and
- the weight assigned to "requiring and providing continuing education for accountants after graduation from college" (PS); "educating state officials about the role and benefits of accounting for economic development" (ES); "having professional accounting examinations and certificates" (PS); "setting auditing standards" (PS); and "setting accounting standards" (PS) were at the bottom of the list of strategies.

These results appear to indicate that Libya is not perceived as being effective in using most of the strategies listed in the perception questionnaire to enhance accounting education and practice.

5.2.2 Inferential Statistics

One-way ANOVA and KW tests of significance were used to analyse significant differences between group mean responses for each broad category and for each individual category. The results are presented in Tables 12 and 13. The location of a significant difference is identified by an asterisk in the one-way ANOVA and KW test result columns. Multiple range tests (Scheffe method with significant level at 5%) were conducted to allocate significant differences among group means. The results of multiple range tests are presented in the final columns in Tables 12 and 13. Location of differences were marked by (>) between each two groups which were significantly different. The multiple range tests results for the main categories and for individual strategies are summarized in Tables 14 and 15 respectively.

From Tables 12 and 14 it can be seen that:

- group mean rankings assigned to category 1 "related professional strategies" ranged from 2.87 (by the OSA group) to 2.49 (by the SA group);
- the highest group mean score assigned to "related educational strategies" was 2.78 (by the OSA group), whereas the lowest one was 2.46 (by the AA group);
- the mean scores assigned by the OSA group to the addressed categories were higher than the mean scores assigned by the other three groups. However, the mean scores assigned by the SA group (for category 1) and the AA group (for category 2) were lower than the mean scores of the other three groups;

Table 14. Summary of Statistically Significant Differences Between Groups (Table 12) At 5% Level.

Group	AA	OSA	SA	LPA	Total*
AA					
OSA	1 and 2		1		3
SA					
LPA	2		1		2
Aggregate number of statistically significant differences identified between the "group response" means at the 5% level.					5

Notes: AA = Accounting Academics; OSA = Oil Sector Accountants; SA = State Accountants; LPA = Licensed Public Accountants; * = Number of statistically significant differences identified between the group and other groups at the 5% level.

Table 15. Summary of Statistically Significant Differences Between Groups (Table 13) At 5% Level.

Group	AA	OSA	SA	LPA	Total*
AA			1, 17 and 21		3
OSA	2, 3 and 5		1	5	5
SA	2, 3 and 10	10			4
LPA			1 and 17		2
Aggregate number of statistically significant differences identified between the "group response" means at the 5% level.					14

Notes: AA = Accounting Academics; OSA = Oil Sector Accountants; SA = State Accountants; LPA = Licensed Public Accountants; * = Number of statistically significant differences identified between the group and other groups at the 5% level

- the group mean of responses indicate that a majority within each of the four groups perceive "related professional strategies" and "related educational strategies" as not being effectively used in enhancing accounting education and accounting practice in Libya;
- for the two main categories "related professional strategies" and "related education strategies", both one way ANOVA and KW tests showed statistically significant differences between group means at the 5% level;
- the mean of responses of the OSA group are statistically significantly different from the mean of responses of the AA group for categories 1 and 2, and the SA group for category 1; and

- the mean rankings of the responses of the LPA group are statistically significantly different from the mean ranking of the AA group for category 2, and the SA group for category 1.

One-way ANOVA and KW tests show that, for seven of the strategies, statistically significant differences were observed between group mean responses at the 5% level. In contrast, for twelve of the strategies both tests indicated that there were no statistically significant differences between groups at the 5% level. For strategies numbered 13 and 21, the one-way ANOVA test of significance indicated statistically significant differences between groups at the 5% level, whereas the KW test did not. For strategy 13, the multiple range test supported the KW test result by showing that no two groups were statistically significantly different at the 5% level. However, for strategy numbered 21, it supported the one-way ANOVA findings by identifying statistically significant relations among the AA and the SA group means at the 5% level. Multiple range tests (Scheffe method) were conducted to identify significant relations among means at the 5% level. The results are presented in Table 13 and summarized in Table 15. An apparently interesting result is that, for strategy 6, both one-way ANOVA and KW tests indicated statistically significant differences between groups at the 5% level. However, the multiple range test (Scheffe method) did not. From Tables 13 and 15:

- the mean rankings of the AA group are statistically significantly different from the mean rankings of the SA group for strategies 1, 17 and 21. Also, the mean rankings of the AA group are higher than the mean rankings of the SA group;
- the mean scores of the OSA group are statistically significantly different from the mean scores of the AA group for strategies 2, 3 and 5; the SA group, for strategy 1; and the LPA group for strategy 5. For all these strategies, the mean scores of the OSA group are greater than the mean scores of the AA, SA and LPA groups;
- the mean responses of the SA group are statistically significantly different from the mean of responses of the AA group for strategies 2, 3 and 10; and the OSA group for strategy 10. For these strategies, the mean responses of the AA and OSA are lower than the mean responses of the SA group; and
- the mean rankings of the LPA group are statistically significantly different from the mean rankings of the SA group, for strategies 1 and 17. The mean rankings of the LPA group for strategies 1 and 17 are higher than the mean rankings of the SA group.

Tables 14 and 15 indicated that, for the two main categories and for seven of the strategies, nineteen statistically significant differences were observed between two or more groups at the 5% level. The results disclose that:

- the mean rankings of the AA group (18.8% or 3) are significantly different and greater than the mean rankings of the SA group for strategies 1, 17 and 21;
- the mean rankings of the OSA group (42.2% or 8) are significantly different and greater than the mean rankings of the AA group (for categories 1 and 2 and for strategies 2, 3 and 5), the SA group (for category 1 and for strategy 1) and the LPA group (for strategy 5);
- the mean rankings of the SA group (21% or 4) are significantly different and greater than the mean rankings of the AA group (for strategies 2, 3 and 10) and the OSA group (for strategy 10); and
- the mean rankings of the LPA group (21% or 4) are significantly different and greater than the mean rankings of the AA (for category 2), SA (for category 1) and the SA (for strategies 1 and 17) groups.

Most of the significant differences which are observed here may not indicate practical differences between groups. For example, OSA's perceptions of "related professional strategies" (mean = 2.87), are statistically significantly different from those of the SA (mean = 2.49) and AA (mean = 2.57). Furthermore, the LPA's perception of the same strategy (mean = 2.7) is statistically significantly different from that of the SA (mean = 2.49) at the 5% level. Considering that a response mean of less than "3" indicates "disagreement" in the response scale used, the mean responses of 2.87, 2.7, 2.57 and 2.49 appear to confirm a common consensus among the groups that "related professional strategies" are not effectively used.

6. SUMMARY AND CONCLUSION

This paper has addressed a question which is central to our understanding of an emerging country's development in the field of accounting education and accounting practice: what factors obstruct this development? By choosing the uniquely interesting State of Libya as the emerging country to be studied, the researchers have extended the research literature contributions of Novin and Baker (1990), and Akathaporn et al. (1993) by testing the robustness of their research methodology in extreme circumstances. Clearly there are problems associated with attempting to generalize findings from such a single country study. But as an exercise which both enhances the research evidence in the area and which also has potential practical significance for Libya, and other developing countries, the research seems valuable.

Eight factors were identified as barriers to the development of accounting education and practice. Surprisingly perhaps, the leading obstructing factors were the "lack of active professional societies", and "inadequate public understanding of the role of accounting". These may be interlinked since a socially active accounting profession could well close any expectations gap in the public mind over the role of accounting. Other leading obstructing factors relate to outmoded accounting curricula and a lack of modern textbooks in Arabic. Libya clearly needs to plan strategically to modernize both its accounting education and practice by ensuring that modern texts which are relevant to the needs of Libya are available for consultation. This modernization process is important since the above analysis has shown that the use of the identified strategies to enhance accounting education and practice in Libya has not been an unqualified success.

There are, however, grounds for optimism in the findings. Both the perceived status of the accounting profession and the availability of accounting educators are not perceived to be obstructing factors. Consequently, it would seem that if the appropriate level of funding, and strategic planning geared to the needs of Libya are established, then the personnel required to implement them would be available. The differences in perceptions between the four groups of respondents may reflect the nature of their respective goals. But on the whole their perceptions are consistent although different groups hold stronger views than the others.

7. THE LIMITATIONS OF THE STUDY

The findings presented above, among other things, were based on the results obtained from analyzing perception questionnaires and bear their limitations. Accordingly, this research has the following limitations:

- a test for non-response bias was not carried out because the questionnaires were collected through the assistance of many individuals and state branches and offices. Consequently, the researchers could not segregate the early and late responses and test for differences between them;
- those whose opinions have been sought with regard to all the addressed issues in the perception questionnaire consist of a sample of accounting academics, state accountants, oil sector accountants and licensed public accountants. Accordingly, there is no way to ascertain whether the views on which the findings are based are representative of the views of the entire population of accounting academics, state accountants, oil sector accountants and licensed public accountants in Libya.

8. FUTURE RESEARCH AVENUES

The preceding results provide some guidance for future research avenues which could be perceived as possible extensions to the present research. The following paragraph highlights some of the areas which might need further research. It is worth mentioning that research avenues suggested in this section are not clear-cut but mainly illustrative of the ways in which this research may serve as a foundation for future research.

Further research is needed to investigate the issues of accounting education and accounting practice in the context of the Libyan "environment" and Libyan needs. For example, researchers could investigate such vital questions as "what should be the accounting objectives in Libya on the basis of its legal, economic and social conditions?" The determination of accounting objectives should lead, among other things, to the specification of micro-and macro-information needs that are consistent with the development needs of Libya. "What type of accounting education is needed for Libya's accounting needs?" and "What accounting principles and auditing standards should be applied to reflect Libya's social, economic and political environment?"

NOTE

1. These development programmes, among other things, aimed mainly at: (a) realizing maximum rates of growth in the non-oil sector; (b) achieving greatest diversity in national income sources so as to reduce Libya's dependence on the oil sector as the first and unique source of income; (c) developing the economic and social infrastructure; (d) attaining a high degree of self-sufficiency and self-reliance and increasing the efficiency of production factors (Libyan Secretariat of Planning, 1963, 1972, 1976, 1980a, b; 1981, 1985, 1986; Libyan Secretariat of Economics and Planning, 1991; Libyan Secretariat of Planning, Trade and Finance, 1993).

ACKNOWLEDGMENT

The authors are extremely grateful to Mr. Donald Sinclair for the assistance he gave with the statistical techniques used in this work.

REFERENCES

African Development Bank, Development Research and Policy Department (CDEP) (1995). *African Development Report 1994*. Abidjan: CDEP.
Akathaporn, P., Novin, A. M., & Abdolmohammadi, M. J. (1993). Accounting Education and Practice in Thailand: Perceived Problems and Effectiveness of Enhancement Strategies. *The International Journal of Accounting, 28*(3), 259–272.

Al-Amari, S. R. (1989). The Development of Accounting Standards in the Kingdom of Saudi Arabia; a doctoral thesis. U.K.: University of Glasgow.

Al-Jalabi, F. M. (1979). *Basic Structural Changes in the International Oil Industry: Selected Studies in the Oil Industry* (in Arabic). Kuwait: OAPEC.

Al-Mousawi, H. M. (1986). The Relevance and Use of International accounting Standards in the State of Kuwait, a doctoral thesis. U.K.: University of Birmingham.

American Accounting Association (January 1986). Special Annual Meeting Views. Revolutionary Changes Ahead in Accounting Education. *Journal of Accounting*, 30–31.

Arab Monetary Fund (1984). *National Accounts of Arab Countries: 1972–1983.*

Arab Monetary Fund (1986a). *Balance of Payments and External public Debt of Arab Countries: 1975–1985.*

Arab Monetary Fund (1986b). *National Accounts of Arab Countries: 1975–1985.*

Arab Monetary Fund (1990). *National Accounts of Arab Countries: 1979–1989.*

Arab Monetary Fund (1993). *Balance of Payments and External public Debt of Arab Countries: 1982–1992.*

Bailey, K. D. (1978). *Methods of Social Research*. New York: The Free Press.

Bait-El-Mall, M. M. et al. (1973). The Development of Accounting in Libya. *International Journal of Accounting: Education and Research*, 8(Spring), 83–102.

Belkaoui, A. R. (1994). *Accounting in the Developing Countries*. Westport, Connecticut, London: Quorum Books.

Central Bank of Libya (1972). *Sixteenth Annual Report of the Board of Directors: Financial Year 1971–1972.* Tripoli: Libyan State Publications.

Central Bank of Libya (1973). *Seventeenth Annual Report of the Board of Directors: Financial Year 1972–1973.* Tripoli: Libyan State Publications.

Central Bank of Libya (1986). *Thirty-first Annual Report of the Board of Directors.* Tripoli: Libyan State Publications.

Central Bank of Libya (1991). *Thirty-fifth Annual Report of the Board of Directors: Financial Year 1990–1991.* Tripoli: Libyan State Publications.

Dau, K. A. (1981). Accounting Education in Libya. In: A. G. Enthoven (Ed.), *Accounting Education in Economic Development*. Amsterdam: North Holland Publishing Company.

El-Sherief, Y. (1978). An Empirical Investigation of Libyan Professional Accounting Services, Ph.D. Dissertation. Columbia, USA: University of Missouri.

Elrifadi, I. S. (1976). A Study in the Economic of the Libyan Oil Sector, Ph.D. Dissertation. USA: University of Pittsburgh.

Enthoven, A. J. H. (1973). *Accounting and Economic Development Policy*. New York, Amsterdam, North Holland: Elsevier.

Enthoven, J. H. A. (1977). Report of the American Accounting Association Committee on International Accounting Operations and Education. *The Accounting Review Supplement*, 66–75.

Enthoven, A. J. H. (1981a). Accounting in Developing Countries. In: C. W. Nobes & R. H. Parker (Eds), *Comparative International Accounting* (1st ed., pp. 217–237). Oxford: Philip Allen.

Enthoven, A. J. H. (1981b). *Accounting Education in Economic Development Management*. Amsterdam: North-Holland.

Enthoven, A. J. H. (1983). U.S. Accounting and the Third World. *Journal of Accountancy*, (June), 110–118.

Farley, R. (1971). *Planning for development in Libya, The Exceptional Economy in the Developing World*. New York: Praeger Publisher Inc.

Fisher, W. B. (1985). *Libya in the Middle East and North Africa* (21st ed.). Europe Publication Limited.

Higgins, B., & Jacqres R. (1967). Economic Development with Unlimited Supplies of Capital. *The Libyan Economic and Business Review, III*(2)(Autumn), 1–50.

Higgins, B. (1968). *Economic Development Principles, Problems and Policies* (Rev. ed.). New York: W. W. Norton & Comp., Inc.

Kilani, K. A. (1988). The Evolution and Status of Accounting in Libya. Ph.D. Dissertation, University of Hull, U.K.

Lee, T. A., & Tweedie, D. P. (1977). *The Private Shareholders and the Corporate Report*. London: The Institute of Chartered Accountants in England and Wales.

Libyan State (1974). *The Official Gazette, Law No. 116 of 1973 to Organise the Accounting Profession in Libya*, (7)(February), 251–268.

Libyan Secretariat of Planning and Economics (1984). Census and Statistical Department. *Results of National Population Census.*

Libyan Secretariat of Planning and Economics (Feb. 1991). *Socio-economic Growth 1970–1990.*

Libyan Secretariat of Planning (1993). Trade and Finance. *National Economy Achievement: 1970–1992.*

Libyan Secretariat of Planning and Economics (1995). Census and Statistical Department, *Estimation of National Population Census: 1991–1995.*

Libyan Secretariat of Planning (1963). *The First Five-year Development Plan*. Tripoli.

Libyan Secretariat of Planning (1972). Department of Census and Statistics. *Population Census-Preliminary Results*. Tripoli.

Libyan Secretariat of Planning (1976). *Social and Economic Transformation Plan: 1976–1980.* Tripoli: Libyan State Publication.

Libyan Secretariat of Planning (1980a). *Great El-Fateh Achievement in Ten Years, The Social and Economic Transformation: 1970–1979.*

Libyan Secretariat of Planning (1980b). *The Fifth Socio-economic Development Plan*. Tripoli.

Libyan Secretariat of Planning (September 1981). *Social and Economic Transformation Plan in Twelve Years of Great El-Fateh Revolution: 1970–1981.*

Libyan Secretariat of Planning (1985). *The Sixth Socio-economic Development Plan*. Tripoli.

Libyan Secretariat of Planning (1986). *Follow-up Report of the 1981–1985 Plan*. Tripoli.

Lindberg, J. (1952). *General Economic Appraisal of Libya*. New York: United Nations Publications.

Mcguire, J. W. (1964). *Theories of Business Behaviour*. Englewood Cliffs, N.J.: Prentice-Hall, Inc.

Novin, A. M., & Baker, J. C. (1990). Enhancing Accounting Education and the Accounting Profession in Developing Countries. *Foreign Trade Review*; (October–December), 247–257.

Nyrop, R. F. (1973). *Area Handbook for Libya*. Washington, D.C.: U.S. Government Printing Office.

Oppenheim, A. N. (1992). *Questionnaire Design, Interviewing and Attitude Measurement*. London: Printer.

Perera, M. H. (1989). Accounting in Developing Countries: A Case for Localised Uniformity. *British Accounting Review, 21*(2), 141–158.

Samuels, J. M. (1990). Accounting for Development: An Alternative Approach. *Research in Third World Accounting, 1*, 67–86.

Sekaran, U. (1992). *Research Methods for Business: A Skill Building Approach* (2nd ed.). New York: John Wiley & Sons Inc.

Shashaah, M. H. (1991). Accounting for Social Responsibility: Implementation in Industrial Jordanian Shareholding Companies, a master thesis. Amman-Jordan: University of Jordan.

Technical Planning Authority (June 1971). *National Accounts of the Libyan Arab Republic, 1962–1969*. Tripoli: Technical Planning Authority.

Wallace, R. S. O. (1988). Corporate Financial Reporting in Nigeria. *Accounting and Business Research*; *18*(72), 352–362.

Wallace, R. S. O. (1993). Development of Accounting Standards For Developing and Newly Industrialised Countries. *Research in Third World Accounting*, 2, 121–165.

Weisberg, H. F., & Bowen, B. D. (1977). *An Introduction to Survey Research and Data Analysis.* New York: Freeman and Co.

APPENDIX A

The Perception Questionnaire

SECTION ONE: GENERAL INFORMATION

Please tick or circle the appropriate letter or letters.

1   Present occupation

A   Accounting Academic

B   Licensed Public Accountant

C   Government Accountant

D   Accountant Working in the Oil Sector (please specify your present occupation)

_____

2   If your present occupation is classified as A, B or C in Question 1, please state whether you are:

A   Interested in oil and gas accounting

B   Involved as an external auditor with oil and gas producing companies

C   Other, please specify

_____

3   Your experience in your present occupation

A   Less than five years

B   5–10 years

C   More than 10 years

4   The latest educational qualification in Accounting

A   Bachelor's degree (or its equivalent)

B   Master's degree (or its equivalent)

C   Ph.D. degree (or its equivalent)

D   Other, please specify

_____

5   The latest place of education

A   Libya

B   U.K.

C   USA

D   Other, please specify

_____

6   Do you have any professional qualifications in Accounting?

A   Yes

B   No

If yes, please specify

_ _

SECTION TWO

Please indicate to what extent you agree or disagree that the following factors have obstructed the development of accounting education and practice in Libya:

	Strongly disagree	1	2	3	4	5	Strongly agree

Educational factors

1   Lack of relevant and effective accounting curricula   1 2 3 4 5

2   Lack of sufficient qualified instructors   1 2 3 4 5

3   Lack of and/or outdated accounting textbooks in Arabic language   1 2 3 4 5

Professional factors

4   Inadequate public understanding of the role of accounting   1 2 3 4 5

5   Lack of active professional accounting societies   1 2 3 4 5

6   Low status of professional ethics   1 2 3 4 5

7   Low status of present accounting publications   1 2 3 4 5

8   Low image of accounting profession   1 2 3 4 5

Other factors[1]

9   Low level of government support   1 2 3 4 5

10   Social and cultural influence   1 2 3 4 5

11   _ _ _ _ _ _ _ _ _ _ _ _ _ _ _ _ _ _ _   1 2 3 4 5

12   _ _ _ _ _ _ _ _ _ _ _ _ _ _ _ _ _ _ _   1 2 3 4 5

13   _ _ _ _ _ _ _ _ _ _ _ _ _ _ _ _ _ _ _   1 2 3 4 5

14   _ _ _ _ _ _ _ _ _ _ _ _ _ _ _ _ _ _ _   1 2 3 4 5

15   _ _ _ _ _ _ _ _ _ _ _ _ _ _ _ _ _ _ _   1 2 3 4 5

[1] Please specify any other significant obstructing factors.

SECTION THREE

Please indicate to what extent you agree or disagree that the following strategies are effectively being utilised in enhancing accounting education and practice in Libya:

	Strongly disagree	1	2	3	4	5	Strongly agree

Related education strategies

1   Developing accounting textbooks in domestic language   1 2 3 4 5

2   Training and upgrading domestic accounting professors   1 2 3 4 5

3	Raising educational requirements for
	accounting	1	2	3	4	5
4	Encouraging profession-university cooperation	1	2	3	4	5
5	Educating decision makers how to use
	accounting information for making
	economic decisions	1	2	3	4	5
6	Providing practical training to accounting
	students during their college education	1	2	3	4	5
7	Educating businessmen about the role and
	benefits of accounting	1	2	3	4	5
8	Encouraging accounting students' association
	activities	1	2	3	4	5
9	Educating government officials about the role
	and benefits of accounting for economic
	development	1	2	3	4	5

Related professional strategies

10	Limiting public accounting to certified
	accountants	1	2	3	4	5
11	Setting auditing standards	1	2	3	4	5
12	Having professional accounting examinations
	and certifications	1	2	3	4	5
13	Setting accounting standards	1	2	3	4	5
14	Using computers for processing accounting data	1	2	3	4	5
15	Setting professional ethics	1	2	3	4	5
16	Determining information needs of users of
	accounting reports	1	2	3	4	5
17	Establishing professional accounting
	organisations	1	2	3	4	5
18	Writing accounting standards into law	1	2	3	4	5
19	Requiring and providing continuing education
	for accountants after graduation from college	1	2	3	4	5
20	Determining number of accountants needed
	by country	1	2	3	4	5
21	Encouraging participation of accountants in
	society activities	1	2	3	4	5

PART III:
ACCOUNTING IN SOUTH ASIA

12. ECONOMIC INTEGRATION AND ACCOUNTING HARMONIZATION OPTIONS IN EMERGING MARKETS: ADOPTING THE IASC/IASB MODEL IN ASEAN

Shahrokh M. Saudagaran and Jeselito G. Diga

ABSTRACT

In this study, we examine the growing trend towards regional economic integration and accounting harmonization options available to developing countries. After reviewing the role of accounting harmonization in the development of emerging markets, we discuss financial reporting issues relevant to emerging markets. We focus on the five original member countries of the Association of South East Asian Nations (ASEAN) – Indonesia, Malaysia, Philippines, Singapore and Thailand. These countries are of interest because of their growing integration into the global economy over the past two decades (something most developing countries aspire to) and a heightened interest in their financial reporting regimes as a result of the ongoing Asian economic crisis. We examine their choice among various alternative harmonization options and explain why these countries have decided to adopt the global harmonization approach mainly through the accounting standards promulgated by the International Accounting

Research in Accounting in Emerging Economies, Volume 5, pages 239–266.
Copyright © 2003 by Elsevier Science Ltd.
ISBN: 0-7623-0901-6

Standards Committee (IASC). Along with examining why the ASEAN countries chose to adopt the IASC model, we also look at the EU's recent decision to switch to the IASC model of harmonization from its original attempt at regional harmonization and the likely effect of the EU's choice on developing countries.

1. INTRODUCTION

During the past decade, the globalization of financial markets has seen institutional investors move large sums of money around the world with unprecedented speed. Much of this "hot money" has moved in and out of emerging markets with dramatic effects. When foreign capital flowed into the emerging markets (EM) it resulted in impressive growth in their economies and a boom in their stock markets. However, the effect of foreign investors withdrawing their capital from the emerging markets in 1997 and 1998, generally with very little warning, had serious negative effects on the economies of many countries. The events in Asia, Russia, Argentina, and Brazil have caused investors, regulators, central bankers, and multilateral agencies such as the International Monetary Fund and the World Bank to reevaluate their policies towards global capital flows, particularly in emerging markets.

The risks of investing in emerging markets are associated not only with structural, political, or economic problems, although admittedly these factors are important. Equally important are informational problems stemming from the difficulty of obtaining adequate and reliable financial information needed to evaluate investment opportunities in these markets. As part of the information generating capacity of emerging markets, financial reporting is a crucial element in creating and sustaining investor confidence in these markets. The quality of corporate financial reporting in emerging markets varies considerably, however, and it has been difficult to ignore the impact of poor financial reporting on the performance of these markets (Kelly, 1998a, b). Financial reporting is increasingly viewed as a vital infrastructure for the growth of emerging markets. As such, greater attention is being devoted to how the quality of financial reporting in these countries can be improved.

While there are several approaches to improving financial reporting, harmonization is frequently offered as one solution. One of the most critical policy issues facing regulators in EMs is whether or not an active program of accounting harmonization ought to be pursued. The issue is particularly important for countries adopting market-oriented economic policies after years of state central planning. Policy makers have to grapple with issues regarding the most appropriate financial reporting system for their country (Samuels & Oliga, 1982; Hove 1986). The alternatives range from adopting aspects of regulation in economically advanced countries to formulating a system uniquely tailored to their particular circumstances (Saudagaran & Meek, 1997). If accounting harmonization emerges as a preferred policy, a choice has to be made from among a variety of policy options on the accounting harmonization model to be pursued. These options range from bilateral agreements to global harmonization. The actual choice, however, will depend, on the concurrent, yet diametrical, effects of regionalization and globalization on individual countries.

There has been a growing tendency for countries that are geographically proximate to work towards economic integration by forming regional economic groups. Examples of these integrative efforts include the European Union (EU), the North American Free Trade Area (NAFTA), the Andean Common Market (ANCOM), the Association of South East Asian Nations (ASEAN), and the South Asian Association for Regional Cooperation (SAARC). This has resulted in increased economic integration around the world with agreements among countries to facilitate the movement of goods, services, capital, and labor across borders. As evidenced by the EU, the creation of a true economic union requires member countries to harmonize monetary policies, economic policies and government spending. It clearly requires countries to give up some measure of national sovereignty and autonomy. Efforts to create regional economic policies will inevitably also draw attention to financial reporting issues, as the experience of the EU has shown (Thorell & Whittington, 1994).

Pursuing accounting harmonization is not a risk-free policy option for EMs. The principal risk relates to the possibility that accounting standards adopted are inappropriate for the particular developing country (Samuels & Oliga, 1982; Hove, 1986). The counter argument, however, is that the greater risk for an emerging market is to become uncompetitive because it does not have a sound basis of accounting that can be understood by investors elsewhere. In an increasingly interdependent and globalized economy, some form of accounting harmonization seems warranted. This assertion is particularly salient for EMs because these markets depend substantially on the inflow of foreign portfolio investments for their continued growth. Rather than have such harmonization occur by default, accounting regulators in EMs might make a deliberate choice of countries with whom they wish to harmonize their domestic accounting standards. The specific choices will depend on existing and planned economic linkages as well as political and socio-cultural similarities between the model country and the adopting country.

In this study, we discuss the accounting harmonization options available to developing countries. After reviewing the role of accounting harmonization in the development of emerging markets, we discuss financial reporting issues relevant to emerging markets. We focus on the five original member countries of the Association of South East Asian Nations (ASEAN) to specifically examine their choice from among alternative harmonization options. These countries – Indonesia, Malaysia, Philippines, Singapore and Thailand – are interesting because of their growing integration into the global economy over the past two decades (something most developing countries aspire to) and a heightened interest in their financial reporting regimes as a result of the Asian economic crisis. We examine their choice among various alternative harmonization options and explain why these countries have decided to adopt the global harmonization approach mainly through the accounting standards promulgated by the International Accounting Standards Committee (IASC). Along with examining why the ASEAN countries selected global harmonization, we also look at the EU's decision to switch to global harmonization (by supporting the IASC) from its previous stance on achieving accounting harmonization through the regional approach.

The remainder of this paper is organized as follows. Section 2 provides an overview of why capital markets are important to developing countries in general. In Section 3, we discuss briefly the important role of financial reporting in emerging markets. In Section 4, we lay out the benefits that accounting harmonization offers to countries with emerging markets. The fifth section discusses the policy options on accounting harmonization available to developing countries including the global approach to harmonization as represented by the IASC's work. Section 6 examines the ASEAN countries' decision to choose the global approach to accounting harmonization over the regional approach. Finally, Section 7 concludes the paper.

2. THE NATURE AND SIGNIFICANCE OF EMERGING MARKETS

The crucial role of financial reporting in EMs can be located more broadly within the policy context of capital market development in developing countries. Currently, an Emerging Market is understood to mean a capital market located in a developing country.[1] At present there are 81 countries whose capital markets are considered EMs by the International Finance Corporation (IFC 2000), the World Bank's investment arm (Table 1). This represents a large increase from 1993 when there were 47 countries classified as EMs by the IFC (IFC 1994). Much of the increase is due to the inclusion in this group of newly independent countries belonging to the former Soviet Union.

Table 1. Emerging Capital Markets.

Argentina	Estonia	Malta	Slovakia
Armenia	Fiji	Mauritius	Slovenia
Azerbaijan	Ghana	Mexico	South Africa
Bahrain	Greece	Moldova	Sri Lanka
Bolivia	Guatemala	Mongolia	Swaziland
Bangladesh	Honduras	Morocco	Taiwan
Barbados	Hungary	Namibia	Tanzania
Bhutan	India	Nepal	Thailand
Botswana	Indonesia	Nigeria	Trinidad & Tobago
Brazil	Iran	Oman	Tunisia
Bulgaria	Israel	Pakistan	Turkey
Chile	Jamaica	Panama	Ukraine
China	Jordan	Paraguay	Uruguay
Columbia	Kazakhstan	Peru	Uzbekistan
Costa Rica	Kenya	Philippines	Venezuela
Cote d'Ivoire	Korea	Poland	West Bank & Gaza
Croatia	Latvia	Portugal	Yugoslavia
Czech Republic	Lebanon	Romania	Zambia
Ecuador	Lithuania	Russia	Zimbabwe
Egypt	Macedonia	Saudi Arabia	
El Salvador	Malaysia		

Source: International Finance Corporation (2000).

The capital markets classified as 'emerging' are quite diverse in terms of their size and history. Some EMs such as those in Korea, Malaysia, Mexico, and South Africa are quite large in terms of market capitalization which, in some cases, approaches or even exceeds the market capitalization of shares traded on the stock exchanges of some developed countries. Moreover, some emerging capital markets, such as those in India, Malaysia, South Africa and Zimbabwe, have existed since these countries' colonial eras, whereas others, such as those in Botswana and Ecuador, were established only in the 1990s (IFC, 1998).

For most developing countries, relying on their stock markets as a means of raising large scale capital is a relatively novel approach to enterprise financing, prompting references to it as a "non-traditional" source of finance to distinguish it from the more "traditional" sources of informal and bank finance (World Bank, 1989; IMF, 1992). The development of active markets for corporate securities is generally seen as a step upward on the ladder of financial development (Frankel, 1993). Multinational lending institutions such as the World Bank as well as development economists have generally agreed that a well-functioning stock market provides the impetus necessary for the economic growth of these countries (Van Agtmael, 1984; ADB, 1986; World Bank, 1990; IMF, 1994). The benefits to developing countries of EMs are varied and help to explain the role of financial reporting within these markets.

First, many developing countries suffer from an investment-savings gap. This gap means that funds available fall far short of the amount needed to stimulate economic development. In this regard, EMs expand the investment options available in the country, which attracts portfolio investments from overseas. Domestic savings are also facilitated by the availability of investment options (Tarumizu, 1991).

Moreover, credit allocation in many developing countries has often been made on bases other than economic efficiency. Consequently, available funds could be misallocated into such things as inefficient state monopolies that sap the financial resources available for productive investments elsewhere. EMs also allow enterprise funds to be raised in a more cost-effective manner (Glen & Pinto, 1995). EMs can also influence positively the 'economic culture' existing in developing countries. Well-functioning markets allow individuals to have a stake in enterprises in their respective countries and help to change cultural attitudes with respect to participating in economic development activities and monitoring the socio-economic contributions of enterprises. In turn, domestic enterprises are encouraged to become more responsive and accountable to a greater number of stakeholders in society (ADB, 1986). These changes are particularly important in the transitional economies, i.e. countries attempting to reform the basis of their economic system from that of relying on state central planning to the free operation of markets (Malle, 1994).

Finally, EMs assist in developing further information flows, a prerequisite for enhancing the allocative efficiency of the economy. By providing market-based signals, EMs assist in channeling funds to most efficient and productive enterprises. Also, active stock markets serve as a barometer for a country's economic health by signaling expectations regarding macroeconomic variables such as economic growth and inflation. In this role, EMs provide important information for government macroeconomic planning (ADB, 1995).

3. THE IMPORTANCE OF FINANCIAL REPORTING IN EMERGING MARKETS

Before EMs can fulfill their developmental roles, it is essential to have in place a set of corporate reporting policies and procedures geared towards supplying the information necessary for making investment decisions. This view is well-recognized by multilateral lending institutions that support the strengthening of the accounting infrastructure in EMs (ADB, 1986, 1995; World Bank,

1989, 1990). In its report on capital market developments in the Asia-Pacific region, the ADB (1995) stressed that "accounting information is an essential element of infrastructure for a financial system" (p. 229). The World Bank (1989), in turn, observed that "in developing countries, accounting and auditing practices are sometimes weak, and financial laws and regulations do not demand accurate and timely reports. Developing an effective accounting and auditing profession is essential for building efficient financial markets" (p. 90). Moreover, a survey of investment institutions dealing on a regular basis with EMs showed that the accounting and legal infrastructure underlying an EM was a major factor for evaluating the investment potential of the market (Van Duyn, 1993).

Financial reporting is central to regulations pertinent to establishing an active market for corporate securities. In particular, it is fairly common practice in EMs to require companies to submit a detailed prospectus of the offer (in compliance with government regulation) and to satisfy the listing requirements of the domestic stock exchange if the company wants its securities to be traded in the exchange. Listing criteria generally consider characteristics such as the company's size, historical performance, and future prospects (*Economist*, 1988). One of the main policy aims in EMs is to ensure that only companies that satisfy minimum 'quality' requirements are allowed to issue publicly-traded securities. At the same time, governments also want to promote so-called entrepreneurial or start-up ventures, which by their nature are riskier than more established companies (IMF, 1992). It is not unusual therefore that a tiered system exists in many EMs with 'speculative' securities being traded on a secondary or over-the-counter market while so-called "blue chip" or premium securities are traded in the main stock exchange (*Economist*, 1988; Price, 1994). Financial reports provide an important basis for formulating an appropriate investment portfolio that could include a combination of these "blue chip" and "second-tier" companies.

Available evidence tends to bolster further claims that the financial reporting system is a crucial component of the infrastructure for developing domestic capital markets. A significant body of research shows that accounting reports are relevant to investors' buy and sell decisions. The importance of accounting reports for stock market investors has been demonstrated through capital market studies conducted in different countries and cross-country surveys of users (Choi & Levich, 1990; Bhushan & Lessard, 1992). Lev (1988) attributes the prevalence of accounting regulations worldwide to the need to maintain the informational efficiency of capital markets. The worldwide pre-eminence of U.S. and U.K. capital markets has been associated, in part, with the stringent nature of financial reporting rules and their strict enforcement in these countries, which, in turn, resulted in the increased availability of information for decisionmaking purposes. The relationship between accounting information and the growth of domestic securities markets is a crucial policy issue for developing countries that aim to boost capital inflows to their economies (Ndubizu, 1992; Larson, 1993). As pointed out by Walter (1993, p. 15), "the nature and extent of information production and disclosure is central to equity market development and the ability to attract cross-border flows . . . The stronger and more independent the information infrastructure, the more attractive an emerging market will be to foreign equity investors".

Due to the immediate need of many developing countries to attract foreign capital, harmonizing domestic accounting requirements with an existing and internationally accepted set of accounting principles is often advocated as an inexpensive way of overcoming the informational barriers faced by foreign investors. The next section considers whether developing countries, including those in ASEAN, should pursue accounting harmonization by evaluating the net benefits of harmonization.

4. BENEFITS OF ACCOUNTING HARMONIZATION

We adopt a broad concept of accounting harmonization under which accounting harmonization could refer either to a global approach, as advocated by the International Accounting Standards Committee (IASC), or a regional approach, as initially pursued by the EU. Most of the perceived benefits of harmonization discussed below can apply equally well to both concepts of accounting harmonization.

Advocates of accounting harmonization, whether on a regional or global basis, outline four primary benefits (IASC, 1983; Aitken & Islam, 1984; ICMG, 1992). These are cost savings accruing to multinational companies (MNCs); enhanced comprehensiveness and comparability of cross-national fmancial reports; widespread dissemination of high quality accounting standards and practices; and, provision of low cost financial accounting standards to countries with limited resources. Prima facie, these benefits provide compelling reasons for EMs to pursue harmonization. It is essential, however, to consider to whom these benefits accrue; and whether other costs or disadvantages are associated with harmonization. We consider all of these issues in this section.

Cost Savings for MNCs

From the viewpoint of MNCs, harmonization potentially provides at least two tangible benefits. The first is reduced compliance costs associated with different sets of national rules. This benefit assumes that one set of general purpose financial reports can be prepared by the MNC to satisfy the information requirements of various users internationally. The second is eliminating potential "competitive disadvantages" arising from differential use of measurement methods or the need to disclose "sensitive" proprietary information. Debates over accounting for goodwill internationally illustrate this point (Dunne & Rollins, 1992; Lee & Choi, 1992). According to advocates of accounting harmonization, differences in accounting for goodwill disadvantage companies in some countries because the companies have to comply with onerous requirements that distort their reported financial condition and performance.

In justifying the pursuit of accounting harmonization, national policy makers will want to know whether benefits derived by MNCs also benefit their domestic economies. In many developing countries, the relationship between host governments and foreign MNCs is one of caution. The information needs of host governments, labor groups and other interest groups are often different from the information that MNCs are inclined to disclose (Fitzgerald & Kelley, 1979; O'Brien & Helleiner, 1980). For example, in ASEAN, government agencies often require specific information in response to uniquely domestic circumstances (Saudagaran & Diga, 1997).

Conversely, in an increasingly globalized environment, governments of most developing countries are anxious to encourage foreign direct investment (FDI). One way of encouraging such investments is to relax the disclosure requirements imposed on MNCs. This condition suggests a subordination of domestic interests to those of MNCs, rather than an inherently harmonious set of interests. For example, the choice of stock market listing location appears to be influenced by the level of domestic listing requirements (Saudagaran & Biddle, 1992, 1995). If so, then accounting harmonization in EMs could help create a level playing field for the listing of foreign MNCs. The nature of financial reporting regimes, however, represents only one factor considered by MNCs and, in most cases, it probably is not the decisive factor. Moreover, no evidence exists that financial reporting requirements influence MNC decisions regarding where to establish production facilities, the principal interest of most host governments with respect to FDI (Dunning, 1993). Consequently, even if accounting harmonization were to provide tangible net benefits to MNCs, it appears improbable that national regulators will view these benefits as a sufficient rationale for pursuing accounting harmonization in the absence of compelling evidence that their domestic economies will benefit, too.

Enhanced Comprehensiveness and Comparability

The second benefit arising from harmonization is that it facilitates the comprehension and comparison of financial reports from different countries. Accounting harmony among ASEAN countries, for example, would allow investors in Singapore to compare the performance and investment opportunities of Indonesian and Thai enterprises. Such understanding is likely to assist in promoting intra-ASEAN trade and investment. As indicated previously, the enhanced comprehensiveness and comparability will also facilitate financial analyses by investors from countries outside the immediate region.

It is arguable whether ASEAN users will benefit equally from harmonization. The benefits will likely be distributed disproportionately because these countries have different information processing capabilities. Currently, Malaysia and Singapore appear to have relatively more sophisticated financial accounting systems than those in Indonesia, Thailand and the Philippines. These differences could encourage regulators to "modernize" their financial accounting systems. Conversely, it could also act as a disincentive to regional accounting harmonization. Those likely to gain minimal benefits from ASEAN accounting harmonization may be less inclined to pursue regional harmonization efforts vigorously.

SGV (1984) suggests that financial reports are an important source of information for users in ASEAN. No compelling evidence exists, however, that the lack of accounting harmony in ASEAN poses a barrier to intra-ASEAN trade and investment. Choi and Levich (1990) and Bhushan and Lessard (1992) found that international users are able to compensate for the effects of financial reporting differences and that their decision processes are not affected adversely by such differences. Such behavior may be suboptimal in the context of efficient capital markets and greater accounting harmony may increase the efficiency of international capital markets. Conversely, the financial reporting differences may themselves be vital sources of information for capital market participants (Meek, 1983; Dye, 1985). Nonetheless, further research into this issue seems warranted in the absence of direct and compelling supporting evidence.

Best Accounting Practices

Since its inception in 1973, the IASC has urged developing countries to harmonize their financial reporting practices in terms of worldwide "best practice." The notion of "best practice", however, is unclear because of the different roles played by financial accounting systems in society (Meek & Saudagaran, 1990). Fundamentally, the notion of "best practice" needs to be assessed in terms of whether a predominantly macro-user or micro-user set of objectives is adopted. The main difference between the two systems relates to the intended users of accounting information. In macro-user oriented systems, government agencies, particularly the tax collection and economic planning agencies, are the principal users of financial reports. In comparison, a diverse set of capital providers is perceived to be the most important user group of accounting reports in micro-user oriented economies.

In the case of the ASEAN countries, all have adopted (or are in the process of adopting) a micro-user oriented financial accounting system, based largely on the international accounting standards (IASs). However, it is debatable whether current IASs represent "best practice" in an accounting sense. IASs are largely a distillation of acceptable practices in Anglo-North American settings (Hoarau, 1995). Until very recently, the IASC has been a follower rather than a leader in worldwide financial reporting developments (Saudagaran & Meek, 1997). Moreover, adoption of IAS does not necessarily imply that domestic financial accounting systems will be perceived to be of "better quality" by international investors (Saudagaran & Diga, 1997) or will lead to tangible macroeconomic benefits (Larson, 1993).

Low Cost Accounting Standards

A fourth benefit cited by proponents of harmonization relates to cost savings for developing countries in formulating relevant and acceptable financial accounting standards. It seems apparent that R&D costs associated with adopting IAS or other foreign accounting standards are minimal. Furthermore, most developing countries do not possess the financial reporting-related research capabilities and resources found in industrialized countries. Given other pressing socioeconomic developmental priorities, it is unlikely that such resources will be made available in the absence of external assistance (e.g. World Bank accounting development project in Indonesia). These factors make it especially attractive for developing countries to "borrow" foreign accounting standards for domestic use. However, the adoption of such standards for cost reasons by developing countries begs the question of whether these are appropriate for their needs.

According to critics of Anglo-North American accounting systems, these systems overemphasize financial reporting for investment purposes to the detriment of other relevant financial reporting objectives (Hove, 1986). Furthermore, accounting education in these countries is geared towards the auditing profession, rather than a more holistic consideration of accounting's role in society (Albrecht & Sack, 2000). These criticisms suggest that while the initial adoption costs of Anglo-North American accounting systems in developing countries may be small, the resulting standards may be irrelevant to the needs of these countries. Policy makers in developing countries need to consider the relevance of a set of standards before adopting them for their countries.

Other Benefits

In addition to the benefits cited above, the process of pursuing accounting harmonization can itself prove advantageous for developing countries. The process of harmonization can assist in creating and sustaining a dynamic environment for change in EMs. Debates on how and what aspects of financial accounting systems to harmonize encourage policy makers to be aware of developments elsewhere. Financial accounting innovations are occurring in industrialized countries whether these adopt a micro-user oriented or macro-user oriented accounting system. With their emphasis on social and economic progress, developing countries cannot afford to neglect these innovations.

The process of pursuing regional harmonization also provides an important developmental opportunity for individual countries within regional blocs, especially for the newer members that are attempting to move from a state-controlled economic system to a market system (e.g. Laos & Vietnam in ASEAN). These countries are typically also in the process of transforming their financial accounting systems. Their participation in regional forums allows them to gain insight to the experiences of other developing countries, not simply as a way of emulating such experiences but also as a way of avoiding costly mistakes.

Pursuing harmonization is beneficial also because it strengthens awareness of the regional organization's collective socio-economic goals. Policy goals such as those embodied by the EU or ASEAN highlight the synergies that could arise from a collective approach to common problems. The role of financial reporting in ensuring enterprise accountability is viewed here as an issue deserving careful consideration. While each country's political, economic and sociocultural circumstances necessarily influence notions of accountability, scope exists for discussing how financial reporting can help address common regional concerns regarding enterprise accountability. Even if regional policy makers decide, for example, that the IASC approach provides the best option for developing their domestic accounting systems, discussion of accounting harmonization within the region encourages a more active approach to IASC deliberations to ensure that the views of the countries in the region are heard.

5. POLICY OPTIONS RELATING TO ACCOUNTING HARMONIZATION

Depending on the specific objective for the research, it is possible to conceptualize accounting harmonization either as a *process* of achieving increasingly greater levels of accounting harmony or part of a range of *policy options* concerning accounting regulation. If accounting harmonization is viewed principally as a linear process, *regional accounting harmony* is merely an intermediate step towards the final goal of achieving *global accounting harmony*. However, there are two important limitations in this view of accounting harmony. First, it tends to focus on the descriptive aspect of the issue, such as in measuring actual levels of accounting harmony or disharmony (Van der Tas, 1988; Tay & Parker, 1990). While description is important, theoretical advancement requires inquiring into the explanations for why harmonization takes place. The second limitation is that the model assumes implicitly that accounting harmony is the appropriate policy goal. In actuality, a program of pursuing accounting harmony is only one of many policy options available to countries intent on developing their accounting systems (Wallace, 1993).

We therefore propose to conceptualize accounting harmonization in this paper in terms of policy options available to a country. The view of harmonization as a distinct policy issue recognizes that the actual choice of whether or not to pursue harmonization is made at the national level. It is also useful, in analytical terms, to distinguish between the various harmonization policy options as distinct policy sub-issues within the broader framework of the harmonization effort. We next discuss the five policy options available in regard to whether or not a country chooses to align its regulatory aims with those of other countries.

Maintain Uniqueness

The first option is to pursue a unique regulatory structure tailored specifically to each country's needs and requirements. While this option does not preclude the use of accounting methods developed elsewhere, it means that policy makers concentrate their efforts on developing internally, accounting regulations that address the unique requirements of their home country. Whether or not these nationally developed accounting standards are "in harmony" with those in other countries is, at most, only a marginal issue. The traditional U.S. approach to accounting regulation is an example of this first approach. Historically, the FASB and its predecessor standard-setting bodies have developed national accounting standards strictly on the basis of U.S. requirements and needs. It is only very recently that the FASB has begun to work with the EU, IASC, and IOSCO while developing new standards and reviewing existing ones (Beresford, 1995). However, recent actions by the FASB, still betray an ambivalence towards cooperating with the IASC (*Accountancy International*, 1999; *Economist*, 1999). Few developing countries, interested in attracting foreign capital, are likely to pursue this option over an extended period.

Peg to Another Country's GAAP

The second policy option related to harmonization is for a country to unilaterally adopt the generally accepted accounting principles (GAAP) of another country. One often observes this in the case of adopting countries that have close economic, political, or colonial ties with the model country. The primary advantage of this approach to the adopting country is that it does not have to devote scarce, and sometimes unavailable, resources to the standard-setting activity. Another advantage is that it facilitates investment from the model country since it makes it less costly for companies from that country to do business in the adopting country. However, in many situations, nationalism and sovereignty concerns make it difficult for countries to adopt the GAAP of another country. As discussed in the next section, the Philippines is an example of a country that has followed this approach by essentially pegging its accounting to that of the United States.

Bilateral Agreements

Under this approach, two or more countries may negotiate mutual agreements which involve harmonizing their standards with certain additional disclosures as part of the arrangement. The Multijurisdictional Disclosure System (MDS) attempted by Canada and the United States was a very visible effort at such an undertaking. This agreement became effective in July 1991 after six years of contentious negotiations. There is some question as to whether MDS will provide the benefits originally envisioned and whether it represents a viable approach to harmonization (Houston & Jones, 1999). The MDS experience is particularly relevant since the two countries attempting the bilateral negotiation approach were Canada and the United States – countries that are not just geographic neighbors but also very similar in their business environments. If six years of negotiations between these two countries produced rather modest results, what chance, one might ask, is there for successful negotiation and implementation of bilateral agreements between dissimilar countries. Critics of this approach point to the MDS process as an example of "how tortuous and relatively fruitless this approach [to accounting harmonization] can be" (Cochrane et al., 1996, p. 259).

Harmonize Regionally

The formation of regional economic groups indicates the growing economic interdependence of countries that are geographically proximate. Regional economic groups such as the European Union (EU), the North American Free Trade Area (NAFTA) and the Association of South East Asian Nations (ASEAN) have become prominent players in the global investment and trade arenas. Efforts at regional economic integration will inevitably draw attention to financial reporting issues, as the experience of the EU has shown (Thorell & Whittington, 1994).

In such a setting, the regional model of accounting harmonization may present an appealing policy option for countries. The regional model, referred to as the 'cluster approach' to accounting harmonization, possesses specific advantages in terms of recognizing the shared interests of the member countries (Choi, 1981). Countries that are geographically proximate often share similar characteristics in terms of their historical, political, economic and cultural backgrounds. Regional accounting harmonization could be pursued to enhance further the level of economic linkages among countries in the region. For many years the European Union (EU) pursued accounting harmonization in the context of the member countries' company laws. Regional accounting groups have likewise been proposed for EMs located in Latin America, Southeast Asia and Francophone Africa (Choi, 1981; Forrester, 1983; Rivera & Salva, 1995).

Harmonize Globally

The fifth policy option, which is global harmonization, refers to a country's conscious effort to harmonize its own accounting requirements in accordance with a global benchmark. Several such benchmarks have been contemplated (see, for example, UNCTC, 1982), although our focus here is on the work of the IASC. In light of the increasing level of integration of global financial markets, globalization of finance is an increasingly significant policy issue for developing and transitional economies seeking to augment their domestic resources with foreign capital. Pressures to revise and transform their financial reporting systems emanate from a variety of international sources. Foreign institutional investors can express their preferences for particular types of accounting regimes, e.g. accounting standards patterned after the U.K. and USA. Multilateral financial institutions such as the World Bank also support particular types of financial reporting. Under such an environment, the global model of accounting harmonization represents a rational policy alternative for EMs (Beresford, 1995).

Adoption of accounting standards established by the International Accounting Standards Committee (IASC)[2] is consistent with moving towards the global concept of harmonization. On the one hand, international accounting standards (IASs) offer credible accounting principles for countries that do not have the resources to develop their own standards or that desire the benefits associated with possessing "globally acceptable accounting standards" (IASC, 1982, 1989). Some IASs, however, could be inappropriate for the needs of EMs. In the long-term, the extent to which developed markets subsequently support IASs is crucial in the decision of EMs to adopt IAS (Purvis et al., 1991). Such reasoning is plausible to the extent that worldwide capital flows are still dominated by the developed capital markets. The juxtaposition of the dominant sources of global capital and requirements of EMs for external sources of capital creates conditions auspicious for the adoption of accounting methods preferred in the leading developed capital markets, particularly Japan, the U.K. and USA. The IASC's set of standards are of pivotal importance in ASEAN because many of the member states have looked towards IASs for guidance in setting national accounting standards.

ASEAN provides a rich setting for studying the contrasting policy options of accounting harmonization. The reason is that ASEAN countries, at one time or another, have at least considered the various alternatives. In particular, the ASEAN Federation of Accountants (AFA) which consists of professional accounting bodies from each of the ASEAN countries has proposed moves for regional accounting harmonization since the mid-1970s (Choi, 1979; Ninsuvannakul, 1986). At the same time, a majority of ASEAN countries have modeled some or all of their accounting requirements on standards issued by the IASC. The direction that harmonization is taking within ASEAN makes for an interesting study, particularly since it affords the opportunity to examine closely the role played by accounting regulation in a crossnational setting.

6. ADOPTING THE IASC MODEL IN ASEAN[3]

The majority of ASEAN's professional accounting bodies have actively promoted programs that reflected a global view of accounting harmonization. Within the global approach, pronouncements of the International Accounting Standards Committee (IASC) played an important role in shaping perceptions of the nature and scope of domestic accounting regulations. Most ASEAN countries either adopt IASs in toto as domestic regulations or they draft domestic regulations that incorporate accounting methods suggested in IASs. The Philippines has not adopted IASs, preferring to peg its financial reporting to U.S. GAAP.

As early as 1977, professional accounting bodies in Malaysia and Singapore endorsed the use of IASs as a basis for their own national accounting standards. In general, international accounting standards were adopted in both countries with little, if any, alteration. Thailand first made use of IASs in 1987 when it issued SFAS 6 "Revenue Recognition" which was based on IAS 18. Prior to this, accounting pronouncements by the Institute of Certified

Accountants and Auditors of Thailand (ICAAT), the Thai professional body, were influenced more by U.S. and U.K. standards. To date, 14 out of 24 accounting pronouncements by ICAAT are adopted from the IASC (now IASB). In the case of Indonesia, it was only in late 1994 that the Indonesian Institute of Accountants (IAI) adopted IASs as the bases for national standards. Almost immediately, however, 21 IASs were adopted for use by Indonesian companies beginning in 1995. In the Philippines, however, except for a recent accounting standard on consolidated financial statements which made reference to IAS 27, no Philippine accounting standard explicitly drew upon IASs. The reason for this is largely historical in that most Philippine standards have traditionally followed U.S. authoritative pronouncements on the subject. This pattern of drawing upon U.S. standards has largely remained intact even for the most recent standards dealing with such issues as consolidated financial statements, accounting for business combinations and statement of cash flows.

In general, government support is strong for the IAS-based accounting standards adopted in Indonesia, Malaysia, Singapore and Thailand. Official and unofficial recognition is provided particularly by securities regulators. Such government approval greatly enhances the level of support given to the standards, particularly by business entities in these countries. Even more significantly, recent amendments to the Company Law in Malaysia and Singapore have incorporated into statute the disclosure requirements found in professional accounting standards. Such developments make it unequivocal that IAS-based accounting standards become an integral part of the fabric of accounting regulation in the country.

An interesting empirical and important policy question is why the majority of ASEAN countries have chosen to adopt IASs as the bases for their national accounting regulations. Here, we highlight some of these forces which explain the principal advantages of IASs over other forms of accounting standards for the adopting ASEAN countries.

Lack of Research Resources

First, all of the ASEAN countries adopting IASs lacked a well-developed and resource-laden agency capable of undertaking research into accounting regulatory issues. In most cases, accounting standardsetting was in the hands of professional accounting bodies, all of which were of relatively recent origin. While government regulators perceived accounting standards as being important for regulating companies, resources were generally not available to develop even a modest research capability patterned after those of standard-setting bodies in the U.K. and U.S. This observation lends credence to the argument of the IASC that its standards provide a low cost option for developing countries that do not have the capability to develop an extensive set of domestic accounting standards (IASC, 1988; Rivera, 1989).

Flexibility of International Accounting Standards

A corollary question, however, is why countries such as Indonesia, Malaysia, Singapore and Thailand specifically adopted IASs rather than, say, standards developed by the U.S. FASB. The reason probably is not the technical merits of the standards themselves since the FASB standards are generally based on more extensive and in-depth research compared to IASs. Neither does the reason relate to innovativeness because again IASs tend to follow, rather than lead, developments from national standard-setting bodies such as those in the U.K. and U.S. Rather, the principal reason for preferring IASs relates to the perceived flexibility and neutrality of international accounting standards vis-à-vis the national standards of some other country. Flexibility means that IASs, given that they incorporate allowable accounting methods in two or more countries (including the USA), are preferable to more standardized accounting require-ments of any one country (Rivera, 1989; Chandler, 1992). They engender less resistance from financial statement preparers in adopting countries, for instance, since the ready availability of accounting options is not threatened by the more flexible IASs. As the IASC tightens its standards, in an effort to get the International Organization of Securities Commissions (IOSCO) to endorse them, IASC standards may lose their ease of implementation.

Nationalism and Sovereignty Concerns

IASs are also perceived to be more "neutral" since they represent accounting methods that are issued by a supranational organization rather than by any one country. As such they are easier to adopt because they do not raise the nation-alism and sovereignty concerns that accompany the adoption of another country's standards. It is therefore less difficult to justify the adoption of IASs from a political standpoint. None of the ASEAN countries that have adopted IASs have been influenced as strongly as the Philippines by the U.S. accounting system. The U.K.-origin of accounting regulation in Malaysia and Singapore features a greater amount of flexibility compared to the U.S. system. Both the Indonesian and Thai accounting systems draw from accounting systems from various countries. Gaining widespread acceptance to use the accounting stan-dards of any one country would therefore be more problematic in these countries. In contrast, accounting practice and thought in the Philippines, as well as commercial and legal systems, have been influenced strongly by the

U.S. (Diga 1996). U.S.-based accounting standards are therefore perceived to be generally acceptable by professional accountants, government agencies and the business community in the country. This is largely a legacy of the colonization of the Philippines by the United States between 1898 and 1946. Similar U.S. influences are also evident in other aspects of the Philippines' infrastructure including its education and business practices.

Leadership Role of National Standard-Setters

Another difference between the adopters of IASs (Indonesia, Malaysia, Singapore and Thailand) and the sole non-adopter (Philippines) relates to the institutional basis for accounting standard setting in each country. In the adopting countries, the professional accounting bodies have the leadership, in some cases unchallenged, role in determining detailed accounting standards. Consequently, the national professional bodies in those countries can focus their efforts on gaining acceptance for IASs as a basis for national standards. In contrast, accounting standard setting in the Philippines is no longer exclusively in the hands of the accounting profession. The standard-setting agency includes representatives from various government and private-sector groups. Given the fact that business regulation in the Philippines in the early part of the twentieth century occurred during the period of U.S. administration and the Filipino dependence on U.S. foreign aid and trade, it is hardly surprising that the Philippines turns to the U.S. for leadership in accounting matters.

Enhancing Credibility of Financial Statements

Finally, one cannot discount the instant respectability gained by adopting IASs. Larson (1993) refers to this as the "bandwagon effect" and observes it particularly among developing countries that have lacked their own accounting standard-setting infrastructure and need to inspire confidence among foreign providers of capital. In the case of ASEAN countries, this motive would appear to apply to a greater degree to Indonesia and Thailand and less to Malaysia and Singapore, given that the latter two countries have stronger professional accounting bodies due to their colonial ties to the United Kingdom. The perception holds that adopting IASs will greatly enhance the credibility of financial statements produced by domestic companies to a largely international audience. However, there are other strong reasons why Malaysia and Singapore, in particular, would find such a perception extremely attractive. In ASEAN, it is precisely these two countries that are competing strongly to become the foremost financial center in the region. It is therefore no coincidence as well that the capital markets in these countries are the largest and most well-developed in ASEAN. Singapore is already a well-known regional financial center presently rivaled only by Hong Kong in terms of importance (Edwards, 1987; Price Waterhouse, 1992b). The Malaysian government has announced its intention to make the country an important regional financial player. In the case of Indonesia, regulatory interest in accounting standards has been spurred by developments in the Indonesian capital market. Since the government implemented deregulation measures in 1988, the market capitalization and volume turnover of the Jakarta Stock Exchange has grown by over tenfold (IFC, 1998). Over 200 Indonesian companies are currently listed on the Jakarta Stock Exchange and, already, some local companies have begun to list on international stock exchanges, including the New York Stock Exchange. These developments are clearly significant in the context of Indonesia considering that it was only in 1988 that the Indonesian stock market was barely functioning with less than 30 listed companies. Thus, the policy goals of governments coupled with the organizational goals of national professional bodies provide strong incentives for the majority of ASEAN countries to adopt IASs.

The evidence suggests that ASEAN countries, on an individual basis, are pursuing a policy of harmonizing their own accounting standards according to a global approach to accounting harmony. This has taken two forms, depending on the particular countries. The vehicle for achieving harmony with global standards, for Indonesia, Malaysia, Singapore and Thailand, is to use IASs as a basis for domestic requirements. In contrast, general adherence to U.S. accounting pronouncements appears to be largely intact in the Philippines. Evidence also suggests that the debate over regional accounting harmonization has been marginalized significantly in ASEAN. Regional harmonization has been reduced to a discussion point in AFA; however, it is currently not a priority goal of the organization.

Global versus Regional Harmonization: ASEAN and EU

What explains the emergence of global harmonization as the dominant choice in ASEAN? Several dimensions of this issue are highlighted here. The first is that, in practical terms, regional harmonization is more difficult to achieve from any one country's vantage point compared to global harmonization. Though this statement may appear to be counter-intuitive, it is quite plausible if the analytical context is the regulatory process of a particular country. Regional harmonization depends on the collective effort and consensus among a group of countries, not all of whom necessarily share the same economic and political goals. The EU's experience in attempting to harmonize company laws of its member countries is enlightening. In particular, the different accounting traditions of the U.K. and Continental European countries, notably France and Germany, transformed the principles of "true and fair" reporting versus "legal compliance" into a highly controversial issue (Nobes, 1992; Thorell & Whittington, 1994). The controversy was only resolved through a compromise that incorporated the U.K.'s notion of "true and fair view" and Continental Europe's preference for "standardized financial reporting" in accordance with statute into the same Directive. This illustrates that achieving regional accounting harmony requires a slow, often painstaking, process of bargaining and compromise (Van Hulle, 1992). In comparison, it only takes one country to unilaterally align its accounting regulations to a recognized global benchmark such as the standards established by the IASC. The advantages of adopting the IASC model from the standpoint of ASEAN countries have already been discussed earlier.

Despite its apparent difficulty, regional accounting harmonization still possesses certain theoretical advantages in terms of ASEAN's broader policy aims of facilitating trade and investment in the region. Why then have the ASEAN members not pursued regional harmonization as a priority policy goal? Once more, it is useful here to draw parallels between the experience of ASEAN and the EU. Regional accounting harmonization has not been seriously pursued in ASEAN because of a number of important factors. These include: (1) the lack of an articulated rationale for regional accounting harmony; (2) a relatively low level of economic integration; (3) the absence of a political infrastructure within which to pursue harmonization; and (4) admission of failure of the regional approach by the EU.

First, unlike the EU, ASEAN has not been able to articulate a clear rationale for why regional harmonization is a preferred course of action for its members. The rationale, while expressed in collective terms, must make the benefits of accounting harmonization explicit for each member state. Accounting systems in ASEAN countries, far from being homogeneous, are characterized by long-standing traditions engendered by each country's colonial history and regulatory preferences. The absence of tangible benefits for member countries has made policy makers, particularly in government and the business community, reluctant to discard traditional approaches to accounting regulation. The EU attempted to overcome resistance to change by presenting a clear case for regional accounting harmonization within the broader framework of common economic policy goals (Nobes, 1992; Van Hulle, 1992). As stipulated in the EU's Common Industrial Policy (1970), the European Commission wanted a level playing field that would allow EU-based companies to remain competitive anywhere in the region. Specifically, the common market was to be achieved, in part, through the harmonization of EU member countries' company law and tax regulations (Van Hulle, 1992). To the extent that the presentation of corporate information was an essential component to maintaining regional competitiveness, it appeared sensible to attempt regional harmonization within the EU.

Second, the current level of economic integration in ASEAN is very low compared to the EU. The notion of creating a regional level playing field in ASEAN is only now beginning to gain acceptance among government policy-makers and industries, many of whom are accustomed to going their own way with regard to national policy (Kondo, 1992). Unlike the EU which already had a significant level of intraregional economic activity, almost 80 percent of ASEAN members' trade and investment activities are with countries outside of ASEAN (ADB, 1995). Currently, ASEAN's most important trade and investment partners are the U.S. and Japan. Moreover, the principal aim for creating the ASEAN Free Trade Area is not so much to make ASEAN a closed trading group, but to encourage greater business interest in ASEAN from major investing countries as the U.S., Japan, EU and the NICs (particularly Hong Kong, South Korea and Taiwan). In the context of accounting harmonization, it appears more compelling from a policy standpoint for ASEAN countries to harmonize their accounting regulations globally in order to further encourage interest from existing and potential economic partners.

The third prerequisite for progress towards regional accounting harmonization is an organizational structure that would support harmonization goals. During the period when the EU initiated its effort toward regional harmonization, support emanated from both the government and the accounting profession. Both were well-represented in deliberations concerning European accounting harmonization. The EU, in particular, had a well-developed infrastructure for regional decision making which included a separate Commission or civil service, Parliament (elected representatives), various consultative committees, and Councils of Ministers (Nobes, 1992; Van Hulle, 1992). ASEAN, on the other hand, has not had a comparable structure although there are ongoing discussions of revamping the organizational structure of ASEAN in order to facilitate regional decision making. Also, the professional accounting bodies in Europe have had a relatively long history of intra-regional cooperation[4] which has influenced the nature and outcome of the Directives concerning company law in Europe (Nobes, 1992; Thorell & Whittington, 1994). The ASEAN Federation of Accountants (AFA), in comparison, is a newcomer in the harmonization debate and has been unable to establish sufficient political clout to influence the agenda regarding the harmonization of corporate accounting regulations in ASEAN.

Finally, the decision of the EU, in November 1995, to cast its lot behind the IASC rather than continue the harmonization effort on its own was a clear indication of the risks of the regional approach to harmonization. This lesson, was in all probability, not lost on policy makers in developing countries, including those in ASEAN. Mueller (1997) provides an insightful and succinct analysis of the reasons for the failure of regional harmonization and the emergence of the IASC as the preferred approach:

As it now appears, though, the strictly regional approach to accounting harmonization has not succeeded. The key reasons [are]:

(1) Internationally active business and finance organizations do not wish to deal with three tiers of accounting standards – national, regional, and global. Two tiers are considered sufficient. The regional tier lost.

(2) European accounting harmonization occurred through political processes and was guided by bureaucrats. This limited inputs from the private sector including practicing professional accountants. As a consequence, non-European corporate executives have expressed frustration time and again over their complete inability to be heard while EU Directives were being proposed, finalized, and implemented. Europeans placed much general trust and acceptance in their governments. Most English-speaking countries place similar trust in markets and end-users of products and services.

(3) In recent years, a degree of competition (or possibly even confrontation) developed between various supra-national accounting developers and standard-setters. At the international level, IASC, IOSCO, OECD, the UN and some World Bank agencies became involved. Regionally, the EU took the lead but ASEAN, the Nordic Federation, and now NAFTA also became involved. All this was costly, confusing, and not results efficient.

Now IASC has evolved as the preferred mechanism for global accounting harmonization.

Around the world national and regional standard setting agencies will increasingly align their standards with the IASs and the model of private-sector IAS-type accounting standard setting appears to have gained the upper hand – at least for the time being (Mueller, 1997, p. 11.30).

7. CONCLUSION

Our overall prognosis is that the global harmonization option as represented by the IASC model will continue to dominate in ASEAN. Even before the recent economic crisis in the region, a genuine notion of regional accounting harmonization in ASEAN did not have much likelihood of becoming a reality since the prerequisites identified earlier were missing. We believe that global accounting harmonization is even more likely to dominate in ASEAN as a result of the region's economic crisis. General acceptance of the IASC approach has already been obtained from regulators, professional accountants and businesses in four out of the five ASEAN countries examined. This means that future changes to IASs will have important implications on the further development of accounting regulation in ASEAN as a whole. To the extent that ASEAN becomes a stronger economic alliance, we expect ASEAN as a whole to move towards a regional consensus favoring the use of IASs. ASEAN convergence towards IASs will probably include the current hold over, the Philippines, and eventually the four newer members, Brunei, Laos, Myanmar, and Vietnam, since the pressure to align cross-border investment regulations will become stronger in the region.

Another recent development that augurs in favor of the IASC and against the regional approach to harmonization is the EU's decision to cast its lot with the IASC rather than continue its efforts at regional accounting harmonization. This is a significant development since it provides a clear lesson for policy makers in ASEAN. If the EU with its far larger resources and economic interdependence has abandoned regional accounting harmonization and instead chosen to work with the IASC then why should ASEAN countries with their lower resources and less interdependence attempt the far riskier approach of going on their own? The regional approach to harmonization has for all intents and purposes been rejected by ASEAN countries. The lesson that most developing countries are likely to take from the failed attempt at accounting harmonization by the EU is that the regional policy option is too costly and time-consuming a process.

Despite the grim outlook for regional harmonization, developing countries can still use their regional organizations such as ASEAN, ANCOM, and SAARC to make their collective voices heard in IASB deliberations in order to ensure that the views and concerns of developing countries are considered in any new international standards that result.

NOTES

1. The World Bank (1998) defined a'developing country' as one whose average income per capita does not exceed a certain level established by the bank. In 1998, the cut-off was set at US$9,600.

2. The IASC was set up in 1973 by professional accounting bodies in nine countries – Australia, Canada, France, Germany, Japan, Mexico, the Netherlands, the U.K., and the U.S. A restructured International Accounting Standards Board (IASB), created to replace the IASC, met for the first time in 2001. As of June 2002, 41 International Accounting Standards (IASs) had been issued.

3. While ASEAN today consists of ten member countries, we focus on the five original members of the group – Indonesia, Malaysia, the Philippines, Singapore, and Thailand. At present, there is a paucity of information on accounting aspects of the newest ASEAN members – Brunei, Cambodia, Laos, Myanmar, and Vietnam. These countries have only recently begun the task of formulating a regulatory policy for

accounting and are at a transitional stage of adopting market-based economic principles. They are still in the process of developing an accounting regulatory framework for privately-owned companies.

4. These European accounting bodies were the Union Europeenne des Experts Comptables set up in 1951, the Groupe d'Etudes set up in 1966, and the Federation des Experts Comptables Europeens (FEE) which took over the roles of the two earlier bodies in 1987.

ACKNOWLEDGMENTS

This paper benefited from comments and materials provided by Gina Aban, Low Aik Meng, Prawit Ninsuvannukul, Pannipa Rodwanna, and Veerinder Singh. We are also grateful for comments on earlier versions of the paper by participants at the 1997 Asia-Pacific Conference on International Accounting Issues in Bangkok and the 1998 Conference of the Hong Kong Society of Accountants-Hong Kong Academic Accounting Association in Hong Kong. We appreciate the able research assistance of Febiana Rinasari.

REFERENCES

Accountancy International (January 1990). IASs are not up to scratch, says FASB member. *Accountancy International, 123*(1265), 9.

Aitken, M. J., & Islam, M. A. (1984). Dispelling arguments against International Accounting Standards. *International Journal of Accounting Education and Research, 19*(2), 35–46.

Albrecht, W. S., & Sack, S. J. (2000). *Accounting education: Charting a course through a perilous future.* Saraosta, FL: American Accounting Association.

Asian Development Bank (ADB) (1986). *Capital Market Development in Selected Developing Member Countries of the Asian Development Bank.* Manila: ADB.

Asian Development Bank (ADB) (1995). *Asian Development Outlook 1995.* Manila: Oxford University Press for the Asian Development Bank.

Beresford, D. (1995). International capital markets: Converging on the horizon. *Finance and Treasury,* (September 11), 3–7.

Bhushan, R., & Lessard, D. R. (1992). Coping with international accounting diversity: Fund managers' views on disclosure, reconciliation, and harmonization. *Journal of International Financial Management and Accounting, 4*(2), 149–164.

Chandler, R. (1992). The international harmonization of accounting: In search of influence. *International Journal of Accounting, 27*(3), 222–233.

Choi, F. D. S. (Fall 1979). ASEAN Federation of Accountants: A new international accounting force. *International Journal of Accounting Education and Research, 14,* 53–75.

Choi, F. D. S. (August 1981). A cluster approach to accounting harmonization. *Management Accounting, 27–31.*

Choi, F. D. S., & Levich, R. M. (1990). *The Capital Market Effects of International Accounting Diversity.* Homewood, Illinois: Dow Jones-Irwin.

Cochrane, J. L., Shapiro, J. E., & Tobin, J. E. (1996). Foreign equities and U.S. investors: Breaking down the barriers separating supply and demand. *Stanford Journal of Law, Business and Finance*, 2(2), 241–263.

Diga, J. G. (1996). Accounting in the Philippines. In: R. Willett & K. Nishimura (Eds), *Accounting in the Asian Pacific Region*. Sydney: Longman.

Dunne, K. M., & Rollins, T. (1992). Accounting for goodwill: A case analysis of the U.S., U.K. and Japan. *Journal of International Accounting Auditing and Taxation*, 1(2), 191–207.

Dunning, J. H. (1993). *Multinational Enterprises and the Global Economy*. Reading, Massachusetts: Addison-Wesley.

Dye, R. A. (1985). Strategic accounting choice and the effects of alternative financial reporting requirements. *Journal of Accounting Research*, 23(2), 544–574.

The Economist (1988). Directory of World Stock Exchanges. R. Bootle (Ed.). London: The Economist Publications.

The Economist (1999). Accounting: Raising standards. (January 30–February 5), 69.

Edwards, A. (1987). *Singapore: A Guide to the Structure, Development and Regulation of Financial Services*. London: Economist Publications.

Fitzgerald, R. D., & Kelley, E. M. (1979). International disclosure standards – The United Nations position. *Journal of Accounting, Auditing and Finance*, 3(1), 5–20.

Forrester, D. (1983). Comment va-t-il in Africa? A study of the influence of French accounting. *AUTA Review*, 15, 230–240.

Frankel, J. A. (1993). Recent Changes in the Financial Systems of Asian and Pacific Countries. Center for International And Development Economics Research Working Paper No. c93031, University of California at Berkeley.

Glen, J., & Pinto, B. (1995). Capital markets and developing country firms. *Finance and Development*, (March), 40–43.

Hoaru, C. (1995). International accounting harmonization: American hegemony or mutual recognition with benchmarks. *European Accounting Review*, 4(2), 217–234.

Houston, C. O., & Jones, R. A. (1999). The Multi-Jurisdictional Disclosure System: Model for Future Cooperation? *Journal of International Financial Management and Accounting*, 10(3), 227–248.

Hove, M. R. (1986). Accounting practices in developing countries: Colonialism's legacy of inappropriate technologies. *International Journal of Accounting*, 21(1), 81–100.

International Accounting Standards Committee (IASC) (1982). *Objectives and Procedures*. London: IASC.

International Accounting Standards Committee (IASC). (1983). *Objectives and Procedures*. London: IASC.

International Accounting Standards Committee (IASC). (1988). *Survey of the Use and Application of International Accounting Standards*. London: IASC.

International Accounting Standards Committee (IASC) (1989). *Exposure Draft No. 32: Comparability of Financial Statements*. London: IASC.

International Capital Markets Group (ICMG) (1992). *Harmonization of International Accounting Standards*. London: ICMG.

International Finance Corporation (IFC) (1994). *Emerging Stock Markets Factbook 1994*. Washington, D.C.: IFC.

International Finance Corporation (IFC) (1998). *Emerging Stock Markets Factbook 1998*. Washington, D.C.: IFC.

International Finance Corporation (IFC) (2000). *Emerging Stock Markets Factbook 2000*. New York: Standard & Poors'.

International Monetary Fund (IMF) (1992). *Private Market Financing for Developing Countries.* Washington, D.C.: IMF.

International Monetary Fund. 1994. International Capital Markets: Developments, Prospects, and Policy Issues. Washington, D.C.: IMF.

Kelly, J. (1998a). World Bank warns Big Five over global audit standards: Action may speed up international code. *Financial Times*, (October 19), 2.

Kelly, J. (1998b). Big Five accountants face UN criticism over audits. *Financial Times*, (October 26), 2.

Kondo, M. (1992). AFTA: A win-win game. *The Asian Manager*, (Nov.–Dec.), 28–32.

Larson, R. K. (1993). An empirical investigation of the relationships between international accounting standards, equity markets and economic growth in developing countries. Unpublished Ph.D. dissertation, University of Utah.

Lee, C., & Choi, F. D. S. (1992). Effects of alternative goodwill treatments on merger premia: Further empirical evidence. *Journal of International Financial Management and Accounting*, *4*(3), 220–236.

Lev, B. (1988). Towards a theory of equitable and efficient accounting policy. *The Accounting Review*, *63*(1), 1–23.

Malle, S. (1994). From market to capitalism: The building of institutional ethics. *Journal of Public Policy*, *14*(1), 1–16.

Meek, G. K. (1983). U.S. securities market responses to alternative earnings disclosures of non-U.S. multinational corporations. *Accounting Review*, *58*(2), 394–402.

Meek, G., & Saudagaran, S. M. (1990). A survey of research on financial reporting in a trans-national context. *Journal of Accounting Literature*, *9*, 145–182.

Mueller, G. G. (1997). Harmonization efforts in the European Union. In: F. D. S. Choi (Ed.), *International Accounting and Finance Handbook* (2nd ed., pp. 11.1–11.34). New York: Wiley.

Ndubizu, G. A. (1992). Accounting disclosure methods and economic development: A criterion for globalizing capital markets. *International Journal of Accounting*, *27*(2), 151–163.

Ninsuvannakul, P. (1986). The Development of the Accounting Profession of the ASEAN Countries: Past, Present, and Future. In: V. K. Zimmerman (Ed.), *Recent Accounting and Economic Developments in the Far East* (pp. 115–148). Urbana-Champaign: University of Illinois.

Nobes, C. (1992). Accounting Harmonization in Europe: Process, Progress and Prospects. London: *Financial Times*.

O'Brien, R. C., & Helleiner, G. K. (1980). The political economy of information in a changing international economic order. *International Organization*, *34*(4), 445–470.

Price, M. M. (1994). *Emerging Stock Markets: A Complete Investment Guide to New Markets Around the World.* New York: McGraw-Hill.

Price Waterhouse (1992a). *Doing Business in Malaysia.* Kuala Lumpur: Price Waterhouse.

Price Waterhouse (1992b). *Doing Business in Singapore.* Singapore: Price Waterhouse.

Purvis, S. E. C., Gernon, H., & Diamond, M. A. (1991). The IASC and its comparability project: Prerequisites for success. *Accounting Horizons*, *5*(June), 25–44.

Rivera, J. M. (1989). The internationalization of accounting standards: Past problems and current prospects. *International Journal of Accounting*, *24*(4), 320–341.

Rivera, J. M., & Salva, A. S. (1995). On the regional approach to accounting principles harmonization: A time for Latin American integration? *Journal of International Accounting Auditing and Taxation*, *4*(1), 87–100.

Samuels, J. M., & Oliga, J. C. (1982). Accounting standards in developing countries. *International Journal of Accounting*, *18*(Fall), 69–88.

Saudagaran S. M., & Biddle, G. C. (1992). Financial disclosure levels and foreign stock exchange listing decisions. *Journal of International Financial Management and Accounting, 4*(2), 106–147.

Saudagaran S. M., & Biddle, G. C. (1995). Foreign Listing Location: A study of MNCs and stock exchanges in eight countries. *Journal of International Business Studies, 26*(2), 319–341.

Saudagaran, S. M., & Diga, J. G. (1997). The impact of capital market developments on accounting regulatory policy in emerging markets: A study of ASEAN. *Research in Accounting Regulation, 11*(Supplement 1), 3–48.

Saudagaran, S. M., & Meek, G. K. (1997). A review of research on the relationship between international capital markets and financial reporting by multinational firms. *Journal of Accounting Literature, 16*, 127–159.

SyCip, Gorres, Velayo & Co (SGV) (1984). *Comparative Accounting Practices in ASEAN.* Manila: SGV Group.

Tarumizu, K. (1991). The role of capital markets in Asian economic development. In: S. G. Rhee & R. P. Chang (Eds), *Pacific Basin Capital Markets Research.* Amsterdam: North-Holland.

Tay, J. S. W., & Parker, R. H. (1990). Measuring international harmonization and standardization. *Abacus*, (March), 71–87.

Thorell, P., & Whittington, G. (1994). The harmonization of accounting within the EU: Problems, perspectives and strategies. *European Accounting Review, 3*(2), 215–239.

United Nations Center on Transnational Corporations (UNCTC) (1982). *Towards International Standardization of Corporate Accounting and Reporting.* New York: United Nations.

Van Agtmael, A. W. (1984). *Emerging Securities Markets.* London: Euromoney.

Van der Tas, L. G. (1988). Measuring harmonization of financial reporting practice. *Accounting and Business Research, 19*(Spring), 157–169.

Van Duyn, A. (1993). Taiwan emerges on top. *Euromoney*, (December), 68–70.

Van Hulle, K. (1992) Harmonization of accounting standards: A view from the European Community. *European Accounting Review, 1*(1), 161–172.

Wallace, R. S. O. (1993). Development of accounting standards for developing and newly industrialized countries. *Research in Third World Accounting, 1*, 121–165.

Walter, I. (1993). Emerging equity markets: Tapping into global investment flows. *ASEAN Economic Bulletin, 10*(1), 1–19.

World Bank (1989). *World Development Report 1989.* New York: Oxford University Press.

World Bank (1990). *Financial Systems and Development.* Washington, D.C.: International Bank for Reconstruction and Development.

World Bank (1998). *World Development Report 1998.* New York: Oxford University Press.

13. ACCOUNTING EDUCATION AND TRAINING IN ASEAN: THE WESTERN INFLUENCE AND THE EXPERIENCE OF SINGAPORE, MALAYSIA, INDONESIA AND BRUNEI DARUSSALAM

P. W. Senarath Yapa

ABSTRACT

In the last two decades, most countries, including ASEAN have begun to take on their own individual identity and have gradually embarked on the social, political and economic routes that they consider best for their future existence and economic development. It seems that many countries that had colonial influence on their accounting education and training systems are now starting to take a closer look at the structures and institutions which they inherited at independence and are studying how these should be reformed. This paper provides an analysis of the nature of accounting education and training in four ASEAN countries – Singapore, Malaysia, Indonesia, and Brunei Darussalam. All these countries were under colonial rule for centuries. Therefore, this paper provides a review of colonial influence on accounting education and training and gives an insight into

Research in Accounting in Emerging Economies, Volume 5, pages 267–292.
ISBN: 0-7623-0901-6

why some countries are still following the colonial system while others have shifted away. However, while Singapore has shown signs of moving away from the colonial system, Malaysia seems to be in the process of such a move. Apparently, Indonesia has moved from the Dutch to the U.S. system in its accounting education and training. Brunei Darussalam is still at the rudimentary stage of its accounting development and is following the British system of accounting education to produce accountants. This paper indicates that if ASEAN countries continue to depend heavily on colonial system of accounting education and training without considering the local environment, institutions and the local economic needs, the consequences would be less than desirable.

INTRODUCTION

During the past two decades, many developing countries including the Association of South East Asian Nations (ASEAN) have shown signs of erosion from colonial influences. In the early years of the colonial period, trade and investment in these countries were set up by British, Dutch and U.S. investors. Therefore, the law enforcement, government administration as well as the education and training in ASEAN, were developed under the direct control of such colonial powers. In recent years, however, there has been tremendous interest in improving the accounting profession in ASEAN mainly due to its impact on economic development (Briston, 1990; Cruz, 1993; World Bank. 1993). A growing body of literature has examined various aspects of the accounting systems and their implications for ASEAN. However, one aspect that has not received adequate attention is the continuing colonial influence on accounting education and training. In ASEAN, accounting was introduced not because it was needed for development, but because it was needed to facilitate the accounting and reporting requirements of Western corporations operating in those countries. An examination of accounting systems of a number of ASEAN countries reveals that colonial influence is very long standing even after several decades of their independence. Apparently, they still follow the same inappropriate systems on their accounting practice and education (Briston, 1978; Hove, 1986: Yapa & Wijewardena, 1996, Yapa, 1999a, 2000). However, some of the countries, particularly Newly Industrialized Countries (NICs) have successfully adopted accounting systems to suit their local needs and to suit international standards[1] (Tang & Tse, 1986; Tipgos, 1987; World Bank, 1993).

The purpose of this paper is to contribute to this debate by presenting available evidence from an analysis of the existing system of accounting education and training initiatives in four ASEAN countries – Singapore, Malaysia,

Brunei Darussalam and Indonesia[2] – and gain insights into why some countries are still following the colonial system while others have gradually shifted away. The choice of Singapore, Malaysia, Brunei, and Indonesia was made because they were countries under two different colonial masters, i.e. British and Dutch for centuries. Eventually, Malaysia, Brunei and Singapore followed the British approach in accounting education and practice while Indonesia, until recent past, followed the Dutch system. Where relevant, the experiences of these countries have been compared and contrasted in order to identify key inferences in a wider perspective. The paper is not intended to be a comprehensive study of the subject, its scope and depth being constrained by limited available evidence. Its modest objective is to lay the groundwork for the conceptualization of further studies and identify direction for future research.

COLONIAL INFLUENCE ON CORPORATE LEGAL ENVIRONMENT

As a regional grouping, ASEAN has attracted much interest because of its remarkable economic growth. The ASEAN was formed on August 8, 1967, as a regional political and economic grouping consisting of Indonesia, Malaysia, the Philippines, Singapore and Thailand. Brunei Darussalam became the sixth member of ASEAN in 1984, and Vietnam which joined in 1995 promises to be an example of a country with rapid economic and social change in the near future. Economic ties between ASEAN countries seem destined to become stronger with ASEAN's commitment to create an ASEAN Free Trade Area (AFTA) by 2003. AFTA's aim is to create minimum barriers to trade and invest-ment among ASEAN member countries. This will be accomplished by reducing tariff on a wide range of products and by harmonizing regulations relating to trade and investment (Craig & Diga, 1996). In order to ensure a sustainable development of trade and investment, a pronounced legal system is essential. The way in which national legal practices developed in these countries is open to conjecture with a number of factors operating in conjunction. Accordingly, ASEAN countries have adopted a legal and microeconomic approach with regard to financial reporting practices and regulations, not only because of their colonial links, but also because it was perceived to be more convenient with the regulatory system of their governments. However, the argument is that most developing countries including ASEAN have adopted legislation of the colonial powers without due regard to their local conditions even after their independence. As stated by Briston:

> In a number of countries, of course the British influence is very long standing, and almost all of the colonial territories in which any substantial degree of industrial development took

place under British rule will have had imposed upon them a British Companies Act with
the usual reporting and auditing requirement (Briston, 1978, p. 108).

In this context, the comparative analysis of national corporate and companies
laws within ASEAN suggests four patterns of development: (1) A British
approach (adopted by Brunei, Malaysia and Singapore); (2) A Dutch approach
(adopted by Indonesia); (3) A U.S. approach (adopted by the Philippines); and
(4) A mixed-country approach (adopted by Thailand) (Craig & Diga, 1996).
Accordingly, Brunei, Malaysia, and Singapore (all former British colonies), have
each adopted a Companies Act modeled on the U.K. Companies Act 1948 and
the Australian Uniform Companies Act 1961 (Pillai, 1984; Price Waterhouse,
1991, 1992a, b). However, the Companies Act of Singapore has undergone
considerable changes since first enacted in 1967 (CCH, 1990). Indonesian
Commercial Code, 1848, was patterned on the early Dutch Commercial Code
with some minor amendments. Under this system, law is codified, and company
legislation prescribes rules in detail for accounting and financial reporting.
Unfortunately, many of the amendments that have been made in the Netherlands
since 1848 were not incorporated in the Commercial Code in Indonesia. As a
result, Indonesia is operating an out of date commercial code adopted in the
nineteenth century that is incompatible with today's commercial environment.
However, a new Companies law was introduced in 1995 to take effect from
1996 (Samidjo, 1985; Briston, 1990; Diga & Yunus, 1997). It is, therefore,
obvious that company laws in ASEAN have been affected strongly by each
country's former colonial links despite the appropriateness of such legislation
to its environment. British group (Brunei, Malaysia, Singapore) was mainly
influenced by Britain and non-British group (mainly the Philippines, Thailand
and Indonesia) was influenced by U.S., Japan, the Netherlands and Germany,
reflecting its important trading links with these major economic powers during
the late 1800s and early 1900s (Maolanond & Yasuda, 1985; Yasuda, 1993).
With this backdrop, it is obvious that accounting practice which is a product
of accounting education and training in ASEAN has been structured based on
the corporate legal environment created by the colonial powers during their
administration without due regard to local needs and conditions.

The theoretical framework is outlined in the next section. There then follows
an analysis and a comparison of the accounting education and training at the
tertiary level of four ASEAN countries which attempts to address the issues
outlined in this present section. The concluding section highlights the issue of
local and regional needs and educational facilities which could be utilized
appropriately to produce accountants to solve problems of economic development.

THEORETICAL FRAMEWORK

In the early 1960s, many researchers both in developed and developing nations held the view that transferring accounting technology from developed countries would be necessary for enhancing accounting education and practice in developing countries (DCs) and it could be achieved through financial and technical assistance from developed countries (Brookner & Heilman, 1960; Engelmann, 1962; Lowe, 1967; Salas, 1967; Chu, 1969). Salas (1967) conducted a comparative survey of accounting education and practice in several Spanish Latin American countries (Argentina, Bolivia, Chile, Colombia, Central Guatemala, Dominican Republic, Ecuador, Mexico, Paraguay, Peru, Uruguay, Venezuela and five other central American countries). In this study involving 136 universities in 17 countries, he concluded that most of the problems associated with accounting education in Spanish Latin America could be satisfactorily overcome by obtaining assistance from American universities. Similarly, in a study by Chu (1969) it was asserted that the shortage of accounting educators was a major barrier to the development of accounting education and practice in Taiwan and it could be overcome by setting up suitable exchange programs with developed countries.

The Committee on international Accounting Operation and Education of the American Accounting Association (AAA) suggested a framework of accounting educational assistance for DCs. The Committee held the opinion that the AAA could play a vital role in improving accounting education and practice in DCs (AAA, 1978, p. 79).

It is evident from numerous studies that accounting technology has been transferred to DCs from developed countries in the West in several different ways. Wallace (1990) has provided four possible explanations for this transfer. His first explanation points to the 'void theory' which suggests that the absence of an organized body of knowledge in one country leads ultimately to the imitation of the systems of another country (Wilkinson, 1965, p. .3). The second explanation is the 'direct investment theory' which suggests that foreign direct investors can easily impose the accounting requirements of their countries in the recipient country (Wilkinson, 1965, p. 12). The third explanation is the 'dependency theory' which suggests that former colonies find themselves bound and/or attached to the systems of the former colonizer (Seidler, 1967; Walton, 1986). The fourth explanation is the "bandwagon effect" which suggests that seemingly independent countries opt to follow the lead of another group of countries.

A study by Zeff (1972) reported that the Mexican accounting practice was influenced to a great extent by the U.S. practice. Similarly, Hardman (1984) pointed out that the many South Pacific countries, especially Fiji and Solomon Islands, have been influenced by Australian and New Zealand accounting education and practice. Bait-el-Mal, Smith and Taylor (1973) observed the British and the U.S. influence on Libyan accounting system. Mepham (1977) in a study on the development of accounting profession in Jamaica revealed how the Institute of Chartered Accountants of Jamaica has been influenced by international and British accounting standards. Markell (1985) observed that university accounting programs in Southern African Development Conference Countries (SADCC) have been heavily biased towards American accounting programs. Carmony (1987) in his study based on the Uruguayan case, reported that the majority of accounting influences originated from the U.S. or the U.K. Although the English influence was strong in Uruguay during 1890s, with the subsequent military government its accounting and reporting practices were upgraded through regulation in accordance with the U.S. accounting standards. Similar U.S. influence was visible in the university accounting education system in Uruguay.

Five types of zones have been identified in the process of transferring accounting technology to DCs: British, Franco-Spanish-Portuguese, Germanic/ Dutch, United States and Communistic (AAA, 1977, 1978; Enthoven, 1983). This division of accounting systems into five historical zones of influence suggests that accounting education and practice underlying financial measurement and disclosure in different countries and regions depend on such historical variables as colonial experience and/or colonial affinity. On the basis of this argument, many scholars asserted that the accounting systems have been moved from developed countries to DCs through colonial influence, political affiliations, powerful investors or multinational companies who invested large amounts of capital in these countries (Wilkinson, 1965; Radebaugh, 1975; Briston, 1978; Perera, 1980; Chandler & Holzer, 1984).

Another important fact is that English has become the second language of many DCs and accounting text books are rarely available in their local languages. Therefore, these countries invariably have to use British, American or Australian texts for accountancy education and training (Wallace & Briston, 1993; Ndzinge, 1994). It is apparent from the reported studies that in most of the DCs, education in accounting was initiated by colonial powers during the periods of their rule. Even after gaining independence most of these countries could not free themselves from these influences. For example, the influence of British accounting is still highly reflected on accounting education and practices in most of the Association of South East Asian Nations (ASEAN), India, Pakistan, Sri Lanka and Bangladesh. Similarly, accounting education and practices in former French colonies like Algeria, Tunisia, and the West African states basically followed the French system of accounting (Briston, 1978; Enthoven, 1979).

Although a growing body of literature has examined various aspects of the accounting systems and their implications for ASEAN, as far as this writer is aware, one aspect that has not received adequate attention is the continuing colonial influence on accounting education and training. This is the task of the sections that follow.

ACCOUNTING EDUCATION AND TRAINING AT TERTIARY AND PROFESSIONAL LEVELS IN ASEAN

Singapore

Historically, except for the brief Japanese occupation in the 1940s, Singapore was a British colony for nearly one and a half centuries until its independence in 1959. Consequently, its general education from primary to university level was inherited from the British education system, and accounting education was no exception. The British system of accounting education was imposed on Singapore during the colonial period in a number of ways: (1) the export of British accounting personnel to Singapore; (2) the export of British accounting qualifications; (3) the establishment of British professional accounting bodies' examination centres; (4) the involvement of British experts in the planning, directing, organizing, teaching and providing assistance in one form or another in the development of academic institutions in Singapore; and (5) the general British influence upon the business, education and administrative environments in the early days of Singapore (Foo, 1988).

Prior to 1956, Singapore did not have any program of studies leading to a local qualification in accounting. The only accounting education available was through the examinations conducted by professional accounting bodies overseas, such as the Association of Certified Corporate Accountants of the United Kingdom (ACCA), the Institute of Cost and Works Accountants of the United Kingdom (ICWA), and the Australian Society of Accountants (ASA). As such, a foreign professional accounting qualification was the only avenue through which a person could expect an accounting job, particularly a job in the public sector. The first local accounting program leading to a Bachelor of Commerce with specialization in accounting was launched by the Nanyang University in 1956. In the following year, the Department of Commerce at the Singapore Polytechnic was established to offer, among other courses, a full-time course leading to the College Diploma in accounting (Fong & Foo, 1992). In 1958, the Department of Cornmerce at the Singapore Polytechnic was replaced by the Departrnent of Accountancy with the objective of offering both full-time and part-time courses leading to a Professional Diploma in Accounting

(Tan et al., 1994). Soon after gaining political independence, the authorities in Singapore realized the importance of producing accountants through their own higher educational institutions without depending on foreign accounting bodies and what was perceived to be out-dated education systems. Consequently, the professional accounting diploma awarded by the Singapore Polytechnic was recognized in 1963 as an adequate qualification for admission to provisional membership of the Singapore Society of Accountants (SSA). The SSA was the local professional accounting body established by the government for the purposes of registering professional accountants and regulating the practice of the profession of accountancy in Singapore. During the 1965–1966 academic year, the Department of Accountancy at the Singapore Polytechnic was renamed the School of Accountancy and the accountancy program was upgraded from a diploma to a university degree to signify the transformation of this poly-technic to a university college. As a result of negotiations between the college and the University of Singapore, the latter agreed to award its accounting degree to students of the Singapore Polytechnic. In 1969, the amalgamation of the School of Accountancy with the Department of Business Administration of the University of Singapore represented another milestone in the historical development of an independent accounting education system in Singapore (Sunday Times, 1968). At the time of the merger, the School of Accountancy was relocated to the University of Singapore campus. As a further development in 1971, the Bachelor of Commerce (Accountancy) program offered by Nanyang University since 1956 also received its professional recognition, subject to prac-tical training, from the Singapore Society of Accountants. In 1978, joint courses in accounting were introduced by the Nanyang University and the University of Singapore. The two schools of accountancy merged in 1980 to form the School of Accountancy at the National University of Singapore.

After the recognition of the Singaporean university system through the forma-tion of the National University of Singapore and the Nanyang Technological Institute, the country's accounting education system achieved its highest growth rate. The School of Accountancy of the National University of Singapore was physically relocated at the Nanyang Technological Institute in 1987 and the School of Accountancy was renamed the School of Accountancy and Business in 1990. In 1991, the Nanyang Technological Institute became a fully-fledged university and is now named the Nanyang Technological University (NTU). The School of Accountancy and Business of this university has gained a reputation today as the leading center for undergraduate and post-graduate accounting education in Southeast Asia. The bachelor of accounting degree awarded by the Nanyang Technological University is based on a 3-year full-time program of study. In addition to its Bachelor of Accountancy degree program, it also offers a professional postgraduate program leading to a Master of Business Administration in Accounting. Both these accounting degrees are recognized by the Institute of Certified Public Accountants of Singapore (ICPAS) for admission to its membership, subject to approved practical experience. The Bachelor of Accountancy program of NTU, at its various stages of development, has produced nearly 10,000 accounting graduates. By the end of 1992, 7,442 of these graduates had become professional accountants by obtaining ICPAS memberships. In addition to the undergraduate degree, the School of Accountancy and Business at NTU also offers two postgraduate research degree programs leading to the Master of Accountancy (M.Acc) and the Doctor of Philosophy (Ph.D.) in Accounting (Wee, 1994).

Since its inception, the Singapore professional accounting body[3] has maintained a close relationship with the university's School of Accountancy. This liaison is evidenced by the fact that the Institute was consulted at each stage of the transition of the School from the Singapore Polytechnic to the present Nanyang Technological University. A representative of the School of Accountancy and Business is appointed by the Minister of Finance as a statutory member of the Council of the ICPAS. Through various committees, the School of Accountancy and Business also maintains close rapport with the professional accounting body, business community and other professional organizations to ensure the continuing relevance of its degree programs (Tan et al., 1994; Wijewardena & Yapa, 1998).

It appears that during the post-independence period as a booming economy, Singapore has been able to consider her national goals, political climate, economic environments and efficiency in utilizing educational resources, including universities and technical colleges, in order to develop a system of accounting education and training more suitable to her local conditions. Further, the coordination between the universities and the ICPAS has improved strong initiatives to manage and improve accounting education and to respond to changing environments by producing adequate numbers of locally qualified accountants.

Indonesia

Accountancy development in Indonesia can be traced back to 1642, the year in which the Dutch Governor General of the Netherlands East Indies issued regulations concerning the administration of accounting for garrisons. Historically, the Dutch system of accounting education was imposed on Indonesia during the colonial period in a number of ways: (1) the involvement of Dutch experts in planning, directing, organizing, teaching, and providing assistance in the development of academic institutions in Indonesia; (2) the export of Dutch accounting qualifications; and (3) compulsory membership of the Netherlands Institute of Accountants (Foo, 1988; Briston et al., 1990; Abdoelkadir & Yunus, 1994).

In 1907 the first government accountant was sent to Indonesia from the Netherlands to open the State Audit Agency. Based on the growing needs in the country, Dutch administration realized that the number of bookkeepers produced by the schools was inadequate. The main reason for such a shortage was that bookkeeping was first taught at high schools and special schools such as the Handelschool or the Middelbare Handelschool (schools specializing in trade). Enrolment in these schools was usually limited to Indonesians with special status, such as the children of the head of a district or the children of a wealthy businessman (Abdoelkadir & Yunus, 1994). Therefore, in 1925, the Trade Teachers Association or Union of Trade/Commerce Education (Bond Van Vereniging Voor Handle Onderwijs) organized two courses on book-keeping classified as Bond A and Bond B equivalent to basic and intermediate accounting courses respectively, to remedy the shortage of accounting personnel. Accordingly, holders of Bond A certificates were mostly employed by small trading companies while Bond B holders were employed by large companies (Sembiring, 1984). The Bond conducted a uniform examination and issued its own certificate. However, Japanese occupation of Indonesia from 1942 to 1945 created a large number of accounting positions which were held by the Dutch in the Ministry of Finance and those positions had to be filled instantly. The Japanese eventually offered four different accounting courses to train Indonesians to take up these positions. These are: course A for the post of assistant inspector for the Ministry of Finance (applicants had to be lawyers and had to undergo six months of training); course B, which was initially divided into course B-1 for Tax controllers and course B-2 for tax offices. The courses were later merged into one course and applicants had to be high school graduates, and the training lasted for one year. Course C was for assistant accountant posts and applicants for this course had to be high school graduates, and the training period was three years. The qualification conferred on successful candidates was equivalent to a Bachelor of Arts degree. Course D was for the position of bookkeeper and applicants had to be graduates from Middlebare Handelschool (schools specializing in trade). The training was only for one year. This certificate was later considered as equivalent to Bond B (Abdoelkadir, 1982; Abdoelkadir & Yunus, 1994). With the surrender of the Japanese in 1945, the Dutch returned to Indonesia and continued the educa-tion system in accounting as before with the Bond A and Bond B courses (Briston et al., 1990). In addition to Bond A and B, another Moderne Bedrijft

Administrative (MBA) certificate was introduced by the Dutch in 1948 and conducted by a private institution mainly for executive positions in Indonesia. These courses mainly combined the curricula of cost accounting and advanced accounting. Later the MBA courses were known as Administrasi Perusahaan Moderen (AMP) and directed by the Ministry of Education (Enthoven, 1974; Hadibroto, 1984).

In 1952, the Economics Faculty of the University of Indonesia established an Accounting Department and it was the first institution in Indonesia to offer a formal accounting program at the higher educational level. Eventually, in 1957 the first four Indonesian accountants graduated. State universities[4] outside Jakarta later offered accounting programs. Moreover, a few private universities such as Universitas Parahiyangan in Bandung (1965), Universitas Trisakti (1969), Universitas Tarumanegara (1972) and Universitas Atmajaya (1973) in Jakarta also offered accounting programs. Some accounting programs in Indonesia are conducted within the Faculty of Economics, where specialization in accountancy occurs after the second or third year of a five-year master's (Sarjana) program which is obviously a typical Dutch approach to accounting education. Upon completion of the Sarjana program, a graduate was awarded a 'doctorandus' degree. Others followed the 'guided study system' which was modeled after the plan used in the U.S. According to this study system, a student could earn both baccalaureate and master's degree in accounting in five years. This dualism in methods of accounting education persisted until recently in Indonesia (Briston et al., 1990; Abdoelkadir & Yunus, 1994).

A new law called 'The Accountancy Law No. 34 of 1954' restricted the use of the designation 'Akuntan' (Accountant) to individuals holding a 'doctorandus' degree from a recognized tertiary academic institution. Before the enactment of the Accountancy Law, it was not possible for Indonesians to qualify as professional accountants unless they studied in the Netherlands and became members of the Netherlands Institute of Accountants (Foo, 1988; Diga & Yunus, 1997). This law enabled any Indonesian to become a registered accountant by obtaining a master's degree (Sarjana) in accounting either from a state university, from an accredited private university or from the State School of Government Accounting (STAN).[5] The vast majority of registered accountants in Indonesia have qualified from the STAN and state universities with accredited accountancy programs. Graduates from unaccredited institutions (mostly private institutions) must pass an examination organized by the 'Committee of Experts' appointed by the Ministry of Education and Culture. Surprisingly, only a few graduates passed the examinations and reached 'Sarjana' level set by the Committee of Experts. For example, out of the 2,536 graduates at the bachelor level, produced by private universities in 1978, only

12 of them have reached the 'Sarjana' level. Those who qualified through these processes are required to register with the Directorate of State Accountancy in the Ministry of Finance. However, before being allowed to establish a public accounting firm, a qualified person must have worked for the government for a period of at least three years. This was required by Act No. 8 of 1961 and the objective was to ensure that the government was able to meet some of its staffing needs in the field of accountancy (Briston et al., 1990). Nevertheless, in Indonesia, the awareness of the accounting profession was formally recognized with the enactment of the foreign investment law of 1967, followed by a domestic investment law in 1968 (Ninsuvannakul, 1988).

The nationalization of Dutch-owned companies in 1957 and the resultant departure of Dutch nationals created a vacuum of adequately qualified and experienced manpower to higher echelons of managerial, accounting and academic positions. This indicates that during the Dutch colonial days, Indonesians had been less motivated for such training and experience and eventually only a few were trained after independence.

The main impact on accounting education in Indonesia due to the departure of the Dutch was the gradual adoption of U.S. accounting systems. With the assistance of the Ford Foundation, the University of California (Berkeley, USA) provided the teaching staff, on a five-year contract, to the University of Indonesia, at the same time providing opportunities for Indonesians to study in the U.S. The Ford Foundation also assisted Gadjah Mada University, which was affiliated with the University of Wisconsin. From that time, the American influence began to gain momentum in Indonesia. However, the Dutch influence did not completely disappear. This state of dualism has continued because graduates of both systems were in demand by the industry and commerce. Moreover, the accountants in senior positions in various organizations preferred to hire junior accountants with Dutch accounting backgrounds. Under the Dutch system of accounting training, the emphasis was more on general and business economics, often using out-of-date, translated Dutch text books. The universities of Airlangga and Pajajaran followed the Dutch system until 1977 when the Consortium of Economics Science (CES) was formed and introduced a common educational system for all universities, based largely upon the American approach (Briston et al., 1990). As a result of these developments, problems of dualism emerged mainly due to poor coordination within the education and training system. In late 1984, to coordinate the accounting education system and to eliminate dualism, the World Bank recommended that the Indonesian government establish a coordinating agency. In 1985, the Ministry of Finance and the Ministry of Education and Culture in a joint decree established the Coordinating Agency for Accounting Development (CAAD) with a full-time executive Secretary. The objectives of CAAD were to improve accounting standards and practices in the government and private sector, to organize the application of accounting standards and practices in stages and to develop a uniform and unified accounting educational system (Abdelkadir & Yunus, 1994). Under these arrangements, extensive feasibility studies were conducted and a principal project was introduced, costing about $165 million covering a five-year period. However, even in this project, there seems to be serious problems such as lack of professional and technical staff that are adequately trained in modern methods of accountancy, the deficiencies in government accounting, shortcomings of the government budget process, scarcity of competent government accountants and auditors, private sector shortage of accountants with up-to-date skills. To some extent this situation can be attributed to a general absence in Indonesian law of regulations relating to accounting. The Indonesian Companies' Act and the Commercial Code, as mentioned earlier, are anachronisms dating back to colonial times and are silent on accounting matters. Thus, there are no statutory reporting requirements and audit requirements except for listed companies. Secondly, Indonesian Accounting Institute (IAI)[6] which is the only recognized professional accountancy body, is relatively young and not well developed. Therefore, Indonesia has to go a long way to seek improvement to these problems (Abdoelkadir & Yunus, 1994). There are currently over 85 universities, institutes and academies in Indonesia and they offer post-secondary accounting programs. Despite these universities and institutions, Indonesia has not been able to produce adequately qualified accountants to meet the demand from commerce, industry and the government sector.

It appears that Indonesia suffers from an acute shortage of well qualified accountants during the post-independence period as a result of inconsistent and uncoordinated adoption of the Anglo-Saxon systems in its economy. It seems that although CAAD is working towards a relevant and feasible solution in the long run, it apparently still requires the proper coordination with many sectors of the economy. Therefore, there seems to be serious doubts about such coordination in accounting education and the desire of CAAD to respond to changing circumstances by producing adequate numbers of locally qualified accountants.

Malaysia

Accounting education and practice in Malaysia have been developed as a result of British influence. As Sheridan (1961) points out, throughout its history, company law in Malaysia has always been geared to its English counterpart even if the imitatory machinery has been somewhat slow in functioning.

Malaysia's accounting education in its recognizable form exists only after independence in 1958. Prior to this, Malaysians were sent to the U.K. for British professional accounting qualifications such as Chartered Accountancy (CA) and Association of Certified and Corporate Accountants (ACCA). However, after independence, twenty local accountants incorporated the Malaysian Association of Certified Public Accountants (MACPA). In 1961, the council of MACPA began setting local examinations and much of the training and education for these examinations was provided through in-house courses and articleship. Formal courses to assist students who were preparing for MACPA examinations were introduced in the seventies. Presently, MACPA has designated some institutions to run accountancy courses on its behalf. They are: Tunku Abdul Rahman College and the Damansara Utama College which are running as private colleges in Malaysia. The government institution to conduct courses on behalf of MACPA is Institute Teknologi MARA (ITM). In 1967, mainly to regulate the accounting profession and accounting practice in Malaysia, the Accountants' Act 1967, which is administered by the Ministry of Finance, was passed by Parliament and eventually the Malaysian Institute of Accountants (MIA) was formed. Until about 1987 this body was rather inactive and its functions were mainly to register accountants who were aspiring to become practicing accountants. However, from 1990, MIA has initiated the setting of its own examinations. The MACPA is a self-regulating professional body and most of the members of this body are holding the membership of MIA.

It was only in the seventies that the new development emerged in accounting education in Malaysia. The local universities and institutions of higher learning began to set up programs offering courses leading to degrees or diplomas in accountancy. Accounting programs are currently offered by University of Malaya (UM), University Kebangsan Malaysia (UKM), Universiti Utara Malaysia (UUM), Institut Teknologi MARA (ITM) and Universiti Pertanian Malaysia (UPM). In broad terms, there are no significant differences between the programs at UKM, UUM, UPM and ITM which tend towards a structure emphasizing general education, followed by specialization in accounting supported by a fair proportion of contextual Business and Economics and related disciplinary studies. UM differs only to the extent that its program concentrates on accounting studies with less emphasis on general education. In all the degree programs, the duration of study is four years, except for ITM which requires a total of five and one half years. UKM, UUM, and ITM require mandatory practical attachment as an integral part of their programs. In addition to this, a student can qualify as an accountant by sitting and passing the examinations set by MACPA. There are three stages of MACPA examinations which consist of Foundation Examination and two Professional Examinations. There are three streams of the professional examinations. Under Stream one, students may work as articled clerks and study for the examination at the same time. Those who are opting for Stream two, qualify through attachment with members in the employment of a commercial, industrial or public sector organization subject to sitting and passing the prescribed examinations. In Stream three, students undertake full-time study prior to articleship. Because of this flexibility in professional accounting education, and with the increase in demand for accounting-related services, more and more students enter into the accounting discipline. At present there are several avenues for aspiring individuals to seek accounting education for purposes of certification to enter the profession in Malaysia. As mentioned above, four local institutions of higher learning provide accounting programs leading to certification (subject to the duration of approved practical training) accepted by the MIA. Apart from this, MIA also accepts qualified members of the local professional body and qualified members from overseas accounting bodies.[7] Therefore, a substantial number of students are enrolled in British professional accounting bodies. Many of the candidates studying for the professional certificate examinations of ACCA and Chartered Institute of Management Accountants (CIMA) in the U.K. do it on a part-time basis whilst continuing with their careers in Malaysia. It has been argued that U.K. accounting is not obviously appropriate for developing nations as solutions to the problems faced by those countries (Wallace, 1990). Although British professional accounting centres were set up in Malaysia in 1935 and continued to conduct examinations purely on the British model, more recently, however, partial adaptation of British professional accounting examinations into Malaysia through formal links has brought up an improvement for their needs. For example, ACCA adapts local law and taxation suitable to Malaysian environment to reflect the local circumstances (Johnson & Caygill, 1971: Briston & Kedslie, 1997). As such, the number of qualified accountants needed to support the economic development of Malaysia has increased substantially.

Given the scenario above, it is obvious that much of the accounting education has been assumed by the universities or institutions of higher learning in coordination with the professional bodies in Malaysia. More and more universities are offering programs leading to degrees in accounting and these programs are apparently, recognized by the local professional body. University of Malaysia and University Kebangsaan Malaysia are encouraging potential local and foreign accounting students to pursue a career in accounting. The MARA Institute of Technology has also started an advanced Diploma in Accountancy course. Moreover, arrangements have been made to obtain accounting degrees from overseas universities through educational link programs with local higher learning institutions. However, professional bodies will accept almost anyone over the age of 18 with minimum entry qualifications. Under the provision of the Accountants Act of 1967, it is stipulated, among other things, that no one can declare himself or practice as an accountant unless he is registered as a member of the MIA.

It appears that during the post-independence period, as an economy that is facing the challenges of the new millennium, Malaysia has been able to consider her national goals, economic environments and efficiency in utilizing educational resources including universities and technical colleges in order to develop a system unique to her own needs and requirements. This has been achieved through the dynamism of the public and private sectors, working in tandem and in collaboration with an international network of institutions of higher leaning. Further, the coordination between the universities and the professional bodies (both local and overseas) has raised the impetus to manage and improve accounting education and to respond to changing circumstances, thus leading to the increase in the number of locally qualified accountants.

Brunei Darussalam

In Brunei Darussalam, public accountants are called registered auditors. The Brunei Institute of Certified Public Accountants (BICPA) is the sole professional accounting body. All the companies are regulated by the Companies Act (Cap 39), which is based on the U.K. 1939 Companies Act. Therefore, Britain has a dominant influence on Brunei due to its historical links with the country. For example, the country's only university revised its undergraduate program in business by introducing, inter alia, a major in accounting and finance in 1995, and established a link program leading to an accounting degree with a major British university. As another recent development, Brunei Shell Petroleum, which is the largest private sector employer with about three thousand employees, has organized for its employees an in-house course leading to the professional qualification of the Association of Accounting Technicians-U.K. (AATUK). Brunei's only technical college produces diploma holders in business and finance. This diploma has the same features as the diploma in business and finance programs offered in the U.K. 'Big Five' firms[8] are also operating in Brunei. In addition to them, another three accounting firms (one local accounting firm, one Singaporean and one Malaysian) are also contributing to the accounting profession in Brunei Darussalam. Since accounting in Brunei is in its rudimentary stage, there seems to be an urgent need to develop domestic accounting standards and secondly, it needs to increase the supply (training and education) of more accounting personnel (Yapa, 1999b).

Comparison of Accounting Education in Singapore, Malaysia, Indonesia and Brunei Darussalam

This study focuses on the basic differences between the accounting education and training systems in Singapore, Malaysia and Brunei Darussalam (British group) and Indonesia (The Dutch, or Non-British group). The analysis on the preceding three sections reveals that, despite the similar colonial influence on the four countries, there exist a number of differences between the British-group and the non-British group in terms of their accounting education systems.

The most remarkable difference is that while Singapore, within only four years of independence, has successfully moved away from the colonial system of producing accountants through professional accounting bodies, Indonesia, even after 53 years of independence, is still trying to adapt a suitable system of producing accountants to meet its local needs. Therefore, the Dutch and the U.S. systems are playing a prominent role in accounting. Although Malaysia initially followed the British colonial model, it is now in the process of producing sufficient number of accountants with a certain amount of coordination among professional bodies and universities. Only the practical training for prospective accountants and the continuing professional development programs are handled by the professional bodies. Moreover, it is interesting to note that formal links have also been set up to offer British professional examinations with a certain degree of adaptation to local needs in Malaysia.

Through a close liaison with the business community and the professional accounting body, the Singaporean university system has developed an accounting degree program which is relevant and appropriate for meeting the cultural and economic needs of the country (Teo & Low, 1993; Fong & Foo, 1992; Wee, 1994). Consequently, the accounting education and training system has enabled the ICPAS to increase its membership from 344 in 1964 to 12,000 in 1992 and concentrate more effectively on the professional development of accountants in the country (Tan et al., 1994).

Similarly, in Malaysia, there are two accounting bodies MIA and MACPA and both require a three-year university degree or equivalent for membership. MACPA is closer to the model of an independent professional body seen in many developed countries than MIA. Both MACPA and MIA have over 10,000 members working in accounting firms, commerce and industry. For example, in addition to providing professional recognition, the MACPA runs its own professional examinations and ethical pronouncements (MacGregor et al., 1997).

However, during the post-independence era, Malaysia has been able to generate required numbers of accountants for the country's needs through its university and professional education. Obviously, with the changes taking place in the environment, the accounting profession and the academia have to make corresponding reforms jointly if they are to contribute effectively and increase their relevance for micro and macro information providing mechanism. Most probably, many countries that had colonial influence on their accounting education and training systems are now starting to take a closer look at the structures and institutions which they inherited at independence and studying how they should best be reformed. In Malaysia and in Singapore, this has been possible mainly because of the proper coordination between the higher educational institutions in accounting and the professional bodies. By getting the university system to provide accounting education required for meeting the academic and professional needs, both Singapore and Malaysia have been able to produce high quality accountants locally in sufficient numbers (Tipgos, 1987; Tan et al., 1994).

However, Brunei is still in the initial stage of accounting development after nearly a decade of its independence from Britain. In academia, of course, there is a very slow growth which is mainly due to lack of local accounting education and training. Among the practicing accountants, two thirds are expatriates from Australia, Malaysia, Singapore and Sri Lanka. They hold professional memberships either from the U.K. or Australia. Therefore, British influence is very strong in Brunei. This fact is attributable to Brunei's small population and the nature of its economy, which is characterized by a relatively small private sector and the absence of a local capital market. Brunei's accounting education and training is still new but government accounting and enterprise accounting techniques and education are replicas of the British model.

In Indonesia, with the liberalization of the economic environment for foreign and domestic enterprises, the accounting profession has become an important force in the business community. As a result of these developments, an increase in the demand for professional accountants has emerged. As revealed by Price Waterhouse, in 1992, there were an estimated 11,500 accredited accountants in Indonesia (Price Waterhouse, 1992c). This is hardly sufficient for the growing demand for accounting services in the country with a population of around 200 million. By contrast, Singapore with only 3 million people has over 8,000 professional accountants today. Malaysia, with a population of 18 million, has over 11,000 locally qualified professional accountants. The shortage of qualified accountants in Indonesia was created mainly by its continuous dependence on the Dutch system even after its independence, without adjusting its education and training to meet local conditions and needs. It is evident that in Indonesia, during the Dutch administration, Indonesians were less motivated to accounting training. Therefore, most accounting positions were held by the Dutch. However, in 1958, with the expulsion of Dutch nationals, a combination of Dutch and U.S. accounting education and training was encouraged. Subsequently, in 1975 by a directive issued by the Ministry of Education and Commerce of Indonesia, accounting education and training were modeled solely on the U.S. system. This transformation gave rise to dualism in accounting practices. Obviously, the dualism resulted in enormous difficulties among employers and academic institutions who were engaged in accounting. For example, on the practical level, the implementation of the American system within an organization encountered severe resistance from senior accountants, who have usually been trained under the Dutch system (Briston et al., 1990). Therefore, there was a severe shortage of accounting personnel in the Indonesian economy. Moreover, with the increase in demand for accounting related services, more and more students realized the importance of accounting and entered into the accounting discipline. However, until the 1990s, all accounting graduates were required to serve for at least three years in government service after their graduation. Hence, there existed a fierce competition for qualified accountants in the private sector because nearly half of the qualified accountants were employed by the government service (Diga & Yunus, 1997). Consequently, the shortage of accounting personnel was further exacerbated. Moreover, it appears that the rate of failure in accounting examinations is also enormously high. As a result, the production of qualified accountants by accounting academic and professional bodies was very limited. For example, from 1980 to 1984 only five students had passed the entire professional examination, which consists of two parts, organized by the Consortium of Economic Sciences (CES). Although approximately five hundred students appeared for professional examination parts one and two in 1990, the pass rate was only 5% for the first part and only 1% for the second part of the examination (Briston et al., 1990). Several reasons seem to have contributed to these poor results by the accounting students. One principal reason is the lack of coordination within the accounting training and educational system. As mentioned earlier, dualism obviously created a tremendous amount of difficulties in the coordination of accounting education and training programs by various educational institutions. Although the route to a professional qualification is relatively straightforward, given the IAI is not an examining body so that entry is possible only through a limited number of universities plus STAN or through the professional organizations organized by the CES, these routes are very narrow and restrictive. Therefore, a large number of accountants of various levels will never have an opportunity to achieve professional recognition. Indonesia desperately needs more accountants, and it is crucial that all the accounting skills and resources available in the country should be coordinated in order to ensure that they are used as efficiently and effectively as possible (Briston et al., 1990). This is confirmed by Abdoelkadir and Yunus in their paper on 'Developments in Indonesian Accountancy' in 1994. According to them, Indonesia has a long way to go to undertake a systematic, coordinated and comprehensive approach towards accountancy development based on local needs. Moreover, the inadequate coverage of subject matter, shortage of qualified teaching staff in the study programs available to candidates, lack of text books, inappropriate curriculum and a host of other problems relating to infrastructure, have created a sombre environment for students (see Briston, 1990). Therefore, a long standing colonial influence has obviously created a severe shortage of accounting personnel in the Indonesian economy.

Another feature of the deep-rooted colonial influence in the accounting education in Indonesia is the heavy emphasis placed on financial reporting. Historically, financial accounting and reporting practices were influenced by the old Dutch systems; but decades later, they have changed significantly following the adoption of U.S. accounting systems. The bulk of graduates from STAN, the government accounting school, are placing heavy emphasis on financial reporting and auditing. This emphasis by the tertiary institutions appears irrelevant as only a handful of corporations provide financial statements and an even smaller number have their accounts audited (Briston, 1990; Diga & Yunus, 1997). Therefore, accounting education at the professional level in Indonesia places a heavy emphasis on financial reporting areas with inadequate attention being devoted to managerial accounting. As a result, accounting education in Indonesia concentrates on the technical or mechanical aspect of accounting. The development of management accounting practice and education in Indonesia is in a rudimentary stage (Diga & Yunus, 1997). In this regard, what Mueller observed in most developing countries seems to be very much applicable to Indonesia. In his study, Mueller (1988) argued that education and training systems developed specifically on the country basis, using indigenous sources, are the real hope for success in accounting education and practice in DCs (Mueller, 1988, p. 81). Referring to the direct transfer of technology, he said that:

> In practice, however, the transfer mechanism is much like yesterday's colonialism – major elements of the Dutch accounting system, for example, were transferred to Indonesia, a former Dutch colony; the French system was transferred to former French colonies in Africa and the South Pacific; the British system to most Commonwealth member countries."

He particularly described the use of foreign training and examination systems for producing local accountants in developing countries and stated that:

> The problem becomes especially acute when a specific domestic training and examination system, geared to produce a domestic professional qualification, is administered in

developed countries to enhance the local supply of qualified accountants. It's really a form of accounting colonialism: these people are "qualifying" on someone else's terms and conditions (Mueller, 1988, p. 83).

He believed that the direct transfer of Anglo-American accounting technology into developing countries has led to an appalling waste of resources. Therefore, given the nature of the Indonesian economy, the infusion of western accounting education systems may be inappropriate at this stage of development. In the area of accounting education and training, the policy decisions ought to be directed towards their relevance to local needs and benefits. As pointed out by Standish (1983), the development of entrepreneurial skills is extremely important for the developing economy like Indonesia. In Singapore, obviously, this picture is entirely different. Although the British influence was very strong in the beginning of the accounting education and training, based on the country's needs, it has been possible for them to adapt to changing environments. They have a well integrated system of accounting education linking both university and the professional body. Eventually, the university education is the first phase of the journey towards attaining the professional status of an accountant. It provides the accountant with a more liberal and broad-based education than the professional training system in the U.K. (Tang & Tse, 1986). As a result of modern amenities and infrastructure in the education system, and well developed library facilities, up-to-date accounting literature is available for wider usage. Plenty of locally developed case studies are available for both undergraduate and graduate students. The development of new technology, and access to the information super highway have especially opened up the way towards achieving the aims of accounting education in Singapore. This fact has been proved by the recent surveys and research works on employers' perceptions about accounting graduates. It states that:

92% of the employers strongly and reasonably agreed that the university education received by accounting graduates had facilitated the process of training these accountants (Teo & Low, 1993).

This situation is quite comparable with other developed and developing countries. Moreover, Singapore has been able to adapt accounting and auditing standards to fit local conditions which proved to be a flexible and cost effective approach to updating the accounting profession. Consequently, they have been able to produce sufficient numbers of accountants required by the country. Recently, the government has been encouraging Singapore companies and entrepreneurs to venture overseas as a step towards further developing the Singapore economy. Therefore, big accounting firms in Singapore are already venturing into countries like China, Vietnam and Indonesia through the setting up of representative offices, branches and joint ventures. Moreover, Singapore enjoys a high standard of living compared to other countries in this study. The successful story of Singapore may be repeated to some extent in many other developing countries with similar social and economic environments (Tang & Tse, 1986; Tipgos, 1987). This indicates how Singapore has adapted accounting education and practice to their changing environment. Therefore, the system that has been adapted by Singapore seems worthwhile and deserves the attention of the planners and policy makers of accounting education in ASEAN.

CONCLUSION

The comparative analysis of accounting education in Singapore, Malaysia, Indonesia and Brunei presented in this paper provides some evidence to confirm the generally held view that some developing countries which were colonies of western countries in the past are still following the same colonial system of accounting education, which is irrelevant and inadequate for producing accountants suitable for their economies. It also shows that Singapore which adopted the same traditional system for producing accountants during the colonial days has been able to move away from it within a few years of independence. In particular, Singapore Society of Accountants (SSA), National University of Singapore (NUS), Nanyang Technological University (NTU) have taken strong initiatives to improve accounting education and responded to changing national needs with sufficient numbers of locally qualified accountants. More importantly, the analysis signals that if a developing country continues to depend very heavily on foreign accounting bodies to produce its accountants, or adopts accounting curricula of developed Western countries for local accounting examinations without designing a curriculum to suit its own economic (particularly with AFTA) and cultural environment, the consequences can be disastrous. However, learning from countries in the region and providing necessary alternatives to improve the existing system may be a valuable effort for a foreseeable development. Therefore, it seems necessary for both political and educational authorities of such countries to pay a greater attention to accounting education and take steps to make it more relevant and appropriate for their needs so that they will be able to produce accountants who can contribute more effectively to solving the problems of economic development.

NOTES

1. Among ASEAN countries, the economies of Singapore, Malaysia and Thailand are the most outwardly oriented, i.e. they place much more emphasis on developing their export capabilities. See World Bank (1993).

2. Indonesia was selected mainly due to its large population and non-British colonial master (mainly Dutch).

3. Initially as the Singapore Society of Accountants (SSA) in 1963 and later as the Institute of Certified Public Accountants of Singapore (ICPAS) in 1987.

4. State universities outside Jakarta are; Universitas Padjadjaran in Bandung (1961), Universitas Sumatera Utara in Medan (1962), Universita Airlangga in Surabaya (1962), Universitas Gadjah Mada in Yogjakarta (1964), and Universitas Brawijaya in Malang (1977) and Universitas Andalas in Padang (1978).

5. The Ministry of Finance in Indonesia also provides accounting education to train accountants to serve the government. In 1957 it established the Sekolah Tinggi Ilmu Keuangan Negara (STIKN), which later became the Institut Ilmu Keuangan (IIK), and is now called Sekolah Tinggi Akuntansi Negara (STAN).

6. Indonesian Accounting Institute or Ikatan Akuntan Indonesia (IAI) was founded in 1957 by the first batch of graduates of the University of Indonesia accounting course. Its objectives, inter alia, are to promote the status of the accounting profession, support the national development of Indonesia, and upgrade the skills and competence of the IAIs.

7. The local professional body is the MACPA and recognized overseas professional bodies include; Institute of Chartered Accountants in England and Wales, Institute of Chartered Accountants of Scotland, Institute of Chartered Accountants of Ireland, Association of Certified Accountants (United Kingdom), Institute of Chartered Accountants in Australia, Australian Society of Accountants, Canadian Institute of Chartered Accountants, Institute of Chartered Accountants of India and Institute of Cost and Management Accountants (United Kingdom).

8. PricewaterhouseCoopers, Arthur Andersen & Co., Deloitte Touche, Tohmatsu International, Ernst & Young, KPMG Peat Marwick.

ACKNOWLEDGMENTS

The author acknowledges the helpful comments of Professor R. J. Briston, of the University of Hull, U.K., and the participants at the 'Eleventh International Conference of Accounting Academics', at the Lingnan University, Hong Kong, June, 2000. The financial support from La Trobe University, Bendigo, to attend the conference is also acknowledged.

REFERENCES

Abdoelkadir, K. K. & Yunus, H. (1994). Developments in Indonesian Accountancy. In: J. O. Burns & B. E. Needles, Jr. (Eds), *Accounting Education for the 21st Century: The Global Challenges, International Accounting Section* (pp. 59–72). AAA.

Abdoelkadir, K. K. (1982). The Perception of Accountants and Accounting Students on the Accounting Profession in Indonesia. Ph.D. Dissertation. Texas A & M University.

American Accounting Association 'AAA' (1977). Report of the Committee on International Accounting Operations and Education, 1975–1976. *Accounting Review*, (Supplement), 65–132.

American Accounting Association, Committee on International Accounting Operations and Education 1976–1978, (1978), *Accounting Education and the Third World*. Sarasota, USA.

Bait-et-Mal, M. M., Smith, C. H., & Taylor, M. E. (1973). The development of accounting in Libya. *The International Journal of Accounting Education and Research*, 8(2), 83–102.

Briston, R. J. (1978). The evaluation of accounting in developing countries. *The International Journal of Accounting Education and Research*, 14(Fall), 105–120.

Briston, R. J. (1990). Accounting in developing countries: Indonesia and the Soloman Islands as case studies for regional development. In: R. S. O. Wallace (Ed.), *Research in Third World Accounting* (Vol. 1, pp. 195–216). Greenwich, CT: JAI Press.

Briston, R. J., Foo, S. L., & Yunus, H. (1990). Accounting Education and Work Force Requirements in Indonesia. In: B. E. Needles, Jr. & V. K. Zimmerman (Eds), *Comparative International Accounting Education Standards* (pp. 147–173). Center for International Education and Research in Accounting, University of Illinois at Urbana-Champaign.

Briston, R. J., & Kedslie, M. J. M. (1997). The internationalization of British professional accounting: The examination exporting bodies. *Accounting, Business and Financial History*, 7(2), 175–194. Chapman & Hall.

Brookner, L., & Heilman, E. (1960). Technical assistance in accounting in Turkey. *The Accounting Review*, (January), 33–36.

Carmony, L. (1987). Accounting in the context of its environment: The Uruguayan Case. *The International Journal of Accounting*, 22(2), 41–56.

Chandler, J., & Holzer, H. P. (1984). Accounting in the Third World. In: H. P. Holzer et al. (Eds), *International Accounting* (Ch. 19). New York: Harper and Row.

Chu, K. C. (1969). Accounting education in the Republic of China. *The International Journal of Accounting Education and Research*, 4(2), 75–91.

CCH Editors (1990). *Guide to Company Law in Malaysia & Singapore*. CCH Asia.

Craig, R. J., & Diga, J. G. (1996). Financial reporting regulation in ASEAN: Features and prospects. *The International Journal of Accounting*, 31(2), 239–259

Cruz, F. B. (1993). Accounting harmonization in ASEAN, Proceedings of the Eighth ASEAN Federation of Accountant Conference, Bangkok, June.

Diga, J., & H. Yunus (1997). Accounting in Indonesia. In: N. Baydoun, A. Nishimura & R. Willet (Eds), *Accounting in the Asia Pacific Region* (pp. 282–302). John Wiley & Sons.

Engelmann, K. (1962). Accounting problems in developing countries. *The Journal of Accountancy*, (January), 53–56.

Enthoven, A. J. H (1974). An Evaluation of the Accountancy Systems, Development and Requirement in Indonesia, January, Unpublished draft report on a Ford Foundation Research Project (p. 31).

Enthoven, A. J. H. (1979). *Accountancy Systems in the Third World Economies*. Amsterdam: North-Holland.

Enthoven, A. J. H. (1983). U.S. accounting and the third world: More needs to be done to improve accounting systems and practice in developing countries. *The Journal of Accountancy*, (June), 110–118.

Foo, S. L. (1988). Accounting educational systems in Southeast Asia: The Indonesian and Singaporean experiences. *The International Journal of Accounting Education and Research*, 23(2), 125–136.

Fong, S. W., & Foo, S. L. (1992). *School of Accountancy and Business: Origin and Development*. Singapore: Nanyang Technological University.

Hardman, D. J. (1984). Accounting development in the Solomon Islands. *The International Journal of Accounting*, 20(1), 141–152.

Hove, M. R. (1986). Accounting practices in developing countries: colonialism's legacy of inappropriate technologies. *The International Journal of Accounting*, (Fall).

Hewison, K., Richard, R., & Garry, R. (Eds) (1993). *Southeast Asia in the 1990s: Authorization, Democracy and Capitalism*. NSW, Australia: Allan & Unwin

Hadibroto, S. (1984). *Accounting Education Development Program in Indonesia Medan*, (September), 131.

Johnson, T. J., & Caygill, M. (1971). The development of accountancy links in the Commonwealth. *Accounting and Business Research, 1.*

Lowe, H. D. (1967). Accounting aid for developing countries. *The Accounting Review*, (April), 356–360.

MacGregor, A., Hossain, M., & Yap, K. (1997). Accounting in Malaysia and Singapore: Culture's Lack of Consequence?, In: N.Bayboun, A. Nishimura & R. Willet (Eds), *Accounting in the Asia Pacific Region* (pp. 99–125). Singapore: John Wiley and Sons, Pte. Ltd. (Asia).

Maolanond, P., & Nobuyuki, Y. (1985). *Corporation Law in ASEAN Countries: A Case Study of Thailand*. Tokyo: Institute of Developing Economies.

Markell, W. (1985). Development of Accounting Education and the Accounting Profession in Third World Countries: Botswana. *The International Journal of Accounting, 21*(1), 99–106.

Mepham, M. J. (1977). The Accountancy Profession in Jamaica. *The Accountant's Magazine*, (November), 468–470.

Mueller, G. G. (1988). Practising Educational Imperialism. *CA Magazine*, (November).

Ndzinge, S. (1994). Aligning Accounting Education and Training to the Skills Needs in Developing Nations: The Case of SADCC. In: J. O. Burns & B. E. Needles, Jr. (Eds), *Accounting Education for the 21st Century: The Global Challenges, International Accounting Section* (pp. 126–133). AAA.

Ninsuvannakul, P. (1988). *The development of the accounting profession of the ASEAN countries: Past, present, and future: Recent Accounting and Economic Developments in the Far East* (pp. 115–148). Champain, IL: Center for International Education and Research in Accounting.

Nobes, C. W. (1984). *International Classification of Financial Reporting*. Croom Helm.

Pillai, P. N. (1984). *Companies and Securities Handbook: Singapore and Malaysia*. Singapore: Butterworths.

Perera, M. H. B. (1980). *Accounting for State Industrial and Commercial Enterprises in a Developing Country*. New York: Arno Press.

Price Waterhouse (1991). *Doing Business in Brunei Darussalam*. Bandar Seri Begawan: Price Waterhouse.

Price Waterhouse (1992a). *Doing Business in Malaysia*. Kuala Lumpur: Price Waterhouse.

Price Waterhouse (1992b). *Doing Business in Singapore*. Singapore: Price Waterhouse.

Price Waterhouse (1992c). *Doing Business in Indonesia*. Jakarta: Price Waterhouse.

Radebaugh, L. H. (1975). Environmental Factors Influencing the Development of Accounting Objectives, Standard, and Practice in Peru. *International Journal of Accounting Education and Research, 11*(1), 39–56.

Roh, M. (1991). Accounting and auditing standards: Towards harmonization in the Asia Pacific region. In: *Proceedings of the Third IGAF Pacific Asia Conference* (June, pp. 72–82). Penang, Malaysia.

Salas, C. A. (1967). Accounting education and practice in Spanish Latin America. *The International Journal of Accounting Education and Research, 3*(1)(Fall), 67–85.

Seidler, L. J. (1967). *The Function of Accounting in Economic Development, Turkey as a Case study*. New York, Praeger.

Sheridan, L. A. (1961). *Malaya, Singapore and the Borneo Territories: Volume 9 of the British Commonwealth, the Development of its Laws and Constitution*. Stevens & Sons

Sembiring. T. (1984). The Matching of Resources Requirement and Their Availability at Regional and International Levels-Indonesia. *Proceedings of Asia and Pacific Conference on*

Accounting Education for Development, International Federation of Accountants, Asian Development Bank and Word Bank (p. 169). Manila.

Samidjo, T. (1985). In: *Pengantar Hukum Indonesia (Introduction to Indonesian Law)* (pp. 254–259). Bandung: C.V. Arminco.

Standish, P. E. M. (1983). Accounting education in Australia: 1982–1983. *Journal of Accounting and Finance, 23*(2)(November), 2–30.

Sunday Times (1968), December 17, Singapore.

Tan, M. M., Pang, Y. H., & Foo, S. L. (1994). Accounting Education and Practice: The Singapore Experience. *International Journal of Accounting, 29*(2), 161–183.

Tang, R. Y. W., & Tse, E. (1986). Accounting technology transfer to less developed countries and the Singapore experience. *Columbia Journal of World Business,* (Summer).

Teo, S., & Low, M. (1993). Employers' perceptions of the education and performance of accounting graduates. *Singapore Accountant,* (October–November), 24.

Tipgos, M. A. (1987). A comprehensive model for improving accounting education in developing countries, In: K. S. Most (Ed.), *Advances in International Accounting* (Vol. 1, pp. 383–404). Greenwich: JAI Press.

Timberman, D. G. (Ed.) (1992). *The Politics of Economic Reform in Southeast Asia.* Manila: Asian Institute of Management.

Wallace, R. S. O. (1990). Accounting in Developing Countries: A Review of the Literature. In: R. S. O. Wallace, J. M. Samuels & R. J. Briston (Eds), *Research in Third World Accounting* (Vol. 1, pp. 3–54). London: JAI Press.

Wallace, R. S. O., & Briston, R. J. (1993). Improving the Accounting Infrastructure in Developing Countries. In: R. S. O. Wallace, J. M. Samuels & R. J. Briston (Eds), *Research in Third World Accounting* (Vol. 2, pp. 201–224). London: JAI Press.

Walton, P. (1986). The export of British accounting legislation to Commonwealth Countries. *Accounting and Business Research, 16,* 353–357.

Wee, L. T. (1994). An innovation in accounting education: the MBA (Accountancy) in Singapore. *Accounting Education, 3*(2), 115–131.

Wilkinson, T. L. (1965). United States Accounting as Viewed by Accountants of Other Countries. *The International Journal of Accounting, 1*(1), 3–14.

Wijewardena, H., & Yapa, P. W. S. (1998). Colonialism and Accounting Education in Developing Countries: The Experience of Singapore and Sri Lanka. *The International Journal of Accounting, 33*(2), 269–281.

World Bank (1993). *The East Asian Miracle: Economic Growth and Public Policy.* Washington, D.C.: Oxford University Press for the IBRD.

Yapa. S., & Wijewardena, H. (1996). The development of accounting systems and accounting education in high income oil exporting countries: An overview. *The International Journal of Accounting and Business Society, 4*(1), 40–54.

Yapa, S. (1999a). Accounting Education in Developing Countries: The case of Sri Lanka. Unpublished Ph.D. thesis. University of Wollongong, NSW, Australia.

Yapa, S. (1999b). Professional accounting environment in Brunei Darussalam. *Accounting, Accountability and Auditing Journal, 13*(3), 328–339.

Yapa. S. (2000). University-Profession partnership in accounting education: The case of Sri Lanka. *Accounting Education, 9*(3).

Yasuda, N. (1993). Law and Development in ASEAN Countries. *ASEAN Economic Bulletin,* (November), 144–154.

Zeff, S. A. (1972). *Forging Accounting Principles in Five Countries.* Champaign, Illinois: Stripes Publishing.